Sikhs in the Diaspora:
A Modern Guide to Practice of the Sikh Faith

ABOUT THE AUTHOR

Dr Surinder Singh Bakhshi was born in Dar es Salaam, Tanzania. He received his medical education in Makerere Medical School, Kampala, Uganda. Post-graduate studies took him to the United States, Scotland and England. He was appointed Consultant in Communicable Disease Control in Birmingham, United Kingdom. He was to manage in the city the last case of smallpox in the world. The World Health Organisation was to describe the control such that there was never any danger of its further spread. Since retiring five years ago he has written a book on tuberculosis. This current book is the first in a trilogy; the second one is a quest for Sikh identity and the third on the relevance of Guru Granth Sahib, not only to Sikhs but also the contemporary world.

To the memory of my Gursikh parents,
Sohan Singh and Amrit Kaur,
who led a life Guru Nanak lived

Author's Note

I read widely and talked to many Sikhs, young and old, as I prepared this book. The more I immersed myself in the writing of this book, the more I felt like a grain of sand in the vast ocean of the treasury of sublime thought and spirituality that is my faith – what Guru Granth says, what tradition teaches, what a Gurdwara is and who decides on its doctrines and practices. What I learnt was the role of Gurdwara and its liturgy as a community hub in the life of a Sikh to help maintain family stability, strengthen social bonds and provide for the devotees their spiritual food.

I have been part of the Sangat of Ramgarhia Sikh Temple, located in the historic jewellery quarter of Birmingham, hub of the Midlands in the United Kingdom, for over three decades. I have witnessed the handover of the chain of responsibility from the founders of the Gurdwara to younger generations born or brought up in this country. The transition has resulted in the moulding of the faith to its time and integration into the rest of the community.

It therefore gives me great pleasure that the Temple has so enthusiastically agreed to sponsor this special edition of the book in the year 2008, in which we celebrate the tercentenary of the bestowal of Guruship on the Granth Sahib by Guru Gobind Singh, the tenth and last Guru of the Sikhs.

Despite my respectful and devoted efforts, there will be unintended errors of omission and commission which Sikhs may find hurtful. Ramgarhia Sikh Temple is not responsible for these errors in any way whatsoever. I alone am responsible for what is written in this book.

I have followed dates in the Nanakshahi calendar for the year 2007-2008, published by SGPC, Amritsar. I have adopted Gurbani quotations, to suit modern conventions, from the six volume *The Sikh Religion* by Max Arthur McAuliffe, first published by the Oxford University Press in London in 1910.

Readers desirous of commenting on this book may do so to the email address provided in the information section. I cannot promise to respond to all comments but I certainly promise to read them and take on board any suggestions made in the messages.

I must now add gratitude and indebtedness to my wife, Rajinder Kaur, a Gursikh, whose insight into Guru Nanak's way of life – and such insight is vouchsafed only to Gursikhs – has so enriched this book, and my life.

Surinder Singh Bakhshi
October 2008

iii

CONTENTS

Author's note   i
Foreword   vi
Tercentenary (1708-2008)   Ix
Introduction   1

PART ONE: Modern Sikh Identity
Chapter 1   Definition of a Sikh   8
Chapter 2   The Rahet Maryada: Code of Sikh Rules of
              Conduct   12
Chapter 3   The Mool Mantar: Creed of the Sikh Faith   14
Chapter 4   The Sikh National Anthem   16
Chapter 5   Symbols of the Sikh Faith   17
Chapter 6   The Sikh Nanakshahi Calendar   22
Chapter 7   Bioethics and Medical Care   29

PART TWO: The Lives of the Gurus
Chapter 8   Guru Nanak Dev, the First Guru (1469-
              1538): Founder of the Sikh Faith   38
Chapter 9   Times of Consolidation: Angad Dev, the
              Second Guru (1504-1552), Amar Das, the
              Third Guru (1479-1574) and Ram Das, the   49
              Fourth Guru
Chapter 10   Arjan Dev, the Fifth Guru (1563-1606): First
              Guru Martyr   55
Chapter 11   Hargobind, the Sixth Guru (1659-1644): Sant
              Sipahi   60
Chapter 12   Interlude: Har Rai, the Seventh Guru (1630-
              1661) and Har Krishan, the Eight Guru   65
              (1656-1664)
Chapter 13   Tegh Bahadur, the Ninth Guru (1621-1675):
              Second Guru Martyr   68
Chapter 14   Gobind Singh, the Tenth Guru (1666-1708)   72

PART THREE: Guru Granth Sahib
Chapter 15   Guru Granth Sahib   82

PART FOUR: The Sikh Way of Life: Beliefs, Values and Moral Conduct

Chapter 16   The Cosmos in Sikh Faith   107
Chapter 17   Guru Nanak Dev: Life Lived   112
Chapter 18   Naam Simran: Meditation upon the Name of
              God   115
Chapter 19   The Sikh Moral Code   120
Chapter 20   The Core Values of the Sikh Faith   125

PART FIVE: SIKH LITURGY

Chapter 21   Recitation of Gurbani   127
Chapter 22   Nit-nem   132
Chapter 23   Sikh Arti   139
Chapter 24   Sangrand   142
Chapter 25   Sikh Ardas   145

PART SIX: Shabad Kirtan

Chapter 26   Shabad Kirtan   152
Chapter 27   Guru Praise of Shabad Kirtan   154
Chapter 28   Genesis of Shabad Kirtan   158
Chapter 29   Shabad Kirtan in Gurdwara   167

PART SEVEN: Gurdwara and Sikh Governance

Chapter 30   Historic Evolution   178
Chapter 31   A Guide for Visitors   184
Chapter 32   Gurdwara in Britain   192
Chapter 33   Sikh Governance   207

PART EIGHT: Stages in a Sikh's Life

Chapter 34	Naam Sanskar (Naming a Child Ceremony)	212
Chapter 35	Dastar Bandi Sanskar (Pagri Tying Ceremony)	219
Chapter 36	Amrit Sanskar (Khalsa Initiation Ceremony)	225
Chapter 37	Anand Sanskar (Lavan – Marriage Ceremony)	229
Chapter 38	Antam Sanskar (Funeral Rites)	241

PART NINE: Gurpurbs, Gurpurb Melas, Festivals and Folk Festivals in Punjab

Chapter 39	Gurpurbs associated with the Lives of the Gurus	248
Chapter 40	Parkash Utsav (Installation of Guru Granth in Harmandir Sahib)	253
Chapter 41	Khalsa Sajna Divas (Vaisakhi Day Celebrations)	257
Chapter 42	Sikh Faith Festivals: Bandi Chhor Divas (Sikh Divali), Hola Mahalla and Maghi Jore Mela	260

Glossary of Sikh faith terms	268

Foreword

In the year 2008, Sikhs commemorate the tercentenary of the investment of eternal spiritual guardianship of their faith in Guru Granth Sahib by Guru Gobind Singh, the tenth and last Guru. Guru Granth is the living embodiment of Sikh Gurus. Guru Gobind Singh ordained the Sikh faith a self-governing nation with belief in equality of all people regardless of race, religion, caste, creed or status. The notion of equality of all under the authority of God has produced a united Sikh faith unhindered by doctrinal or social conflicts.

Sikhs are deeply conservative but their genius for absorption and adaptation makes them an enlightened society.

Guru Nanak Dev, founder of the Sikh faith, visited, in search of universal truth, seats of learning of Hindu, Muslim and Buddhist thought in India, Nepal, Sri Lanka, Arabia, Iraq, Iran and Afghanistan in the sixteenth century. He made three great journeys lasting twenty-five years. He stayed for over a year in Baghdad, then the supreme centre of Islamic learning.

Japji, Guru Nanak's meditation on the unity of the creation, states that the abundance of nature on our earth is finite, however otherwise it may appear to us. Man is a mere grain of sand in the immense order of the universe. He is not its master. If he abuses the abundance that nature provides him, he will be wiped out with no more than the flicker of an eyelid. While man will be forgotten, the earth will in time once more regain its pristine beauty. Written half a millennium ago, when Europe was still struggling to throw off its yoke of mediaevalism, these prescient words are today a warning to us all about the fragility of our earth. The only truth that counts, Guru Nanak further tells us, is the love that we have for each other in the service to humanity. To help those who need our assistance is to experience the presence of God within us. This is real. The rest is mirage.

Much doubt is expressed about the role and place of multinational cultures in achieving British cohesiveness in the twenty-first century. Sikhs do not lay claim to the superiority of their faith over others. Sikhs believe that a Christian, a Hindu or a Muslim should rather become a better Christian, Hindu or Muslim than convert to another religion. No religion has a monopoly on truth. Nor can a religious tradition survive if it remains static. Those who reject progress do a disservice to their faith.

We live in a country which is proud of its hard-won liberties. Adoption of these values enhances the relevance of our faith to Sikhs born and brought up in the United Kingdom. British Sikh is a proud label to bear. It does not efface Sikh faith but strengthens it by combining two freedom-loving societies.

That indeed is the message of this book. It shows how living in harmony with other faiths has immeasurably strengthened Sikh faith. More Sikhs attend their Gurdwara today than they ever did before. The 250 Gurdwara in Britain are like mini states that provide an umbrella under which Sikhs may look forward to a confident future.

'Sikhs in the Diaspora: A Modern Guide to Practice of the Sikh Faith' takes a contemporary view of Sikh faith. It is a role model for celebration of diversity in Britain. Dr Surinder Singh Bakhshi, a thoughtful Sikh, has done us a timely service in putting this volume together for our benefit.

Ramgarhia Sikh Temple in Birmingham is proud to count Dr Surinder Bakhshi a member of its Sangat. It is pleased to publish this special edition in the tercentenary year of the appointment of Guru Granth by Guru Gobind Singh, the living embodiment of the ten Sikh Gurus. We commend the book to all Sikhs and non-Sikhs who seek a fresh insight into how we can lead a better life together in harmony with each other.

Tercentenary (1708-2008)
Gurtagaddi: Guru Gobind Singh Anoints Granth Sahib Guru of the Sikhs and declares Khalsa Panth a Self-Governing Nation

As his end neared, Guru Gobind Singh called together his disciples to recite Gurbani with him. After a short while, he smiled and bestowed his blessings on his beloved Sikhs. With folded hands, his strength ebbing away, he asked them to come close to him. Guru Gobind Singh declared,

'Waheguruji ka khalsa, Waheguruji di Fateh!'

Guruji then said,

'The one thing that man dreads most is death. I have always lived in its shadow and I have looked at it in the eye. Do not grieve for me. For whensoever five of my Amritdhari Sikhs gather, there in the Sangat you will feel my presence.'

Asked in sorrow who was to succeed him to the Gurtagaddi, the throne of Guru Nanak, when he was no more, Guruji said,

'The ten Gurus have now after 250 years fulfilled their mission. I have given my life so that you have it in abundance. I will now deliver the Khalsa Panth to God and his judgement'.

Guru Gobind Singh then proclaimed,

'O, my beloved Khalsa, let him who desires to behold me behold Guru Granth. Obey Granth Sahib. It is the visible body of the Gurus. And let him who desires to meet me, search me in its Gurbani.'

He then added,

'My mission is accomplished

The spark of Khalsa Panth is lit
It shall not be extinguished
The Guru will dwell with the Khalsa
All power be his'.

The final words of Guru Gobind Singh were,

'Let us now meditate and honour His name [God].'

At dawn, Guruji left his earthly abode in Nanded, on the banks of the river Godavri, in Maharashtra, in the year 1708. Guru Gobind Singh was destined to live a short life but immortal glory was his forever. Sikhs recall his final words in the following verse recited at the conclusion of Ardas, prayers,

'Under orders of the Immortal Being, the Panth was created
All the Sikhs are enjoined to accept the Granth as their Guru
Consider Guru Granth as embodiment of the Guru
Those who want to meet God can find Him in its Shabad
The Khalsa shall rule and its opponents will be no more
Those separated will unite and all shall be saved.'

On 20 October 2008, Sikhs celebrate the tercentenary of the bestowal of the Gurtagaddi on Guru Granth in Nanded, India.

Introduction

Sikh migration to Britain began at first because of Britain's colonial relationship with the Punjab, India. From the very beginning of this relationship in the mid nineteenth century, Sikhs were recruited into the British Army to safeguard the interests of the British Empire in India and abroad.

The movement of British subjects within the Empire was unrestricted until the Commonwealth Immigration Act of 1962. Sikh males began migrating from the Punjab to post-war Britain in the early 1950s, but mass migration did not take place until the 1960s. Sikhs came to Britain due to pressure on their land and shortage of jobs. A labour shortage and an economic boom in Britain meant that jobs, mainly unskilled, were not hard to find in foundries and textile industries. The new arrivals settled mostly in London, the Midlands and West Yorkshire. Now they have spread to all urban areas of the country.

In the 1970s, a further wave of Sikh migration came from East Africa. These second- and third-generation skilled migrants had initially gone to Africa to build and support the African railroad industry in the 1930s.

The British Sikh community is now in its third and fourth generation and has firmly established its roots in Britain. Sikhs in Britain number only about half a million, and yet they have made a remarkable impact on the economy, culture and social life. Hard working and resourceful, Sikhs have taken up positions as MPs, lawyers, mayors, doctors, engineers, teachers and civil servants. Sikhs have become industry leaders and have applied their entrepreneurial spirit to both revive moribund businesses and start new ones. The Sikh spirit is also manifest at community level. There are over 250 Sikh Gurdwara around the country serving their communities and providing services to the elderly, disabled and needy.

Guru Nanak Dev, founder of the Sikh faith, was born in 1469, a time when the mediaeval excesses in Europe were slowly beginning to give way to the age of enlightenment. Guru Nanak also lived at a dark period in the history of India but his own early life was an idyllic one surrounded by loving parents, family and friends. From a young age, his leanings were unworldly and he spent much of his time with Sants, holy and learned men, in his village.

The young Guru Nanak embarked upon a journey of quest for truth and knowledge, a journey that took him to countries of South Asia and the Middle East. In his twenty-five years of travel, Guru Nanak spent about two years in the Arabian countries, mostly in Baghdad, then the centre of Islamic culture and science. A tablet marks the place he stayed at, stating

Here lived the holy man, Nanak, when he visited Baghdad

Like all travellers, Guru Nanak had an enquiring mind. He visited holy places where he met and discoursed with men of great erudition and learning. He absorbed much knowledge and his learning spanned across land barriers, languages and cultures. He gave his message in verse set to music played by his faithful companion, Mardana. Guru Nanak believed music was a common language which transcended all human barriers to understanding. His compositions are recorded in Guru Granth, the scriptures of the Sikh faith.

Guru Nanak claimed that in his travels, talking to people of all ages and levels of education, he had come to the conclusion that all men were born equal and were all worthy of respect and honour. It is a sign of his learning and humility that when the time came to hand over Gurtagaddi, Guruship, to his successor, Angad, it was passing on the Pothis, records of his writings, that marked the transition rather than any show of worldly display.

The Sikh faith is one of the most dynamic in the world today. It is also the youngest and the last of the world's major faiths to be founded in the past 1,500 years.

Sikhs are known for their martial prowess. Guru Gobind Singh, who carried the mantle of Guru Nanak as the last Guru of the Sikhs, sensed the danger of genocide of his people by the Mughal rulers of India. He bestowed upon his Sikhs warrior traditions drawn from the ancient, mystical, heroic times of the Indian people, to create the order of the Khalsa Panth. The Guru ordered his Sikhs to wear a sword to fight the just war and to protect the innocent. He ordered them to maintain their faith, whatever the challenge facing them. He asked his Sikhs to be sentient in the observance of their faith and not molest the women and children of their adversaries, or appropriate the property of their enemies, as was the practice of marauding armies in mediaeval times. These strictures became the foundation of the principles of Sikh morality.

This was proclaimed at the time when Guru Gobind Singh had lost his four sons to the enemy. Sikhs, despite having fought many wars, have no history of committing atrocities, murder, plunder or rape.

Sikhs thrive in Western democracies, with their ethos of individual freedom and personal rights. Guru Nanak said that Sikhs should respect fair rulers and not betray them after eating their nimak, salt. Sikhs have a history of cordial relationships with the people of Britain going back over 150 years. Sikhs are an accommodating people. They show their loyalty by their hard work, honesty and patriotism.

What are the historic roots of this non-Christian faith in Britain today?

The Dignity of Man

Religion and culture are an integral part of the well-being of Sikhs. Sikhs must discharge their obligation towards family, neighbours and society. There is no place for renunciation or asceticism in their faith. Religion has no meaning if it is divorced from life.

All facets of life are diverse revelations of the divine order. From such recognition of diversity has arisen pluralism, an essential attribute for social order in the ideology of Sikh faith. Thus Guru Nanak laid the foundation of a faith grounded in equality, mutual respect, truthfulness, honest living and sharing the fruits of one's efforts with others. Guru Nanak believed that each of us was a divine gift and the practice of untouchability was human degradation. He felt that such acts devalued people and he found them unacceptable.

Guru Nanak observed that the priest craft was corrupt and depraved. He declined to accept priests as an agency for interpretation and enforcement of divine will. He abhorred a priesthood that invoked divine interventions and stood in the way of freedom for the people, and the defeatism and political terror that characterised it at the time.

As mediators between man and God, priests' lives must be free of superstition and taboo. To revitalise his defeated and demoralised people, Guru Nanak showed that priests had no superior authority over that of the common man.

Freedom from Fear

Guru Nanak believed freedom of human action was a divine attribute. Freedom from fear was an essential stage on the path to the dignity of man. Only a man free from fear achieves Grace. Freedom from fear of rulers and release from bondage is essential to a decent political order. Freedom from fear of priests delivers man from bondage to chains of superstition and corrupt rituals.

Indian traditions dictated that man was inherently evil. Kings were divinely anointed. Rulers preserved social order and stressed the discharge of duties in a stratified social order. Guru Nanak declared it an evil system with which there was no scope for reconciliation.

The master-slave relationship was dehumanising for both. In Babar Bani, a composition in Guru Granth, the hordes of Babar, the Mughal conqueror, are described as the marriage procession of evil, forcibly demanding the hand of the helpless bride, the people of India. Alienation, coercion, persecution and abject submission of the people result in disintegration of the human personality.

Guru Nanak exhorted his people to return to simplicity of faith and commit themselves to truth and honest living. A Sikh endeavours to establish the identity of a human being as someone possessing honour and dignity. Individual consciousness emerges out of divine light, which shines through the individual. Spirituality is truth, freedom and the integration of one's self. Evil is not instilled in human beings. They are not sinful by nature.

Guru Nanak set the goal for his followers as the practice of spirituality in a self-determined endeavour towards truthful behaviour. Guruji said it would not serve God's purpose if people lost their identity by self-abnegation and their consciousness and personality through dissolution. However, by good deeds, God is awakened within an individual, who then returns to worldly consciousness in the transformed state through selfless service to others.

Guru Nanak defined his new individual acting in two ways. First, the spiritual struggle for self-awareness and, second, human accord. Combined, these two dynamics engendered a society free from prejudice of caste, birth or creed.

The Universality of the Presence of God

Gurbani says,

'Presence of God in one's own soul, and perception of it in others. Relate to God not by mysticism, asceticism or passive faith. But the presence of God within man in an interactive way'.

Grace arises out of the human soul rather than descending from the heavens. Guru Nanak could not accept the finality of revelation by one faith and the concept of the chosen people by another. Guru Nanak did not reject any faiths but protested against the distortion of their practice by their followers.

He wanted people to adhere to the vision and value of their faith and accept diversity in their relationship with others. Guru Nanak in his twenty-five years of travels promoted dialogue between different faiths to further understanding and mutual respect.

Guru Nanak accepted the need for dialogue between faiths, in order to recognise each faith as ordained by God rather than to generate conflict. He promoted freedom of conscience. Guru Nanak liberated his disciples from a passive, fragmented state of inaction towards an active spiritual and morally integrated state.

The institutions developed during the time of the Gurus, upon which the practice of the Sikh faith is based, reflect the social ideals of a free society. Within modern society, Sikh institutions have evolved to serve the social, cultural and religious needs of its people. These institutions are not divisive, but regulate the relationship first between individuals and second in social groups to promote mutual benefit and peaceful living.

PART ONE
Modern Sikh Identity

CHAPTER 1
Definition of a Sikh

Legal, religious and social definitions are the foundation of Sikh identity.

Legal Definition

1. The Sikh Gurdwara Act 1925 Section 3(9)
Sikh – 'Sikh' means a person who professes the Sikh faith.

If any question arises as to whether a living person is or is not a Sikh, he shall be deemed respectively to be or not to be a Sikh according to whether he makes or refuses to make, in such manner as the State may prescribe, the following declaration:

I solemnly affirm that I am a Sikh, that I believe in Guru Granth Sahib, that I believe in the ten Gurus and that I have no other religion.

2. The Delhi Sikh Gurdwara Act 1971 Part 1 (2) k
I solemnly affirm that I am a Keshdhari Sikh, that I believe in and follow the teachings of Sri Guru Granth Sahib and the ten Gurus only, and that I have no other religion.

The first definition is legally applicable at present to the state of Punjab and some adjoining areas. However, in practice, the definition is universal not only in India but throughout the world and accepted as such in the absence of a local definition, of which the Delhi definition is an example.

Definition of Faith

The SGPC (the elected Sikh supreme authority) Sikh Rahet Maryada, the code of Sikh Rules and Conduct, definition in Section One, Chapter 1, Article One

Any human being who faithfully believes in:
i.   One Immortal Being
ii. The Ten Gurus
iii. Guru Granth Sahib
iv. The utterances and teachings of the ten Gurus
v.   The *Amrit* bequeathed by the tenth Guru
And who does not owe allegiance to any other religion,
Such a person is a Sikh.

UK Race Relations Act 1976

The Sikh community has an "ethnic origin" under section 3(1) of the Race Relations Act 1976 and, therefore, in seeking to prevent a pupil from wearing his Pagri, turban, a school was acting contrary to race relations legislation. The Sikh community qualifies as a racial group for the purposes of the 1976 Race Relations Act (House of Lords, *Mandla v. Dowell Lee* [1983] 2 AC 548).

In the judgement of the House of Lords, if members of a group shared history, a distinctive cultural tradition, a common geographical origin or descent, common language and literature, a common religion and a minority status and also saw itself as a distinct community and was so regarded by others, then the group could constitute an ethnic group.

The Lords emphasised the cultural dimension of ethnic groups and, at the same time, argued that the notion of common descent gave members of an ethnic group something akin to a racial aspect. Although the Sikhs did not qualify as a separate race just because of that, they were more than a religious sect, 'almost a race, almost a nation'.

USA Patriot Act 2001: Title X Miscellaneous Section 1002 (Sense of Congress)

(a) Congress finds that–
(1) all Americans are united in condemning, in the strongest possible terms, the terrorists who planned and carried out the attacks against the United States on September 11, 2001, and in pursuing all those responsible for those attacks and their sponsors until they are brought to justice
(2) Sikh-Americans form a vibrant, peaceful, and law-abiding part of America's people
(3) approximately 500,000 Sikhs reside in the United States and are a vital part of the Nation
(4) Sikh-Americans stand resolutely in support of the commitment of our Government to bring the terrorists and those that harbour them to justice
(5) the Sikh faith is a distinct religion with a distinct religious and ethnic identity that has its own places of worship and a distinct holy text and religious tenets
(6) many Sikh-Americans, who are easily recognizable by their turbans and beards, which are required articles of their faith, have suffered both verbal and physical assaults as a result of misguided anger toward Arab-Americans and Muslim-Americans in the wake of the September 11, 2001 terrorist attack
(7) Sikh-Americans, as do all Americans, condemn acts of prejudice against any American
(8) Congress is seriously concerned by the number of crimes against Sikh-Americans and other Americans all across the Nation that have been reported in the wake of the tragic events that unfolded on September 11, 2001.
(b) Congress–
(1) declares that, in the quest to identify, locate, and bring to justice the perpetrators and sponsors of the terrorist attacks on the United States on September 11, 2001, the civil rights and civil liberties of all Americans, including Sikh-Americans, should be protected

(2)   condemns bigotry and any acts of violence or discrimination against any Americans, including Sikh-Americans

(3)   calls upon local and Federal law enforcement authorities to work to prevent crimes against all Americans, including Sikh-Americans; and

(4)   calls upon local and Federal law enforcement authorities to prosecute to the fullest extent of the law all those who commit crimes.

The legal 1925 definition galvanised the Sikh Panth. The Rahet Maryada introduced the additional faith qualification of a Sikh having to be Amritdhari. The Delhi definition was legal, but was compromised by specifying a Keshdhari Sikh rather than an Amritdhari one. The Indian constitution described people of all religions founded in India as originating in Hinduism. The UK definition gave Sikhs an ethnic mantle, something Sikhs have demanded and have continued to demand, but have been denied in India. The Americans recognised the 1925 legal definition. Sikhs are the only people who receive a mention in the Patriot Act. Modern Sikh identity has been fashioned by these definitions.

CHAPTER 2
The Rahet Maryada:
Code of Sikh Rules of Conduct

The Shiromani Gurdwara Parbandhak [management] Committee (SGPC) based in Amritsar, Punjab, is the supreme temporal and spiritual authority of the Sikhs. It is elected by an electorate of the Sikh Panth, nation, who are registered as voters under the provisions of the laws governing the Committee. Apart from the management of Gurdwara, it is responsible for many Sikh educational, health and charitable institutions in India.

The Committee appointed a group of learned Sikhs of all persuasions to codify rules of conduct for the faith, compatible with practice in the modern world. The only condition laid down was that these must comply with the faith's religious, moral and social tenets. The object of the Rahet Maryada was to promote uniformity in religious conduct and observances, in the interests of peaceful cohesion.

The need for a Code was widely accepted and agreed practices began to be accumulated and brought together for the purpose. The Panth was conscious that any imposition of rules from above would be counterproductive and resented by the faith. It had the foresight to decide that the Code should provide basic guidance that the Panth could build upon, to suit local, regional and national needs. This was to avoid the type of conflict that had been observed in other religions when they promulgated canon laws, resulting in splits and irreconcilable differences within the practice of their religions.

Thus, the Sikh Rahet Maryada is the product of collective Panthic wisdom, the faith agreeing to allow it to take precedence in sectional beliefs and preferences. In a wider context, the contents of the Rahet Maryada are taken as the final word in the matters they deal with.

The approved version was agreed in 1945 and published in 1950, after fourteen years of consultation within the Panth. It is a slim document, numbering only twenty pages. The status of this document lies in its authorship and its acceptance by Sikhs. It sets out the procedure for Amrit, the Sikh initiation ceremony, the order of service in Gurdwara, details of four life ceremonies, instruction on what Sikhs should and should not do and a list of daily prayers. It emphasises the faith's most profound moral convictions, the result of 500 years of the Sikhs' bloodstained history. The sense of an obligation to the poor and the less fortunate, a belief that everyone is equal in the eyes of God, and respect for people of other faiths have their roots firmly planted in Sikh faith.

The English version of the Rahet Maryada was published in 1994. The Rahet Maryada is a progressive document. It helps the Sikh faith to be a progressive faith and be part of an aspirational, inclusive, multi-dimensional society. Sikhs can be a role model in their adopted countries. They do not find themselves in conflict with local governance and are prepared to work hard, seize every opportunity and move upwards in society.

The Rahet Maryada succeeded in its purpose far beyond what its proponents in 1932 could have hoped for. Sikhs may visit a Gurdwara anywhere in the world where they will always receive a warm welcome and find that they are no stranger to the act of worship that they find there. The Sikhs are the most united of the religions of the world. There are no sectarian differences or enmity within the Panth. The Rahet Maryada is as relevant today as it was the day it was produced, if not more so. Individual and shared values among Sikhs grow stronger by the day. The Sikh Rahet Maryada must take all credit for it.

CHAPTER 3
The Mool Mantar: Creed of the Sikh Faith

The Mool Mantar is the Sikh creed of faith. Guru Granth begins with the Mool Mantar. The literal meaning is as follows:

Ek Onkar	There is only One God
Sat Naam	Truth is his name
Karta Purkh	He is the Creator
Nir Bhau	He is without fear
Nir Vair	He is without hate
Akaal Moorat	He is immortal, without form
Ajooni	He is beyond birth and death
Saibhang	He is self-illuminated
Gur Parsaad	He is realised by the kindness of the true Guru.

Guru Nanak states this creed at the beginning of his sublime composition, Japji. It describes the universe as a magical place, a self-created fantasy, revealing the presence of the Creator both within and outside his creation. The universe is infinite and has existed for an infinite time. We do not know what was there before it, what will happen in the present or what will follow it. The earth is a blip in the scheme of creation. Man is but a grain of sand. We may enjoy the abundance of provision we find on this finite earth. However, we must leave it as we find it. To do so, we must not be led astray from the order of the universe. To be worthy of this creation, individuals must always stay in Grace by being submerged in God's name – Naam Simran.

Pride has no place in our armament. If we fail to obey the laws of the universe, we will be as easily wiped off the face of the earth as we are put here. There is no mercy for degrading what God has put on earth, for sowing disorder and mayhem. The reality of our existence is no more than a stage that could be dismantled at any moment. That is the surreal truth of our existence.

Have Guru Nanak's prophetic words 500 years ago come to bear fruit? Will soon nothing be left of man's presence in the universe? If it does, it would make no difference to the universe. Humanity may disappear. The earth would renew itself to its pristine self in other millennia. Perhaps it could be one step in the creation that did not work, as there must have been many such examples in the past.

Is it not the time for humanity to return to our spiritual roots, the true corridor into the real world, instead of the illusionary one, without which Guru Nanak saw no hope for humanity? Or is it too late? Have we passed the point of no return?

CHAPTER 4
The Sikh National Anthem

The Sikh national anthem is drawn from stanza 231 of Chandi Charitar Ukat Bilas in the Dasam Granth (the Granth of Guru Gobind Singh, the tenth Guru). It is a battle hymn, praying to God to give Sikhs strength to fight injustice and tyranny. Guru Gobind Singh lost his father and four sons at the hands of the tyrants. Despite these supreme sacrifices, he was undeterred and continued to instil pride, courage and strength in the Khalsa. The verse became popular during the twentieth century when Sikhs began to defy British colonial rule in India. The stirring martial verse is sung at Sikh celebrations associated with Guru Gobind Singh and other suitable occasions.

Deh Shiva bar mohe ihai	Grant me this boon, O God
Shubh karman the kabhu na taroo	May I never refrain from righteous acts
Na daroo ar siyoo jab jah laroon	May I fight without fear all foes in life's battles
Nischai kar apni jeet koroo	With confident courage claiming the victory
Ar Sikh hao apne hi mum ko	May thy glory be ingrained in my mind
Eh lalch hou guna tau uchroo	And my highest ambition be singing thy praises
Jab aav di audh nidhann nanay	When this mortal life comes to end
Aut he rann me tab joojh maroo	May I die fighting with limitless courage.

CHAPTER 5
Symbols of the Sikh Faith

Sikh emblems are of great symbolic and spiritual importance in the faith.

Ek Onkar

ੴ

Ek Onkar means one God. Ek Onkar is a central tenet of the Sikh faith. It is also a symbol of the unity of God in the faith. Ek Onkar in the Gurmukhi script is a combination of two letters: Ek, one, and Onkar, God. The double arch over the second letter (which is the first letter of the Gurmukhi alphabet) signifies the timelessness and eternal presence of the Creator. Ek Onkar is the first phrase in the Mool Mantar, the Sikh creed of faith.

The Khanda

The Khanda is the insignia of the Sikhs, a symbol of universal creative power. In the centre is a straight double-edged sword, symbol of the primal power of the Creator. The Chakar, quoit, defines infinity. The two curved swords on the outside symbolise the spiritual (piri) and temporal (miri) balance in the universe.

Nishan Sahib

Nishan Sahib is the Sikh holy flag, which is made of a triangular cotton or silk cloth. The colour of the Nishan Sahib is usually saffron but variation from red to yellow may also occur. It was first hoisted by Guru Hargobind at Akal Takht Sahib, the Sikhs' throne of authority, next to the Harmandir, Golden Temple, at Amritsar, in 1609. The Nishan Sahib is placed outside every Sikh Gurdwara and is supported by a pole of timber or metal. The Khanda is depicted on the flag. A steel Khanda may also be placed at the top of the pole. Great respect is shown to this flag; the flagpole is washed every year at Vaisakhi using milk and water, and the flag and pole clothing replaced at the same time.

The Five Kakars, 5Ks

Guru Gobind Singh ordained that Sikhs initiated into the Khalsa Panth must wear the five accoutrements at all times to mark their faith. These are the five Kakars or the five Ks because they all begin with the letter K in Punjabi. All the symbols remind Sikhs of the need to be sentient in the practice of the faith in their mind and body.

Kesh: uncut hair, including body hair – reflects obedience to God's gift of hair to humanity.

Kanga: a small wooden comb tucked into the hair on the head to keep it clean and tidy. It reminds Sikhs of the importance of discipline of mind and body.

Kara: a steel bracelet worn on the right wrist. Its circular shape tells Sikhs of the continuity of the flow of love of God in the Khalsa Panth. It is an eternal relationship with no beginning or end. It also reminds Sikhs that most sins and crimes are committed through the hands.

Kirpan: a curved sword with a single cutting edge. It represents courage to live and fight for justice. While a full length Kirpan is worn for ceremonial purposes, a smaller Kirpan, about 15 centimetres long, is usually worn on the left side under or over the outer clothes, in a sheath slung over the shoulders. Others prefer to wear it as a miniature device embedded in their Kanga. The Kirpan signifies a Sikh's responsibility to protect the defenceless.

Kachera: a loose fitting pair of drawers made of cotton, worn as underwear, symbolising continence of thought and self-restraint of the body. A garment of practical importance in battle. It ensured briskness during action and freedom of movement at all times.

The five Ks are applicable equally to Amritdhari men and women. When first introduced in the seventeenth century, the symbols were also important as a uniform, as all Sikhs were expected to be warriors when the Mughals, sworn enemies of the Sikhs, threatened their faith with annihilation.

The five Ks represent a Sikh's bearing in life, to remind them of the virtues of honest living, truthful behaviour and respect for humankind. Above all, Sikhs follow this dress code because Guru Gobind Singh ordained them to do so. All the Gurus and their devotees wore Pagri, turbans, and this too has become an integral part of the faith.

Difficulties with following the Sikh dress code in Britain

When Sikhs first began to arrive in numbers in Britain after the Second World War, difficulties arose relating to their dress code, especially the Pagri. The problem became acute for Sikhs at work and in education. Nowadays, the situation regarding the Pagri, the main cause of discrimination against Sikhs, has been largely resolved in Britain. Sikhs are also exempted from wearing protective helmets. Discrimination against the turban at work and in education is now unlawful and it is accepted without comment in public institutions and society in general. However, discrimination still occurs and the Panth has to be on constant guard to protect its disciples from indiscriminate violations of law and human rights.

The Kirpan can still cause concern in schools. Most schools will accept the practice provided it is unobtrusive. In aeroplanes, Sikhs may be asked to hand the Kirpan over to flight staff for safe custody until the flight is over. The Kara is also often the cause of dispute. Sikhs always endeavour to resolve these matters peacefully or by recourse to a court of law.

In general terms, the five Ks do not pose problems in any free democratic country, though the wearing of a turban in French schools has recently become an issue, because of the country's conflict with Islamic dress. At the time of writing, the matter remains to be resolved in the courts.

Hospital staff often ask patients to remove, or sometimes even interfere with, one or more of the Ks. Sikhs are frequently asked to shave hair for some procedures, or remove their Kara, but both are usually unnecessary. Hospitals need to discuss and accede to Sikhs' request to retain their Ks. The Kara can be taped with insulating tapes when required. The latter can also be used in sports or places of work where this item is considered a risk; however, it has not been shown to be so in practice. As a retired medical practitioner, I have never found, in forty years of medical practice, the Sikhs' dress code to be a hindrance in medical, or indeed in any other, practice.

It is true to say that, except in France, there are no restrictions in wearing the five Ks in any democratic country of the world. In matters of essential health and safety, compromise can be achieved without violating the sense of religious practice among Sikhs. It may be noted that, even when bathing, Sikhs will keep on their Kachera. They remove it only when they are ready to wear a fresh one. Sikhs, with their dress code intact, are free to join the police and armed forces in almost all the free countries.

Sikh girls and boys are not forbidden to wear school uniforms, provided the modesty required is preserved. Sikh girls may wish to wear a headscarf, and this is now an accepted practice for Sikh women in schools and at work.

Unemployment rates are generally much lower among Sikhs than other minority ethnic groups in Britain. This at least shows a lack of overt discrimination against Sikhs. Even when the dress code is considered the cause of discrimination, it will be found that it is generally a pretext for discrimination against all minorities.

The wearing of the Ks for Sikhs is a help rather than hindrance, as Sikhs are respected for their hard work and diligence all over the world. To be wearing the five Ks is a guarantee of honesty and law-abiding citizenship.

CHAPTER 6
The Sikh Nanakshahi Calendar

Important dates in Sikh history have followed the Hindu Bikrami solar-lunar calendar to determine religious anniversaries. While the Bikrami solar calendar varies only slightly from its Western counterpart, the Indian custom of tagging religious dates onto the lunar calendar has sown great confusion in the past. Gurpurbs and other festivals were movable from days to months, even years, in the Bikrami calendar. The lunar dates, phases of the moon, are fixed but because the lunar year is shorter than the solar year the difference has to be taken into account in determining dates. An extra month is added to the lunar calendar every few years to bring it in line with its solar counterpart. Indeed, we have to rely on complex astrological calculations to predict dates correctly. Such is the variation in following a lunar calendar that is calibrated to the solar calendar that some anniversaries may not show in a particular year, while appearing twice in the subsequent calendar year.

The length of the solar year of the Bikrami Samat, calendar, conforms to but does not exactly match the Western Gregorian calendar. The Bikrami year consists of 365 days, 6 hours, 9 minutes and 10 seconds, while the Gregorian calendar is based on a length of 365 days, 5 hours, 48 minutes and 46 seconds. The latter allows for consistency in matching days to the movement of the sun. The difference of about twenty minutes between the two calendars builds up over centuries. The Bikrami calendar has an error of one day in about seventy years. There is no self-correction within the Bikrami calendar. The Bikrami calendar is in advance of the Gregorian calendar by 56 years 8 months and 17 days (for calculations 56.7 years). While the Gregorian calendar was corrected in the eighteenth century by the introduction of a leap year, this has not been carried out in the Bikrami calendar.

The days of the month in the Bikrami calendar are not fixed. The number can vary from 31-32 days for the summer months and from 29-30 days for winter months. The rules for determination of Sankrantis, first days of the month, are complicated and reliance has to be placed on astrological Jantris (almanacs) to calculate such a simple thing as the beginning of a month.

The lunar portion of the calendar, according to which the religious festivals were fixed, is based on twelve months of the lunar cycle (full-moon-to-full-moon or new-moon-to-new-moon). The year length would be about eleven days shorter than the solar year. Therefore, the lunar year begins eleven days earlier in the following year, in relation to the solar year. This is why Gurpurb dates shifted by about eleven days from one year to the other in the Bikrami calendar.

Confusion is compounded when lunar dates are described in the Bikrami mode, which is a solar calendar. The word Sudi (the days following the rising moon) or Wadi (the days following Puranmashi, the full moon) are lunar dates and are independent of the solar calendar, though unfortunately both are linked in a complicated way to calculate dates of festivals. Astrologers rather than scientists calculate the dates. It would not be in the interest of astrologers, in the practice of their esoteric art, to be more explicit, to avoid closer rational scrutiny. Whenever readers see Sudi or Wadi added to a date, it is a lunar date. The solar dates do not have these additions.

An extra month is added every two or three years to keep the lunar year in step with the solar year. This month is called malmas, intercalary month. In years that have the added month there will be 384 or so days. This makes the Gurpurb dates occur about eighteen or nineteen days later when such a month is introduced.

Sikhs had historically followed the Bikrami Samat, one of several in the Hindu religion. The Bikrami calendar is the official calendar in Nepal. Besides the wide variation experienced in this calendar, there were also time shifts, so that the seasons lineated by Guru Nanak in the Barah Maha, the twelve months composition in the Granth, no longer synchronise with the weather experienced now because of the time shift over centuries.

Sikhs have attempted in the past to reform the calendar but have met with great resistance. A bizarre situation arose when Sikhs realised that in the year 1999, when Vaisakhi day would mark the tercentenary of the birth of the Khalsa, the birth date of Guru Gobind Singh himself would be entirely missing. Vaisakhi was always celebrated on 13 April in the solar calendar but the birthday of Guru Gobind Singh, in contrast, was celebrated according to the lunar calendar. The Gurpurb to celebrate the birthday of Guru Gobind Singh did not occur in the years 1991, 1993 and 1996. However, it occurred twice in 1992, 1995 and 1998. It was not supposed to occur in the year 1999, the year of the 300th anniversary of the creation of the Khalsa.

The Vaisakhi date for 1469, in the year of the birth of Guru Nanak, was 27 March; in 1899 it was 12 April and in 2100 it will be 15 April. Moreover, intercalary months are inauspicious in the Hindu calendar and no festival can take place in those months. This makes prediction of dates even more complex. The Panth recognised the idiocy of the situation and has hence finally agreed, although very reluctantly, to reform its calendar.

In 1999, a new solar Sikh calendar was introduced, called Nanakshahi, based on the Western calendar, and it was brought into broader use in 2004. The Nanakshahi calendar was readily accepted in Great Britain, as it fixed dates of Sikh festivals, which had had such variation in the past. Sikh historic days will no longer move about the calendar from year to year. Gurpurbs will now always take place on the same date, and will occur only once each calendar year.

However, Sikhs could not bring themselves to completely abandon the ancient calendar. A simple conversion to the Western calendar would have solved the problem in one reform, but they had to a strike a compromise to please, if not all Sikhs, then most of them. They did so by beginning their calendar in the year of the birth of Guru Nanak in 1469 in the month of Chet, which is the first month described in

Barah Maha Bani. The first day of the year in the Nanakshahi calendar is therefore 14 March. It was also agreed that the birthday of Guru Nanak should continue to be celebrated on Katik Puranmashi, the full moon, in the lunar calendar. Hola Mahalla and Sikh Divali will also continue to follow the lunar calendar.

Features of the Nanakshahi Calendar

- it is a solar calendar
- year one is the year of Guru Nanak's birth in 1469 and the year length is the same as the Western calendar (365 days 5 hours 48 minutes 45 seconds)
- it contains five months of 31 days followed by seven months of 30 days
- there is a leap year every four years in which the last month (Phagun) has an extra day

Otherwise, the Nanakshahi calendar is standardised with the Western calendar and will help Sikhs to arrange their dates related to Sikh history without having to refer to Jantris, Hindu manuals that are used to work out dates of festival. The new Nanakshahi calendar conforms to Gurbani compositions related to the seasons. Sankrantis, the first day of the month, will occur on the same dates in the year, every year. These days, called Sangrand, linked to the lunar calendar in the past with variable dates, will now have fixed dates for the first day of every month.

The days still celebrated according to the lunar calendar are called moveable and the three most important have been mentioned. Those that are celebrated in the Nanakshahi calendar are called fixed. The months in the Nanakshahi calendar are as follows:

Month	Number of days	Begins on (Sangrand)
Chet (March-April)	31 days	14 March (New Year's Day)
Vaisakh (April-May)	31 days	14 April
Jeth (May-June)	31 days	15 May
Harh (June-July)	31 days	15 June
Savan (July-August)	31 days	16 July
Bhadon (August-September)	30 days	16 August
Asu (September-October)	30 days	15 September
Katik (October-November)	30 days	15 October
Maghar (November-December)	30 days	14 November
Poh (December-January)	30 days	14 December
Magh (January-February)	30 days	13 January
Phagun* (February-March)	30/31 days	12 February

*Phagun: in a leap year the dates from 1 to 13 March will differ by one day from those of the same month in a non leap year.

The dates of the Gurpurbs in the Nanakshahi calendar are as follows:

Guru	Birthdate	Gurtagaddi (date of installation as Guru)	Jyoti Jot (date of death)
Nanak Dev*	30 Katik, 13 Nov (in 2008)		8 Asu, 22 December
Angad Dev	5 Vaisakh, 18 April	4 Asu, 18 Sept	3 Vaisakh, 16 Apr
Amar Das	9 Jeth, 23 May	3 Vaisakh, 16 April	2 Asu, 16 Sept
Ram Das	25 Asu, 9 October	2 Asu, 16 Sept	2 Asu, 16 Sept
Arjan Dev	19 Vaisakh, 2 May	2 Asu, 16 Sept	2 Harh, 16 June
Hargobind	21 Harh, 5 July	28 Jeth, 11 June	6 Chet, 19 March
Har Rai	19 Magh, 31 January	1 Chet, 14 March	6 Katik, 20 Oct
Har Krishan	8 Savan, 23 July	6 Katik, 20 October	3 Vaisakh, 16 Apr
Tegh Bahadur	5 Vaisakh, 18 April	3 Vaisakh, 6 April	11 Maghar, 24 Nov
Gobind Singh	23 Poh, 5 January	11 Maghar, 4 Nov	7 Katik, 21 Oct

*Although it is now accepted that historically Guru Nanak was born on 15 April, for traditional reasons the birthday Gurpurb is celebrated on Katik (October-November) Puranmashi, the day of the full moon in the month of Katik. This date varies from year to year. At present, it falls in November. The next generation will see the Gurpurb appearing sometimes twice a year or not appearing at all in the subsequent year. The day of Guru Nanak's birthday is also the day of his Gurtagaddi.

Other dates in the Sikh calendar are:

Event	Date
First Parkash Granth Sahib	17 Bhadon, 1 September
Gurtagaddi Guru Granth Sahib	6 Katik, 20 October
Vaisakhi Day	1 Vaisakh, 14 April
Hola Mahalla	9 Chet, 22 March (in 2008)
Bandi Chhor Divas (Sikh Divali)	14 Katik, 28 October

CHAPTER 7
Bioethics and Medical Care

Bioethics

Sikh faith is about compassion, love and justice. It is not a prescriptive religion. However, it will not under the guise of tolerance discard the values and standards of a decent society. Sikh faith reinforces personal discipline and behaviour, which are essential for a responsible society. It refuses to encourage personal lawlessness and irresponsible attitudes, which are rapidly destroying the claim of Western civilisation to be a civilised society. The Panth will not allow the destruction of all that made the Sikh faith great. We now live in a predominant culture with family breakdown leading to social disintegration, lowered educational standards and a criminal culture.

Sikhs take a duty-based rather than rights-based approach to ethical decision making. There is no body of written Sikh canon law to decide on these matters. There is no metaphysical dispute between the faith and its practice of bioethics. Precedence of practice based on the Granth and actions of the Gurus and their followers is woven into the Sikh way of life and is not separately codified. Sikh traditions affirm the importance of family, faith and culture within a spiritual dimension. Cultural and religious assumptions regarding human nature, purity, health and illness, life and death, intermingle in varying formats. Sikh beliefs are not ideological, as Sikhs will accept logical explanations and act flexibly. Nothing is pre-ordained or forbidden. The key to Sikh bioethics is the importance of individual decision making rather than a collective one. Sikhs accept that precedence is open to interpretation, and changes with the needs of the times.

Sikh bioethics is no different from those of a civil society. However, the Sikh faith, in common with other world religions, respects human life. Its approach to bioethics is prevention. It is important to appreciate the very strict disciplinary code on which the Sikh family is based. The absence, for example, of abortion for social reasons, teenage pregnancies, illegitimate births and sexual diseases (including Aids) are conspicuous by their absence among Sikhs in Britain.

Sikh bioethical values, in general, do not differ from their Western counterparts. Sikhs normally find no objection in following medical advice and usually see no contradictions with their faith, when it is in the best individual interest. The author, in a lifetime practice of medicine, has not come across any objections to the acceptance of blood donation, transplantation, artificial insemination, birth control or other modern medical practice that enhances human life.

Sikhs born in India, even educated ones, generally value the practice of traditional medicine, which is freely used in conjunction with Western medicine. They see no contraindication in this practice. Cultural beliefs about health, disease and treatment often differ significantly from Western medical practice. Sikhs somehow manage to reconcile their widely differing beliefs as to the causation of illness, and accept modern treatment without prejudice. A clue to the strength of rational beliefs is to be alert for the term nazar, evil eye, to suggest a more traditional view of medical care. There may be reservations about Western medicine. It does not mean a particular bar because of faith beliefs.

Sikh patients will expect the same level of care as other patients. Cultural and religious prejudices are few and should not be assumed, unless there is evidence for it. This is double jeopardy. Indeed, an attendant may do more harm and offend his or her patients and be accused of prejudice in approaching a patient from a pre-conceived notion of racial beliefs.

More importantly, there are likely to be differing dietary practices, to which attention must be paid. Sikhs do not eat beef, though some will accept chicken, fish and mutton. Sikhs tend not to eat pork, but practices vary. Nevertheless, vegetarianism is much more common, especially in women.

Ethical decisions for Sikhs are grounded in both religious beliefs and cultural values. In contrast to the contemporary secular approach to bioethics, which is predominantly rights-based, Sikh bioethics is primarily duty-based. Indeed, there is no word for 'rights' among Sikhs. Traditional teachings deal with the duties of individuals and families to maintain a lifestyle conducive to good physical and mental health.

The Sikh faith is a separate religion, yet nevertheless it shares ancient Indian cultural values that include ideas of fate and rebirth, and collective consciousness versus individualism. Although there are profound differences between the Hindu and Sikh religions, and even considerable diversity within them, the notion of fate and a belief in rebirth will be important for many Sikh patients as they make ethical decisions surrounding matters of life and death. However, Sikhs believe a person is able to, and indeed should, exercise free will and this, with the additions and deletions made through free choice in the current life, will influence the hereafter.

From this perspective, the moment of conception is the beginning of life from a practical point of view; life is sacred to Sikhs, as indeed it is to all religions. That is the sole basis on which medical procedures are considered. Abortion for social reasons is certainly unacceptable to Sikhs, but there will be no hesitation in saving a mother's life if an abortion will achieve that end. Sikhs will expect every effort to be made to save premature babies. Because of the emphasis on the sanctity of life and insistence on maximum medical intervention, the clinical and ethical approach may come into conflict with the wishes of the Sikh parents. On balance, Sikhs will accept advice on a healthy outcome.

Another difference between Sikh and Western cultures concerns the question of identity. Who is the ethical agent in decision making: the patient or the family? In Western society, a person is viewed as having autonomy in ethical decision making. With Sikhs, this is not always so – the person is not autonomous but is intimately integrated within the family. This requires a sensitive approach to matters such as informed consent, which include the patient's societal context. Again, even in Sikh faith individual consent must be the paramount consideration. It is a matter of great sensitivity; on the surface, tradition should be respected but underlying this is the sense that individual rights are the only ones that matter.

Purity is an important concept in Sikh culture. There are two terms for purity, 'shuud', the human body within nature in its perfect state, and 'suuch', physical purity, as in personal cleanliness. Sikhs do not consider, as the Hindu religion does, the discharges of one's body, during menstruation or at birth, to be impure. For Sikhs, childbirth is auspicious and the act of childbirth itself, involving the discharge of bodily fluids, does not render the mother impure. Even if some Sikhs harbour such cultural beliefs, the faith utterly rejects these notions and certainly forbids rituals relating to the purification of the mother or the baby.

Sikhs born in Western countries accept Western ethical values in health care regarding issues such as abortion, organ donation and post mortems. Yet Sikh notions with respect to life and death may pose problems to recent immigrants, particularly older people, who apply the duty-based approach of their own tradition when considering treatment options.

It is important to be aware of these differences among Sikhs. Much more misunderstanding arises when set beliefs are attributed to a community when its members are open-minded and expect options to be put before them.

It is important to involve the family, but it is essential to ensure that the wishes of the individual are respected and are paramount, as a family may put pressure on a vulnerable member, a young daughter-in-law for example, to act in a traditional way. Confidentiality is as important to Sikhs as to Western people, sometimes more so, as

Sikhs may not wish to discuss certain illnesses with others, even with close relatives.

In theory the complexity of the religious and cultural traditions of Sikhs and the diversity of beliefs and practices within the same community may overwhelm practitioners of Western medicine. Individual patients' reactions to a particular clinical situation could be influenced by a number of factors, including how recently they or their families arrived in the West, their level of education, if their roots are rural or urban, their socioeconomic status, and their religious stance.

In practice, provided the practitioners hold an open mind, do not believe in stereotypical notions and are willing to discuss medical management with their patients, they will not find Sikhs to be any different from their other patients, however different their thinking is regarding the same problem.

Patients may be able to explain the traditional herbal medicines, but they may not be familiar with uncommon metals and other organic chemicals contained in them. Sikhs suffering from chronic conditions are more likely to accept traditional medicine, but will not abandon Western prescribed treatment. The adverse effects of the combination of traditional treatment with Western medicine are not uncommon, and should be looked for in unusual circumstances. Patients will readily admit to such orthodox treatment if questioned. It may be prudent in the treatment of a chronic or unexpected illness to investigate this aspect of culture. Patients should always be asked to bring in all medicines, including traditional ones, used at home. Traditional treatment should always be treated as a neutral subject. No amount of chastisement will deter patients who have a strong belief in it.

Medical and Nursing Care

An essential aspect of health care is the provider's role in understanding the concerns of patients and their families, and their transmitting these concerns to all those involved in their care. It is useful to establish a relationship with a local Gurdwara for advice and assistance.

New immigrant Sikhs may have language problems. Great caution needs to be exercised in the use of interpreters. If trained interpreters are not available, it is preferable to ask a relative to accompany a patient who does not speak English. This usually happens in practice, as a friend or relative will accompany a patient anyway. Again, balance must be struck in confidentiality and convenience of communication. The attendant must decide the options in each case and must not assume a standard approach.

The Sikh faith does not ban treatment provided by a practitioner of the opposite sex, though a request for a practitioner of the same sex for elderly men and women should be respected, especially for urological, rectal and gynaecological examinations. Sikh women may insist on covering their bodies with more than a hospital gown and this should be allowed. It is important to avoid unnecessary touching.

During times of illness, Sikhs pray to seek spiritual solace. Meditation and recitation of prayers is their way of doing this. Sikh patients consider illness to be the will of God, and believe that God is merciful and benevolent, but one has to make an effort too to get well, which includes acceptance of medical treatment. Do not interrupt a praying patient without consent. A prayer room for Sikhs should be quiet, clean and carpeted. It need contain no religious symbols. An inter-religious space, free of religious artefacts, is acceptable.

Practices subject to discussion include maintaining a terminal patient on artificial life support for a prolonged period in a vegetative state. Abortion is not advised, except for medical reasons. Sikhs do not readily accept an autopsy, but there is no religious bar to it.

The most important issue for practising Sikhs is respect for their symbols of faith. The dress code of the Sikh faith is unique, and it is sacrosanct to them at all times. Great sensitivity is required in dealing with it. Even infants, toddlers and children keep their hair uncut and wear a Kara. No attempt must be made to remove these, without absolute permission. If necessary, a Kara can be covered with an adhesive tape to provide insulation.

A Pagri must not be touched or removed without permission. If it is desirable to do so, Sikh patients may wish to keep their head covered with a small turban, a scarf or, if acceptable, a surgical cap. If it is necessary to remove the Pagri, the family should be given responsibility for it. The patient may accept that it be put together with his personal belongings. If it is essential to remove hair, then full and agreed consent must be sought prior to removing it from any part of the patient's body. If there is access to a Sikh religious authority, advice should be automatically sought. Such support is invaluable.

Cleanliness is part of the Sikh way of life. Daily bathing and personal hygiene care should be provided, unless advised otherwise for a medical reason. Families will usually take care of hair washing, combing, and tying into a knot for men. Relatives will take similar care for the women. Help may be offered. Although body discharges do not have a connotation of impurity, this may be so for elderly women.

Family and friends regard it as a duty to visit Sikh patients in hospitals, but they will accept hospital rules.

Sikhs, especially women, tend to be vegetarians, but vegetarian or non-vegetarian meals are individual preferences. Sikhs must not be given Halal food, especially animal products. Meat prepared according to Western practice is acceptable to Sikhs. The eating of eggs varies among vegetarians. Sikhs do not observe fasting for religious reasons.

Sikhs accept general terminal care. Relatives and family will recite prayers before and after the last moments. The body should be covered with clean white linen. The five Ks must remain with the body. Sikhs cremate their dead (except foetuses or small children) and this is carried out expeditiously, though no time limit is set for this purpose. Often, families wait for the arrival of relatives from other countries. The family will follow Sikh traditions for preparing the body in a funeral parlour for its final journey.

PART TWO
The Lives of the Gurus

CHAPTER 8
Guru Nanak Dev, the First Guru (1469-1539): Founder of the Sikh Faith

Guru Nanak Dev was born to a Hindu family on 15 April 1469 in Nankana Sahib in the Sheikhupura district, near Lahore, now Pakistan. Mehta Kalu, his father, was a land agent in the employment of a local Muslim property owner; his mother was Mata Tripta and Bibi Nanki, an only, older, sister. At the age of six, Guru Nanak was sent to the village school to learn reading, writing and arithmetic. A Muslim teacher then schooled him in the study of Persian, the language of the Muslim rulers. Guru Nanak also studied Sanskrit, the sacred language of Hindu scriptures. He was a gifted and an inquisitive child who learned quickly and often asked searching questions of his teachers.

At age thirteen, it was time for Guru Nanak to be invested with the sacred thread according to the Hindu custom. At the ceremony attended by family and friends, Guru Nanak declined to accept the sacred cotton thread as an empty and foolish ritual. Guru Nanak said,

'Let mercy be the cotton, contentment the thread
Continence the knot and truth the twist
O priest! If you have such a thread, do give it to me
It will not wear out, nor be soiled, nor burnt, nor lost
Says Nanak, blessed are those who go about wearing
such a thread.'

Asked, since he had declined to wear the thread, whether he would accept Islam instead, Guru Nanak replied,

'Let God's grace be the mosque and devotion the prayer mat
Let the Qur'an be the good conduct.
Let modesty be compassion, good manners fasting
You should be a Muslim the like of this
Let good deeds be your Kaaba and truth be your mentor

Your Kalma be your creed and prayer
God would then vindicate your honour.'

As a young man, herding the family cattle, Guru Nanak spent long hours absorbed in meditation and in religious discussions with Hindu holy men who lived in the forest near the village. He became acquainted with the teachings of Indian philosophers and reformers. He developed a deep understanding of the Hindu scriptures as well as those of the Muslims. He was well versed in Persian and Sanskrit as is shown by his use of these languages in his compositions.

His parents perceived a lack of interest in work. Thinking that if bound in marriage Guru Nanak would start taking an interest in worldly affairs, a suitable match was found and in 1487, at age eighteen, he was married to Sulakhni, daughter of Moolchand, a trader. They had two sons, Sri Chand born in 1491 and Lakshmi Das, born in 1496. Guru Nanak pronounced that marriage was part of his sacred duty and did not conflict with spiritual pursuits.

Jai Ram, the husband of his sister Nanki, obtained employment for him in Sultanpur, a neighbouring district, as a supervisor of the government granary. Guru Nanak moved to Sultanpur with his family and an old Muslim childhood friend, Mardana, a rabab (rebec, a bowed string musical instrument) player. Guru Nanak worked during the day, but early in the mornings and in the evenings he spent long hours in meditation and singing Shabads, devotional works he composed himself, accompanied by Mardana on the rabab. These sessions became popular with local villagers, who would gather in large numbers to listen to Guru Nanak.

Early one morning, in 1496, when he was twenty-seven years of age, Guru Nanak Dev went as usual to the river to bathe and meditate. He had a vision while submerged in the water. Guru Nanak lost track of time but when he emerged he said that he had been in communion with God. God had spoken to him in words now enshrined in the Mool Mantar, creed of Sikh faith, the prayer at the beginning of Guru Granth. The words were,

'There is but One God, His name is Truth
He is the Creator, He fears none, and He is without hate
He never dies, He is beyond the cycle of birth and death
He is self-illuminated; He is realised by the kindness of
the true Guru
He was True in the beginning, He was True when the
ages commenced
And has ever been True, He is also True now.'

The Mool Mantar was his message and lifelong mission to preach to others.

Guru Nanak abandoned his worldly pursuits to follow the path of truth. Devotees asked him if he was a Muslim or a Hindu. Guru Nanak replied,

'I now know there is no Hindu, there is no Muslim
We are all one with God
God does not recognise caste, rituals, idol worship
And beliefs that have no virtuous content.'

The next stage of his life began, despite the hazards of travel in mediaeval times, with three (four, as some claim) long Udasis, journeys, which started in 1496 and lasted twenty-five years. Guru Nanak travelled across India and then crossed oceans to go to Sri Lanka, the Middle East and Iran. From the latter journey, he returned via Afghanistan and Nepal. He discoursed with scholars, Buddhists, Hindus, Jains and Muslims, in their holy places.

Accompanied by his companion Mardana for company, Guru Nanak conveyed his message to the people in Shabads he composed himself. Guru Nanak chose music to preach his message as then the devotees who came to listen to him easily understood it. He would stay in one place long enough to know the people and learn their language. He would then use the local language to convey the message of his Shabads to the people.

Guru Nanak first journeyed east and southward. This journey lasted a decade in which he visited the Hindu and Muslim pilgrimage centres, especially the shrines along the river Ganges. He then continued his journey to Bengal and Assam, and then most probably ended his journey in Sri Lanka before retracing his steps back to the Punjab, his home. On his second journey, he travelled north and visited the Kashmir valley, the Himalayan ranges further north and then Tibet. Guru Nanak mentions Simar Parbat in the Kailash Mountains in one of his Shabads.

It was on his return from the second journey that he visited Punja Sahib, now in Pakistan. Punja Sahib is one of the most sacred Sikh shrines. It is claimed that a palm print etched in the face of a rock (Punj means five, a hand) is that of Guru Nanak, who had stopped it when an angry holy man rolled it towards him from a hill. A spring has gushed water at the bottom of the rock since the times of Guru Nanak. The third journey was west to the Middle Eastern countries of Arabia, Iraq, Iran and Afghanistan. He returned after crossing the Khyber Pass into Peshawar and back to the Punjab.

After the completion of his second journey, he founded a settlement named Kartarpur at a beautiful spot on the Western banks of the Ravi river. Guru Nanak would one day settle down here when his missionary journeys were over. It was also here that he would meet his successor, the second Guru, and Baba Buddha, the most revered of the devotees of Guru Nanak. Baba Buddha would go on to serve the next four Gurus. Guru Nanak lived at Kartarpur for many years. His fame had spread everywhere. A constant stream of seekers of spiritual knowledge visited Kartarpur.

It was at Kartarpur that Guru Nanak organised the Shabads into an orderly compendium. The Gurmukhi script in which the Bani were recorded was developed by him at Kartarpur, the task later completed by Angad, the second Guru. Sikhs regard Gurmukhi as their holy script bequeathed to them first by Guru Nanak and then Guru Angad.

Wherever he travelled, Guru Nanak set up Gurdwara, many of which have survived the past 500 years. The descendants of those devotees from the times of Guru Nanak, Muslim and Hindu, still gather and recite the Shabads of Guru Nanak at these places. Guru Nanak chose to live with people of the lowest castes, an unheard of step in the then prevailing, rigid Hindu caste system with its notions of untouchability and pollution. He practised what he preached.

The offerings he received were first distributed among the poor and the rest given to his hosts to feed devotees so that all would sit and eat together. This institution, Langar, was a nucleus for establishing equality and sharing with others who were less fortunate than they were. The institution of Langar established by Guru Nanak is today at the heart of Sikh faith.

It is said that on one journey he stayed in the home of a low caste artisan, Bhai Lalo, instead of accepting the invitation of a high caste landowner, Malik Bhago. This angered the rich man, who asked Guru Nanak why he had scorned the comfort of his place to stay at the abode of a poor man.

Guru Nanak asked for food to be brought from both houses. Guru Nanak squeezed in one hand the coarse bread from Lalo's hut and in the other the fancy food from Bhago's house. Milk gushed forth from the loaf and blood from the delicacies of Bhago. Malik Bhago was put to shame that his riches had been amassed by exploiting the poor, while what Lalo offered was the milk of honest work.

This prescription for honest living and the condemnation of exploitation, coupled with the Guru's dictum that 'Riches cannot be gathered without sin and evil means', have since the very beginning been the founding moral tenet of the Sikh faith.

Guru Nanak told his devotees not to expect rewards for their meditation. A story is told that while he was resting at a town devotees would come every day to listen to Guru Nanak preach. One of them while on the way to see the Guru came across a street woman and was allured by her. He would leave home on the pretext of going to see the Guru but instead visited the woman.

A few days later, a thorn pricked a devotee who came every day to pay homage to the Guru while his neighbour, who instead visited the woman, found a gold coin in the street. The incident bewildered the Guru's devotee. He mentioned it in the morning prayer meeting. Guru Nanak said,

'Your friend was destined to come across a treasure but due to his evil ways, it has been reduced to a single coin, while you were to have been impaled with a stake, but have been let off with the mere prick of a thorn.'

Guru Nanak was preaching that meditation was God's way. It was not for gratification or reward.

A story illustrates how Guru Nanak preached his message of honest living, free of cant and hypocrisy, with ordinary examples of daily life. When the Guru visited Kurukshetra in Haryana, India, a holy fair was in progress to celebrate the solar eclipse. On his arrival, Guru Nanak asked Mardana to pretend to prepare and cook animal flesh. Upon seeing these preparations, an angry crowd gathered to attack the Guru for the sacrilege. Guru Nanak responded,

'Only fools argue whether to eat meat or not. They do not understand truth nor do they meditate on it. Who can define what is meat and what is a plant? Who knows where the sin lies, in eating one or the other?'

At Hardwar, a place of Hindu pilgrimage, Guru Nanak found people throwing water from the Ganges upstream towards the sun as oblations to their ancestors. Guru Nanak started throwing water downriver towards the west, in the direction of his fields in Punjab. When ridiculed about his folly, he replied,

'If Ganges water will reach your ancestors in heaven, why should the water I throw not reach my fields in the Punjab, which are at a far shorter distance?'

Guru Nanak insisted that peace in life is not achieved by renunciation of this world. God has sent people to this earth with a purpose and the purpose was not to abandon one's duties. Guru Nanak visited Gorakhmata where he discussed the true meaning of asceticism with yogis,

'Asceticism does not lie in ascetic robes, in a walking staff, or in the ashes
Asceticism does not lie in the earrings, in the shaven head, or blowing a conch
Asceticism lies in remaining pure amidst the impurities of life.'

And

'Asceticism does not lie in mere words
An ascetic is one who treats everyone alike
Asceticism does not lie in visiting burial places
It lies not in wandering about or in bathing at places of pilgrimage
Asceticism is to remain pure amidst the impurities of life'.

On his second journey, Guru Nanak travelled as far north as Tibet. Before he did so, he visited Sheikh Ibrahim, the Muslim successor of Baba Farid, the great Sufi dervish of the twelfth century and founder of poetry in Punjabi. When asked by Ibrahim which of the two religions was the true way to attain God, Guru Nanak replied,

'If there is one God, then there is only His way to attain Him, not another
One must follow that way and reject the other
Worship not him who is born only to die
But Him who is eternal and is the master of our universe.'

On his third and longest journey, Guru Nanak visited the Arabian countries of the Middle East. These included stoppages at Medina, the holy Muslim city, and Baghdad, the learned capital of Islam in Iraq.

It is recorded that in Baghdad, Muslim scholars told Guru Nanak that the heavens and earth were composed of seven upper and as many lower regions. Guru Nanak replied,

'There are worlds and more worlds below them
And there are a hundred thousand skies over them
No one has been able to find the limits and boundaries of God
If there is any account of God, then the mortal being can attempt to it
But God's account will not finish and the mortal dies
while still writing
Nanak says, God Himself alone knows His own self.'

In 1916, a tablet with the following inscription was uncovered in Baghdad, 'In memory of the holy man, Baba Nanak, king of holy men. This monument has been raised anew with the help of the seven pious men.' The date on the tablet, 927 Hijri, corresponds to AD 1520-1521.

On his return and final journey home, Guru Nanak stopped at Saidpur in Western Punjab, during the invasion of Babar, the first Mughal emperor of India. On seeing the massacre of the population by the invaders, Mardana asked Guru Nanak why so many innocent people were put to death. Guru Nanak told Mardana to wait under a banyan tree and after a while he would return to answer his question. While sitting under the tree, Mardana was bitten by an ant. In anger, Mardana killed as many ants as he could with his feet. Guru Nanak said to him,

'You know now, Mardana, why do the innocents suffer along with the guilty?'

The soldiers of Babar took both Guru Nanak and Mardana prisoners. While in jail, Guru Nanak composed a Shabad about the senseless slaughter of the innocents by the Mughal invaders. It is a most heart-rending description of the terrible sufferings people had to endure at the hand of the Mughal tyrants. Guru Nanak was later set free after having had to perform many unpleasant tasks on the orders of the soldiers.

This was Guru Nanak's last journey. After having spent a lifetime travelling and setting up Gurdwara, Guru Nanak returned home to the Punjab. He settled down at Kartarpur with his family. Guru Nanak then resumed the life of a peasant farmer. Devotees from all over the land came to visit and even settle in Kartarpur to worship in his company. The devotees became known as the Sikhs, the learners.

His message, simple, but revolutionary for his times, was a belief in equality and a refusal to accept distinctions based on birthright, religion or sex. Guru Nanak made Langar a part of Sikh faith. Here all were required to sit together and share a common meal, whether they were kings or beggars.

Guru Nanak composed most of his Bani, writings, in Kartarpur. The Shabads dealt with spirituality and provided his observations and responses to the situations and incidents that he came across in his travels and daily living.

Guru Nanak never asked his devotees to change their religion. He only wanted them to reflect on what he preached. His only message was to meditate on the true name. Guru Nanak wished to impart his message of meditation on the name of God, true and simple living and care of the poor. The devotees on return to their villages set up their own Gurdwara for their gatherings, worship and provision of Langar for the poor. Thus arose the institution of Gurdwara and now wherever there are Sikhs one finds a Gurdwara.

Guru Nanak asked devotees not to shirk family life. There was no priest or hermit in his faith to be intermediaries between God and his disciples. Life was not a burden but a privilege. The family was the medium of spiritual training and expression.

Guru Nanak said the home of each Sikh was a Gurdwara too. All Sikhs were brothers and God was their father. Sikhs do not practise false rituals and believe in superstition. That was the Sikh way of life.

Bhai Gurdas, the scribe of Guru Granth Sahib, was born twelve years after the demise of Guru Nanak. Being a near contemporary of Guru Nanak, his writings are accepted as a reliable record of the times. He writes that Guru Nanak lived the eighteen final years of his life in Kartarpur Sahib.

While working the fields one day in 1532, Guru Nanak was approached by a devotee who said, 'I am Lehna'. Lehna means a creditor. Guru Nanak looked at him and replied,

'So you have arrived, Lehna. I have been waiting for you all these days. I must pay your debt.'

Lehna became the constant and ardent companion of Guru Nanak. Lehna's devotion to Guru Nanak was absolute. When he was not working in the fields with Guru Nanak, he would devote his time to attending to the needs of the Guru.

Guru Nanak put Lehna's devotion to many tests. Once, accompanied by Lehna and his two sons, Guru Nanak came across what looked like a corpse covered with a sheet. Turning to his companions Guru Nanak asked,

'Who would eat the flesh of this corpse?'

His sons, thinking that their father was not in his senses, quickly departed from the scene. But Lehna removed the cover. He found that it was filled with fruit and nuts, instead of a dead body. Thus Guru Nanak tested his successor in this and many other tests of faith. Guru Nanak said,

'Lehna, you were blessed with the sacred food because you could share it with others. If people use the wealth bestowed on them by God for themselves alone or for hoarding it, it is like a corpse. However, if they share it with others, it becomes sacred. You have known the secret. You are my image.'

Guru Nanak then blessed Lehna with his ang, hand, and gave him a new name, Angad, saying,

'You are a part of me.'

Guru Nanak bestowed his Pothis – books of his collected compositions – on Angad.

Knowing his end was near, Guru Nanak gathered his followers for prayer and invited Angad to occupy the seat of the Guru. Thus, Guru Angad was ordained as the successor to Guru Nanak. Guru Nana gave this last message to his Sikhs,

'I know for certain this world must perish, and the end must come
I know this and nothing else
Neither spouse, nor son, neither father, nor brothers shall help
I must go alone in the end; none can undo what is my fate
I have spent days and nights in vanity
But, says Nanak, I am yours [God's], the dust of the feet of your
servants.'

Guru Nanak then put himself to rest. Guru Angad covered him with a white sheet. On 22 December 1539, at the age of seventy years, Guru Nanak gave up his earthly abode.

It is said that after his death Muslims wanted to bury him but Hindu devotees insisted on disposing of his remains by fire instead. When the sheet was lifted, the remains of Guru Nanak were not there. Devotees of both religions divided the white shroud and disposed of it according to the rites of their respective faiths.

In his own lifetime, Guru Nanak determined the direction of his faith and laid the foundation of Sikh institutions, which became the Sikh way of life. A moral life was the sole human spiritual recognition and quest. Guru Nanak declared that God was at one with the affairs of man. We live in this God's world. There was no other world to aspire to. This is the way Sikhs must live their life.

CHAPTER 9
Time of Consolidation:
Angad Dev, the Second Guru (1504-1552),
Amar Das, the Third Guru (1479-1574) and
Ram Das, the Fourth Guru (1534-1581)

The second, third and fourth Gurus were of humble origin. They led their lives by example rather than command. So great was their humility that they completely submerged themselves in Guru Nanak and his Sangat, congregation. It is not surprising that Sikhs regard their Gurus as the embodiment of the spirit of Guru Nanak. The Gurus had no wish to construct new precepts or propound afresh upon good or evil in the world. The Gurus followed the path of Guru Nanak and emulated the life he lived.

The Gurus gave meaning to the word that Sikh faith was a practical religion. It was a way of life. It is the way a Gursikh, Sikh devotee, follows. It was reserved for Guru Nanak's successors to build upon his foundation. That is how the Gurus saw their mission.

Being respectively long time companions of their predecessor Gurus, they absorbed Guru Nanak's Gurbani in turn and then themselves became composers of Gurbani. We owe to these three Gurus for giving us insight into Guru Nanak's teachings.

The Gurus consolidated the institutions of Sikh faith, adding seamlessly to the work of their predecessors. To them could be applied the epitaph, one jyoti, soul, three beings. Chroniclers claim that we can identify the way the saplings of the faith grew with the three Gurus into a rich foliage to lend a distinct identity to Sikh faith.

The period of their Guruship was a crucial one. The Sikh faith in its infancy had to face two dangers. The first one they faced is still very much alive today. It was the danger that the Hindu religion would swallow the newly founded Sikh faith as it had done to others that emerged in the past in India. The Sikh faith had to establish its own identity.

The second danger was to confront Sikhs throughout the times of the Gurus. Indigenous Muslims had ruled Punjab in Guru Nanak's early life. Then ferocious Mughals invaded India during the latter part of his life. Indeed, Guru Nanak was made a prisoner while passing through a town during the invasion. Guru Nanak saw the difficult times his people faced and tried to comfort them that all tyrannies perish in the end. The Sikh faith would survive. All Sikh Gurus had to contend with the Mughal rule of Punjab. The Mughal rulers brought up in the harsh life of the central Asian steppes never completely reconciled themselves to the people of India, product of an ancient and gentler culture. The Gurus gave the rulers no cause for concern but the Mughal rulers refused to accept the founding of a new faith. Sikh faith was to be tested by the Mughals to its limits but the faith prevailed to flourish today all over the world, while Moguls, the mighty rulers, are no more.

Guru compositions strengthened the bonds between the faith and its followers. Sikhs would forever seek communion with their Gurus through their writings in the Granth. Towards the end of the time of the three Gurus, the Sikh faith had established itself as a distinct system of thought. The Gurus had firmly implanted in Sikh liturgy institutions of Langar, Sangat and Shabad Kirtan. The fellowship of the Sikh Panth, which is the essence of Sikh social and moral life, had taken root.

The Gurus felt the need to give structure to Sikh faith and established a network of faith centres. They codified the Sikh identity, and reinforced the integrity of the Sikh faith founded by Guru Nanak.

Guru Angad (1504-1552)

Guru Angad (Bhai Lehna) was born on 18 April 1504. Bhai Lehna married Mata Khivi in January 1520 and had two sons and two daughters. The family were devout Hindus. Bhai Lehna worked as a small trader. After the marauding Mughal army ransacked his ancestral village, the family settled in Khadur village beside the Beas river, in Tarn Taran, a small town near Amritsar City.

Bhai Lehna had on occasion heard Shabads at religious gatherings. He was enchanted with them. He became a disciple of the Sikh faith, dedicated himself to Guru Nanak and came to live at Kartarpur. He spent seven years in the service of Guru Nanak and became his close companion and carer. Guru Nanak tested his devotions in many ways. He found in him the embodiment of obedience and service. Guru Nanak installed Bhai Lehna the second Sikh Guru on 18 September 1539. He gave him a new name, Angad. After the death of Guru Nanak on 22 December 1539, Guru Angad left Kartarpur to set up his ministry in his home village of Khadur.

Guru Nanak did not follow the Hindu convention of recording his verses in Sanskrit. He composed them in several dialects of the ordinary people. He had begun to experiment with Punjabi to construct a new alphabet. Guru Angad then standardised the script and named it Gurmukhi. Now Sikhs had their own written language. It was an important step to reinforce the identity of the Sikhs as a faith separate from both the Hindus and the Muslims.

Guru Angad wrote sixty-three Saloks, which are included in Guru Granth. He made the practice of Langar a formal part of Sikh ritual and gave it the name Guru Ka Langar, Guru's Langar.

Guru Angad revisited many places Guru Nanak had travelled to in Punjab to renew the faith. He established new Sangats to further strengthen the base of Sikh faith.

Guru Angad followed the example of Guru Nanak and nominated Amar Das, a pious Sikh, his successor. He presented the books of Gurbani Pothis to Guru Amar Das.

Guru Angad lived an austere life, devoid of show and ostentation. His Guruship of thirteen years experienced turbulent times but he guided the Sikh Panth with care and dedication. His humility should not obscure the firm foundation he set down for continuing Guru

Nanak's mission. The Sikh faith was greatly strengthened during his time. Guru Angad died at the age of forty-seven in April 1552.

Guru Amar Das (1479-1574)

Guru Amar Das, the third successor to the Guruship, was born in 1479. He was married to Mansa Devi at the age twenty-four. They had two sons and two daughters.

Amar Das became a companion of Guru Angad at the older age of sixty-two years, but he showed utter devotion to his Guru, taking care of his every need. He would get up early in the morning and walk to the river to bring water for the ablutions of Guru Angad. One stormy night, Amar Das fell into a pit and badly injured one of his legs. He held on to the water, not letting even a drop spill out. When Guru Angad came to know of the incident from the villagers, he felt that, with this and many other acts of service, Amar Das had demonstrated his devotion, the qualities required to lead the Sikh faith. Guru Angad announced the ascension of Amar Das to the Guruship in 1552. Guru Amar Das moved his ministry to his home village of Goindwal, which he had already established as a new village on the instruction of Guru Angad.

If Guru Angad was a consolidator, then Guru Amar Das was a social reformer, organiser and thinker. Guru Nanak and then Guru Angad had established many Sangats in their travels. The Sangats were scattered and lacked links with the Gurus. Guru Amar Das set up an organisation to develop cohesiveness and continuity. He divided the Sikh faith into fifty-two spiritual domains – Manjis – extending from Kabul in Afghanistan to Bengal in the East. A pious Sikh was placed in charge of each Manji, seat of authority. Its occupiers were called Manjidar. The Manjis provided a regular link to the Gurus. Guru Amar Das held two gatherings of the Sikhs a year on Divali and Vaisakhi days in Amritsar, which have continued to this day.

Guru Amar Das emphasised, like his predecessors, the importance of Langar to Sikhs. The Guru would not worship with anyone who would not first eat in Langar in the company of the Sangat. The practice emphasised the faith's commitment to a casteless society. People of all castes prepared the food. To expect people of high caste to share food was to break customs set in stone for thousands of years. This is an example of how the Gurus made changes to society. There was no direct pressure or threats. This was a courageous concept to introduce in a caste-ridden society. Charity also became an essential part of the Sikh faith.

Guru Amar Das prescribed simple ceremonies to mark birth, marriage and death, free of superstition and cant. Priests were no longer required to conduct these events. Guruji paid attention to the place of women in society. He strengthened equality for women by appointing some women as his Manjidars. Guruji condemned sati, the self-immolation of widows on their husbands' funeral pyres. He encouraged widows to remarry. He forbade the wearing of veils by Sikh women. He also preached against purdah. The acceptance of equality between men and women was another mark of distinctiveness from the Hindu and Muslim faiths.

Guru Amar Das composed hymns of vivid spiritual insight. Part of Anand Sahib, the Song of Bliss, is recited at the end of all Sikh ceremonies. It is an exposition of gurmat sahaj marg, the path of equipoise, of joy at finding the true way. Meditation, altruism and supplication are ways to Grace. Grace banishes sorrow and fear of death. Inner bliss is achieved. A person who practises these virtues is called a Gursikh. Gursikhs feel the presence of God within them and without at all times.

Guru Amar Das composed 874 Shabads in seven Raags, musical modes, nine of which were new musical measures. His compositions reiterate the faith's opposition to the prejudices of caste. Guru Amar Das then collected the compositions of the first two Gurus and his own in the form of a hymnody, the first step to the compilation of the Granth by Arjan Dev, the fifth Guru.

He died at the age of ninety-five on 16 September 1574. His Guruship had lasted twenty-two years.

Guru Ram Das (1534-1581)

Bhai Jetha, born in 1534, was a street vendor. He lost his parents at the age of seven, and was brought up by his grandmother. He was married to Bibi Bhani, the younger daughter of Guru Amar Das, in 1553. They had three children, all sons. He was a companion of Guru Amar Das for twenty-one years from 1553 to 1574. He was nominated to the Guruship in 1574. He submerged himself with his Guru, Sangat and missionary work for the rest of his life.

Guru Ram Das introduced Masands, representatives, to replace the Manji system, with greater responsibility in a rapidly growing faith. The Masands supervised the Sikh Sangat and Gurdwara in matters concerning Sikh faith. They preached the Sikh faith and collected donations for the upkeep of the faith and for the poor.

Guru Ram Das also established rules for the mode of worship for Sikhs. The rules were the basis of the framework of the Rahet Maryada for the Sikhs of the future.

Guru Ram Das was a poet of great distinction. He introduced eleven new Raags, musical modes. The Bani of Guru Ram Das reflect his immense understanding of Indian poetics and prosody. He composed Lavan, the marriage ceremony of the Sikhs. He introduced folk lyrical genre in Gurbani, which received spiritual recognition in the Granth. Ghorian, the Shabad sung before marriage Lavan, is a great favourite of the Sikhs.

Guru Ram Das established the new missionary centre of Ram Das Pur in 1577 and laid the foundation of Amrit Sarovar, which means pool of nectar. Arjan Dev, the next Guru, was to use it as the nucleus of development of Amritsar, the most important place of worship for Sikhs. The fourth Guruship lasted seven years from 1574 to 1581. Guru Amar Das died in 1581 after bestowing the fifth Guruship on his youngest son, Arjan Dev.

CHAPTER 10
Arjan Dev, the Fifth Guru (1563-1606):
First Guru Martyr

Arjan Dev was the third and youngest son of Guru Ram Das. He was born on 2 May 1563. In 1579, Arjan Dev married Mata Ganga Devi and their only child, a son, Hargobind, was born to them in 1595. Arjan Dev was installed Guru at the age of eighteen years. His ministry lasted twenty-five years.

Guru Arjan Dev settled in Ram Das Pur (later Amritsar) to complete the building works started there by his father. He first finished the construction of the Amrit Sarovar, and then laid the foundation stone of the Harmandir shrine (Golden Temple) in the middle of the Amrit Sarovar. To help raise money for these monumental projects, the Guru asked Sikhs to donate daswandh, a tenth of their earnings, to their Masands who in turn brought it to the Guru. The money was used for the purchase of materials and the upkeep of his devotees who gave free labour. The shrine was completed in 1591. A new town, Amritsar, city of nectar, grew up around the shrine. Amritsar is now the holiest city of the Sikhs.

The construction of the original simple brick and mortar lined building of the Harmandir was to evolve over the centuries to the present world-renowned architectural jewel. Generations of Sikhs lavished their wealth and labour on it. However, Guru Arjan Dev had stated that the Harmandir was for spiritual worship and not to be admired just for the beauty of its construction. The shrine was to have no images, idols or statutes within it for worship. The focus was the Granth and the mode of worship was the recitation and singing of Gurbani from it.

This remains today the purpose of the shrine. The Harmandir is a magnificent monument to the faith, but worship at all hours of the day and night holds primacy of its use. Sikhs can now hear its services all over the world thanks to modern technology.

Harmandir Sahib is not a lofty, towering structure, as other religious monuments tend to be. In old pictures, one can readily see towers of other religious shrines rising above the Harmandir on all sides. The shrine is small in scale and design and the plinth on which it is built is lower than the surrounding land. The edifice combines taste and beauty without extravagance. It has four doors, one on each side, a sign of welcome to all people who enter it. Guru Arjan Dev stated,

'My faith is for the people of all castes and creeds from whichever direction they come and to whichever direction they bow.'

The symmetric scale of the shrine is visible from all sides without having to look upwards or having to arch one's neck around it to catch its glory. The whole is viewed at a glance. The perfect symmetry between the Sarovar and the Harmandir, the latter reflected in its gentle waves from whichever point you look at it, induces a mood of serenity and calm. Those who visit it once return to it repeatedly, drawn by its mystic allure.

Guru Arjan Dev next undertook, like his predecessors, missionary tours of the Punjab. He set up many Sangats and strengthened the Masand system by new appointments. Guruji emphasised their role as his representatives within their jurisdiction and their responsibility for welcoming people to the Sikh faith. Their collective offerings provided a regular flow of income for the development of new townships and projects of public welfare like water, roads, rest houses, supply of food in scarcity areas and the opening of new Gurdwara. Guru Arjan Dev also built a leprosarium to care for victims of the disease.

Guru Arjan Dev attended to the spiritual needs of the large numbers of Sikhs who came to see him daily. He loved to perform Kirtan at which he sang his own compositions and the Shabads of other Gurus.

The most important act of this Guru was the compilation of Guru Granth with Bhai Gurdas, a learned Sikh companion, as its scribe. In it, he included the compositions of the first four Gurus and his own

Shabads. Guru Arjan Dev also included compositions of Hindu Bhagats and Muslim Sants, which had been recorded by Guru Nanak. Guru Arjan Dev added verses of Bhatts, bards, who were the Guru minstrels. Guru Arjan Dev organised the sacred compositions under a musical notation system of which Raag was the centrepiece.

Guruji then added an epilogue, Mundawani, his seal upon the Granth. Apart from its universal spiritual message, it speaks out against injustice and the cruelty of man to others. The scriptures were not just a collection of fine writings and a display of erudition of the times, but they emphasised above all the message that we should honour all those who show compassion for their fellow beings, regardless of religious persuasion.

The Sikhs revere the Granth because it contains the teachings of their Gurus. It is a compendium of divine wisdom and meditation. While the Gurus claimed no kinship to God, Gurbani is divine revelation.

Guru Granth took three years to complete. It was named the Pothi. The more popular name was Adi Granth, the prime Granth. After Gobind Singh, the tenth Guru, bestowed upon it status of perpetual Guru of the Sikhs, it became known by its present title, Guru Granth, to reflect upon its place in Sikh faith.

Guru Arjan Dev ceremoniously placed Guru Granth, after its completion, on a high pedestal in Harmandir Sahib in August 1604. He instructed Sikhs to revere the Granth, not as an idol, but because it was a store of divinely inspired messages which instructed them in the ways of God and moral life. Unlike the Hindu scriptures, the Granth was open to be read by devotees of any caste, creed or sex. Baba Buddha was appointed the first Granthi, custodian of the Granth. The first Granth, Kartarpur Sahib Bir, is still in existence today.

On 17 October 1605, the third Mughal emperor, Akbar, died and was succeeded by Jahangir. He was an intolerant ruler and decided to put an end to the Sikh faith. Jahangir wrote in his memoirs called Tuzak-i-Jehangiri,

'At Goindwal on the banks of the river Beas lives a Hindu, Arjan by name, in the garb of a Pir or Sheikh. For a long time I had harboured the wish that I should bring him into the fold of Islam. So I ordered that he be brought into my presence.'

When Guru Arjan Dev received the summons to appear before Jahangir, he knew what his fate would be, as he was not going to renounce his faith. The Guru bestowed the Gurtagaddi on his son, Hargobind, before he left for his fateful meeting with Jahangir in Lahore, Punjab.

Jahangir demanded that Guru Arjan Dev remove all references to Islam in the Granth and then accept the Islamic faith himself. Guru Arjan Dev declared that he was only prepared to accept orders from God as to his faith. Jahangir, on hearing these words and angry at the defiance shown by the Guru, ordered Guru Arjan Dev to be tortured to death.

Guruji was stripped and bound to a huge gridiron with red hot coals under it. The Sikhs forced to watch his agony noted that he appeared to be illuminated by an extraordinary light. Despite hot sand being poured over his naked body there was no smell of charred flesh; instead a heavenly scent appeared to permeate the air. Gursikhs say he was protected from intense pain by the fire of divine love which burned more fiercely within his breast than the embers which so disfigured his flesh.

On 16 June 1606, after five long days, the torturers dragged Guruji to the Ravi river. Thousands of followers, keeping vigil for their Guru, watched him, barely able to recognise his tortured body, with charred skin covered with blisters. Seeing his disciples numb beyond grief, Guru Arjan Dev smiled and bade farewell to his followers, thus,

'Sweet is your will, O God
The gift of your Name alone I seek
I bear all this pain in the True Name
Let no one, in his affliction, lose patience in faith.'

The Guru was then thrown into the raging waters of the river and the strong currents swiftly carried his tormented body within its folds. The devotees could see him no more. Guru Arjan Dev was the first martyr in the cause of the Sikh faith. He sacrificed his life to uphold the sovereignty of his faith and refused to alter the Granth to please the Mughal emperor. His sacrifice for his principles lives on in the heart of Sikhs who have forever drawn upon it as an inspiration to stand firm for their rights as free people. The martyrdom was to change the course of Sikh history. A peaceful faith was to turn into a fearless defender of its faith, resolved to take an uncompromising stand against tyranny for the next two centuries and triumph in the end.

CHAPTER 11
Hargobind, the Sixth Guru (1595-1644):
Sant Sipahi

Guru Hargobind, the only son of Guru Arjan Dev, was born on 5 July 1595. He married three times and had six children. Guru Hargobind succeeded Guru Arjan Dev in 1606, at the age of eleven years.

The Sikhs were profoundly affected by the martyrdom of Guru Arjan Dev. It was a turning point for them. A change began to take place in the character of the Sikh Panth. It was not enough to just practise the faith but there was a need to adapt to the ways of the world by adding a political and defensive dimension to protect the Panth. The martyrdom made the Panth reassess its relationship with the Mughals. The trust between the Panth and the Mughals was never restored again.

Guru Hargobind wore two swords, one of spiritual power – piri – and the other of physical prowess – miri. The Guru became a Sant Sipahi, holy warrior. The sword was for Sikhs emblematic of justice as well as a signal to its detractors that Sikhs would protect their faith with force. A chronicler states that Guru Hargobind had a trained force of 700 cavalry and sixty artillerymen at his command to add martial valour to his religious spirit. Bravery in battle was necessary to save the faith from the enemies wishing to destroy it. Dhadhis, poets, wrote and sang Vaars, martial songs, to inspire the Sikhs with tales of heroic deeds in battles in times past. The Guru himself learnt riding and the use of different weapons. The Panth added the ethos of armed resistance to the peace-loving spiritual faith, ready to defend its interests with the sword in its hour of need.

Guru Hargobind built Akal Takht, the Eternal Throne, the seat of Sikh temporal authority, beside the Harmandir in 1609. Its purpose was to introduce a formal institution to make moral and secular decisions affecting the Sikhs. It was a forum to plan the struggle for the survival of the Sikh Panth. Decisions made by representatives of the Sikhs assembled at Akal Takht were binding on all Sikhs. This was an example of consensual decision making, which continues to be the hallmark of contemporary Sikh governance. It also reflects, importantly, that the Sikh Panth is not separable from its moral and secular practice.

The emperor Jahangir did not tolerate this policy of self-sufficiency and preparation for self-preservation. He thought it was the creation of a state within a state. Jahangir imprisoned Guru Hargobind in the Gwalior Fort, a massive, impregnable structure on top of a hill. The prison had been chosen well. Sikhs were unable to breech its walls to free their Guru. However, so strong was the agitation against his imprisonment, coming so soon after the martyrdom of his father, that the emperor felt obliged to release Guru Hargobind after holding him prisoner for three years.

Before he accepted his own freedom, the Guru insisted that Jahangir release fifty-two Hindu princes also incarcerated in the fort. The princes had committed no crime. They had done no wrong except Jahangir felt they threatened the suzerainty of his empire. They had sought the protection of the Guru.

Jahangir was compelled to release the princes at the same time as the Guru. The Guru is known by the title of 'Bandi Chhor Baba', freedom crusader, for his noble deed and self-sacrifice. Guruji reached Amritsar on the day of Divali. Baba Buddha, the Sikh sage, lit thousands of oil lamps in the city to welcome the Guru back to their fold after his long incarceration. Guru Hargobind had refused to bow before the mightiest ruler of India. The Panth was now stronger than ever before. Sikhs celebrate the Divali festival at Amritsar as 'Bandi Chhor Divas', the day of liberation.

The Guru resumed his interrupted consolidation of the Panthic force to be ready to face the continuing threat to their well-being. He insisted on the freedom to practise the Sikh faith without fear of retribution.

Guruji also undertook Dharam Parchar, missionary work, to preach the faith of Guru Nanak to the people of the land. He travelled to many parts of India. Whole regions of the Punjab embraced the faith under his aegis. The Guru made a memorable visit to Kashmir in 1620 when a large number of Hindus embraced the Sikh faith, increasing his followers to manyfold the number they had been when he assumed the Gurtagaddi. The Kashmiri Hindus were later to seek the protection of Tegh Bahadur, the ninth Guru, who was to give his life in their cause.

Jahangir was powerless to persecute the Guru and his Sikhs. Not only was he afraid that he would be unsuccessful in doing so, but he was confronted, as the Mughal emperors were wont to be, by the threat to his throne from his own sons. Not until his death in 1627 when he was succeeded by Shahjahan, the fifth Mughal emperor, who had little knowledge of Sikhs and who lacked the caution of his father, did Guru Hargobind feel obliged to embark upon a series of battles to defend his faith. The emperor had ordered his commanders to destroy the faith by whatever means necessary.

Guruji fought five battles from 1628 to 1634 with Shahjahan. The Guru survived all battles, despite overwhelming forces confronting him. He often had to move from one battlefield to another, but he always recovered and was ready again to battle the imperial forces, by whatever meagre means he had at his command.

The first confrontation, in 1628, a year after Shahjahan became emperor, was a skirmish, obviously to test the willingness of the Guru to face the emperor. Shahjahan was soon to learn that he faced a determined foe that would not be defeated easily. In the second and the most serious conflict between the Guru and the Mughal forces, Shahjahan dispatched 10,000 soldiers to exterminate the Sikhs for once and for all time.

The Guru had built a defensive wall around Amritsar city and constructed a small fort named 'Lohgarh', iron fort, on its outskirts. Guru Hargobind prepared himself to defend from the fort. The Sikhs, though much smaller in number, put up a heroic struggle. The attackers had the upper hand over the Sikhs on the first day of the battle. On the second day, the Sikhs retaliated in small groups with such ferociousness that panic spread among the soldiers and as their senior commanders fell one by one to the swords of the Sikhs they made an ignominious retreat and left the theatre of war in disarray.

The imperial army had destroyed much of the city of Amritsar. Guru Hargobind decided to abandon its safety, as he feared that staying there would put Harmandir Sahib in danger. Guruji said that it was essential that the Sikhs' spiritual centre remained intact to serve its people.

Guru Hargobind had also suffered heavy loss of life and injury of his warriors. He retreated to the semi desert wastelands of the Malwa region of Punjab to recuperate and build a new force. The imperial army, now numbering 22,000 soldiers, once more surrounded him in the Malwa Jungle, for the third attack in 1631. The Sikhs had only the protection of the dense forest. They made full use of it. They embarked upon guerrilla attacks on Mughal forces at night, creating as much mayhem as possible and then dispersing and vanishing at daybreak. The imperial forces could not find an enemy to fight with but continued to sustain heavy causalities at nightfall. The enemy lost morale and were not willing to fight any more. Guruji lost 1,200 Sant Sipahis, a very large loss for him, but he routed the army, which ran from the scene of the battle leaving behind thousands of their own dead and wounded. The Guru built a shrine at the site of the battle, Gursar, place of the Guru, to commemorate his memorable third victory over the enemy. Guru Hargobind established his mission at a place he named Kartarpur, in memory of the town established by Guru Nanak. Guru Hargobind was not to return to Amritsar during his lifetime.

The imperial forces made their last foray against Guru Hargobind in 1634. The Sikhs now had an experienced army of 5,000 warriors, better prepared and equipped to face the enemy. Once more, the Mughal force was overwhelmed as Sikhs showed no fear of fighting large numbers. They were swift and fleeting and the lumbering Mughal soldiers could never catch up with them. The Sikhs showed no mercy in their fury and speed. The imperial army lost its commander in the field and felt obliged to retreat once more from the battle scene.

In all the battles Sikh Gurus fought, the scale was always small compared to other imperial forays against powerful kings and enemies in the land. However, Sikhs rejected the writ of the tyrants, however powerful, and scorned their authority. A mood of defiance was in the making of the Sikh character, which is what made the Mughals so helpless against them and their ability to establish hegemony wherever they wished. It was to slowly sap the very foundations of the Mughal empire and lead to its ultimate decay.

After the battle of Kartarpur, the Guru decided to leave the plains of Punjab and established a new town in the foothills of the Himalayas. He named the town Kiratpur, where the ninth and the tenth Gurus were also to establish their mission centre. The town is now called Anandpur Sahib. Guruji spent the last decade of his life, from 1635 to 1644 at Kiratpur. The Guru breathed his last on 19 March 1644. Before his death, he nominated his grandson Har Rai as his successor.

CHAPTER 12
Interlude: Har Rai, the Seventh Guru (1630-1661) and Har Krishan, the Eighth Guru (1656-1664)

Guru Har Rai

Guru Hargobind anointed Har Rai, his grandson, at the tender age of fourteen, as his successor, the seventh Guru, in March 1644. The succession to Guruship at such an age, and one more such appointment was to follow, may have reflected disappointment with elder sons or the need for a generational change to allow for a fresh start to development of the faith in changing times. Guru Har Rai, born in 1630, was the son of Baba Gurditta, the oldest son of Guru Hargobind. Guru Har Rai married Mata Sulakhni and had two sons, Ram Rai and Har Krishan.

Guru Har Rai was a pious man who spent his time in meditation and the service of his faith. He continued the missionary work of the earlier Gurus. He travelled across India, to Kashmir and Afghanistan as well as to all corners of the Punjab.

During the last days of Guru Hargobind, Emperor Shahjahan was engaged in a long fraternal, internecine war with his sons. Aurangzeb, who eventually succeeded him, blinded his father and threw him in a dungeon. Aurangzeb was an utterly fanatic and zealous man. During the battle for power, there was a lull of an uneasy peace. Guru Har Rai and his Sikhs once more had an opportunity to lead as uneventful a life as the times allowed. However, as soon as Aurangzeb felt safe to do so, he was to turn his attention to the Sikhs. After two decades of relative peace, Sikhs were once more the target of Mughal hate.

Aurangzeb ordered Guru Har Rai to attend his court. Guru Har Rai refused. The Guru sent instead his elder son, Ram Rai. Aurangzeb demanded the deletion of the word beiman (dishonest) as a metaphor for corrupt Muslims in Gurbani, which he thought was derogatory to Islam.

The verse in the Gurbani says that the human soul is not bound to the corporeal body of a person. The physical matter of the body whether of a Hindus or Muslim faces the same fate in the end. This, the verse says, is the eternal truth. The soul leaves the body after death. It does not await the judgement of doomsday. The earth consumes a soulless body in the course of time and reduces it to dust.

Ram Rai, in order to please the emperor, replied that the text had been corrupted by some ignorant person and inserted the word Muselman instead of beiman in the Gurbani. When Guru Har Rai learnt of this change, he was mortified, as no mortal being was allowed to alter Gurbani, the word of God. The Guru called his son an apostate and never spoke to him again.

Guru Har Krishan

Knowing that his end was near due to serious illness, Guru Har Rai could not bring himself to forgive his erring elder son who had so offended him by his attempted compromise with the Mughal rulers, which could have shaken the very foundations of the Sikh faith. Guru Har Rai instead installed his younger son, Har Krishan, at the age of five years, as the eighth Guru. Guru Har Rai passed away on 20 October 1661, at the age of thirty-one years at Kiratpur.

Guru Har Krishan was born on 23 July 1656 at Kiratpur. The decision to appoint Har Krishan to the Guruship infuriated Ram Rai, his elder brother. He complained to Aurangzeb against his father's decision. The emperor ordered the presence of the Guru in his court.

When the Guru arrived in Delhi accompanied by a large number of his disciples, he was made a charge of Raja Jai Singh, from the Rajput social group and one of the ministers of Aurangzeb. Aurangzeb himself was away from Delhi engaged in one of his intermittent wars against his fellow Muslims. The presence of Guru

Har Krishan was a matter of great excitement in the capital and people from all faiths flocked to the palace to pay their respects.

At the time, epidemics of cholera and smallpox were rife in Delhi. The young Guru and his disciples attended the sufferers of the epidemics. The local Muslim population was much impressed with the humanitarian deeds of the Guru and named him Bala Pir, child prophet.

While serving the ill people, the Guru himself contracted smallpox. When his condition became serious, he called his disciples and told them that his end was drawing near. When asked to name his successor, he named 'Baba Bakala', pious man of Bakala, a village near the river Beas. Tegh Bahadur, his great-uncle and youngest son of Guru Hargobind, his grandfather, lived in Bakala.

Guru Har Krishan passed away on 16 April 1664. Guru Gobind Singh, in recognition of his self-sacrifice at such a tender age, paid tribute to Guru Har Krishan in his composition Vaar Sri Bhagauti Ji Ki,

'Let us think of the holy Har Krishan, Whose sight dispels all sorrows'.

Sikhs recite this tribute to the eighth Guru in their daily Ardas.

CHAPTER 13
Tegh Bahadur, the Ninth Guru (1621-1675): Second Guru Martyr

Tyag Mal was born to Guru Hargobind and his second wife Mata Nanaki in Amritsar on 18 April 1621. He was one of five brothers. During his childhood, he learnt to read and write Gurmukhi, Hindi and Sanskrit and mastered martial arts, archery, equestrian skills and swordsmanship during his teenage years.

Tyag Mal lived under the shadow of the martyrdom of Guru Arjan Dev, his grandfather, at the hands of Mughal rulers in Lahore in 1606. Emperor Aurangzeb, a Muslim fanatic, was forcibly spreading Islam all over the country. He not only had his own father imprisoned but also eliminated his brothers. He even incarcerated for a time his own son and heir, Bahadur Shah. He destroyed Hindu temples and would not let them practise their faith in public. His cruel reign was to last forty-nine years, from 1658 to 1707.

The Sikh faith was treated with increasing hostility for the next two centuries and this was to colour the faith to adapt to circumstances and not succumb to religious bigotry. Earlier, the Mughal rulers had imprisoned Guru Hargobind, who had found it necessary to form his own army to protect Sikhs. In a battle, Tyag Mal had joined with his father when he was only thirteen years of age and he showed such bravery that Guru Hargobind named him Tegh Bahadur, warrior of the sword.

In 1632 Tegh Bahadur married Mata Gujri, who bore him one son, Gobind. After the death of Guru Hargobind, Tegh Bahadur, then twenty-three years old, went to stay with his maternal grandfather in the village of Bakala, Punjab. He was to spend the next two decades of his life there. Tegh Bahadur sought solitude and led a pious life. During these years he made his first journey to distant parts of India, including Kashmir, Assam and Hindu holy places, to preach the message of Guru Nanak. As persecution against Sikhs increased, he decided to move away from the Punjab and make his home in Patna, a city in central India. From there he made his second journey to visit Bengal and Assam taking Guru Nanak's message to the further reaches of the country. Gobind Singh, his only child, was born in Patna, during his absence in 1666. Guru Har Krishan had nominated Baba Bakala, as Tegh Bahadur was known, his successor as the ninth Guru of the Sikhs. This was in the year 1664.

Guru Tegh Bahadur at the end of his travels to the east settled in Kiratpur, founded by his grandfather, and named it Anandpur in 1665. The city at the foothills of the remote Shivalik hills was built in the shape of a fortress. He then began his third journey visiting cities in the north to continue to preach and convert devotees to the Sikh faith.

Guruji returned to Anandpur Sahib in 1670. During his Guruship, Anandpur became an important place of pilgrimage for Sikhs. As conditions in the Punjab continued to worsen and persecution of Sikhs became widespread, he embarked on his fourth and last journey to the Punjab to be with his disciples in their time of need.

Sher Khan, Mughal governor of Kashmir province, started forcefully converting Kashmiri Hindus to Islam. Persecuted by the oppressors, the Hindus travelled to Anandpur Sahib to seek the protection of Guru Tegh Bahadur against their Muslim ruler.

Guruji instructed the Kashmiri pundits to go to Delhi and tell Aurangzeb that if Tegh Bahadur were to convert to Islam, they would follow suit. Guru Tegh Bahadur then embarked on his fateful journey with five devotees to Delhi. Aurangzeb ordered the Guru and his Sikhs to be put in chains in cages. They were tortured mercilessly and asked to renounce their faith and accept Islam. The Kazis, learned scholars of Islam, told Guruji that the emperor had ordered that if he accepted Islam, he would be freed and granted what money and land he wished for.

In reply, Guruji said that he already had everything he could wish for and did not need riches earned through tyranny and oppression. His faith was in the Creator who loved his creation. In reply to questions put by the Kazis, Guruji proclaimed that only that rule was just that allowed followers of other religions to practise their faith unhindered.

Emissaries from his son Gobind Singh reached Guru Tegh Bahadur in prison. After hearing about the anguish of his family and devotees, Guru Tegh Bahadur said,

'If you do not worship Him [God], consider your life a waste
A devotee goes on chanting His name
Like a fish continually splashing in water'.

Then he addressed Mata Gujri, Gobind's mother:

'Even Ram [Hindu God] with his immense kingdom
Too went away to exile
O Nanak, everything is transient in this world
Since the world is but a dream.'

Further, in this letter, pointing towards the helpless condition of his compatriots, he wrote to his son Gobind,

'We are powerless today,
Trapped in chains and cannot find the way out,
O Nanak, it is only He, who will give us shelter and lead the way'.

In reply to this, Gobind Singh, at the age of nine, sent a message to his father reassuring him that his devotees were steadfast, accepted God's will and were content in his Grace.

After Aurangzeb had exhausted coercion to convert him to Islam, he gave orders for the execution of Guru Tegh Bahadur. Guruji and his devotees were brought out to Chandni Chowk, Old Delhi, in chains, where crowds had gathered to witness the execution. According to chronicles, Guruji and the devotees were reciting Gurbani until their last breath. First, the executioners sliced with saws the five devotees accompanying Guru Tegh Bahadur, tore off their limbs and then beheaded them in the presence of Guru Tegh Bahadur.

The Kazis once more ordered him to accept Islam as the true faith. Guruji smiled and said he was ready to face the truth. The Kazis jeered and asked why he was called Tegh Bahadur. Guruji replied,

'You will know when you wield the sword.'

The Kazis got tired of their tirades, ordered the execution and left Guruji to his fate. The executioner, using a blunt sword, struck repeatedly at the neck of the Guru to behead him and prolong his agony. This took place in November 1675. Bhai Jaita, a Ranghreta, an untouchable devotee, waiting in the crowd, picked up the severed head, covered it with a cloth, and set out for Anandpur Sahib. As he, with shaking hands, proffered the head to Gobind Singh, Guruji hugged Bhai Jaita and said,

'Ranghreta, Guru Ka beta [You are Guru's son, Ranghreta]'.

Gobind cremated the revered head of his father in Anandpur Sahib. A shrine stands at the site of the cremation. In Delhi, Lakhi Shah Vanjara, another low-caste Sikh, took care of the body of Guru Tegh Bahadur. He put it in his house and then set fire to it. Gurdwara Sis Ganj, shrine of the revered martyr, stands at the place where the Guru was beheaded in Chandni Chowk, Delhi. It is one of the most revered shrines of the Sikhs. Sikhs had to wait another two hundred years until, with the help of the British imperial forces, they were to destroy the last remnants of the Mughals in India for ever and raise the Khalsa flag at the Delhi shrine, which still flies today to proclaim the righteousness of the Sikh cause.

In Sikh history, the martyrdom of Guru Tegh Bahadur was to lead to the birth of the Khalsa Panth we see today.

CHAPTER 14
Gobind Singh, the Tenth Guru (1666-1708):
Param Manukh, First among Men

'He gave us music, martial art and Shabad. In him, we find a Sant singing Shabads, a soldier striking martial music, a householder singing virtues of a good life and an artist creating wonderful pictures in prose'(*Anonymous, eighteenth century*).

Guru Gobind Singh was the tenth and last Guru of the Sikhs. His life was short and tragic. He founded the Khalsa Panth and led it through its baptism of fire. Guru Gobind Singh was a colossus – a Param Manukh, first among men – whose inspired leadership put an indelible a stamp on his faith.

An uneasy childhood

Guru Tegh Bahadur, who had made Patna in Bihar his temporary home, was away on Dharm Parchar, a missionary tour, when Guru Gobind Singh was born to Mata Gujri on 5 January 1666. On the site of the place of birth, where he also spent his early childhood, now stands Patna Sahib shrine and one of the five Takhts, thrones, of the Sikh faith. Guru Gobind Singh was an only child.

Guru Tegh Bahadur continued his tour for the next four years. Following his return in 1700, and after a short stay in Patna, he moved his family to Anandpur Sahib in the foothills of the Shivaliks, a range of hills marking the end of Himalayas in Punjab. Guru Gobind Singh was then four years old.

It was an uneasy time. Born in a loving home but in a strange land, in the absence of a father and then travelling long distances at a tender age, was a harbinger of a life, short but full of prophetic events. The family was much safer in Anandpur Sahib than it would have been in the plains of Punjab because of the then uncertainty facing Sikhs.

A fatherless Guru

Gobind's life was abruptly interrupted at the age of nine years when Aurangzeb, the Mughal emperor, martyred Guru Tegh Bahadur in Delhi in 1675. Guru Tegh Bahadur anointed his son the tenth Guru as his end neared. Guru Gobind Singh was formally installed as the last Guru of the Sikhs at the age of nine years.

The martyrdom of Guru Tegh Bahadur had left the Sikhs bereft of a leader, as Guru Gobind Singh was still only a child. The Mughal rulers decided to leave the Sikhs alone, because not only were they afraid of provoking the Sikhs further, but also because Aurangzeb felt that the Sikhs would not survive without their martyred Guru. Moreover, Aurangzeb ruled by terror and waged constant wars against belligerents. He had many enemies to contend with in his empire. Sikhs posed a perceived religious but not a territorial threat to him.

During this period of uneasy calm, Guru Gobind Singh grew up under the care of his mother. Guru Gobind Singh's early education included reading and writing of Punjabi, Hindi, Sanskrit and Persian. As he continued his education, he also began receiving instruction in martial arts. Trained in soldierly pursuits, he became acknowledged for his equestrian mastery and swordsmanship. Guru Gobind Singh was destined to become a great warrior and a leader of immense repute.

Battles: Pre Khalsa Period, 1682-1696

Anandpur Sahib 1682-1685
The neighbouring Rajput Hill rulers had grown restless seeing Sikhs once more had a confident leader. They did not appreciate Guruji telling them to stop colluding with the Mughal rulers and the practice of giving their daughters to them as a price for holding on to their power as Rajas. The Hill Rajas decided to attack and destroy Anandpur Sahib, then the centre of Sikh faith.

In all, eight battles were fought in and around Anandpur Sahib between the years 1682 and 1696. In these skirmishes, the Hill Rajas sought the assistance of nearby Mughal governors. Guru Gobind Singh and his warriors, though puny in numbers, frustrated all attempts to dislodge them from Anandpur Sahib. Guruji never initiated an attack; instead, he urged the Rajas to recognise who their real enemy was and work with him for the freedom of their people. The Rajas refused to accept the offer. Guru Gobind Singh was only sixteen years old at the time of the first battle.

Paonta Sahib 1685-1888
Guru Gobind Singh thought it prudent to move away from Anandpur Sahib for a short while to avoid further conflicts with the Mughals and Hill Rajas. He left Anandpur Sahib for a small village on the banks of the river Jamuna in 1685. He named the village Paonta. There is now a historic Gurdwara, called Paonta Sahib, at the site.

Guru Gobind Singh had begun to compose Bani while still in Anandpur Sahib. Paonta Sahib gave him the opportunity to devote more time to it. He inaugurated a centre of learning in Paonta Sahib. Most of Guru Gobind Singh's literary work was done at Paonta Sahib. It is said that at one time there were fifty-two poets and writers at his court whose task it was to compose religious poetry and translate the Vedic epics. Tales of ancient heroes were transcribed from Sanskrit into Punjabi in order to remind Sikhs of their ancient heritage and instil the martial spirit in them. The glorification of the sword that he eulogised as Bhagauti was to secure fulfilment of justice for the Sikhs in God's name. The sword was never meant as a symbol of aggression. It was the emblem of freedom, to be used only as a last resort in the cause of justice.

The Vaar Sri Bhagauti Ji Ki, a Vedic battle epic, popularly called Chandi Ki Vaar, depicts the legendary contest between Gods and demons as described in the Markandeya Purana epic. The choice of a warlike theme for this and a number of later compositions such as the two Chandi Charitars showed the parallel with the predicament in which Guru Gobind Singh found himself in his time. It reflects on the time Guruji spent planning on the future course the Sikh faith should adopt to defend itself. It is now agreed that poets who lived in the time of Guru Gobind Singh wrote most of the epics compiled together in the Dasam Granth (the tenth Guru's Granth).

The Guru also composed in rousing verse Bani, part of which, though not included in Guru Granth, is recited in Nit-nem, Sikh daily prayers. These are Jaap Sahib, Akal Ustat, Swayyae and Benati Chaupai. These allegorical compositions reveal the vision of the Supreme Being that had been vouchsafed to Guru Gobind Singh. His writings emphasise love of God and equality of mankind governed by an ethical and moral code of conduct. Guru Gobind Singh deprecated idolatry and superstitious beliefs.

The Hill Rajas did not intend to leave Guru Gobind Singh alone. He had to fight again another battle with the combined might of the Hill Rajas at a place called Bhangani. Having once more overcome the enemy, Guru Gobind Singh returned to Anandpur Sahib, as Paonta Sahib was not as defensible as Anandpur Sahib.

Anandpur Sahib 1688-1696
The Mughal rulers turned against their allies and began to attack the Hill Rajas themselves. Guru Gobind, ever a defender of his compatriots, came to their aid. The Guru and his Sikhs were involved in a battle with a Mughal commander, Alif Khan, at Nadaun, on the left bank of the river Beas, about thirty kilometres south east of Kangra Hills, India, in March 1690. Describing the battle in stirring verse in Bachitar Natak, Guruji's allegorical autobiography, he said that Alif Khan fled in utter disarray,

'W*ithout a care to the fate of the rest of his camp'.*

The Hill Rajas again returned to warfare and engaged Guruji in three further battles from 1691 to 1696. Once more, the Mughals joined the Hill Rajas, but a battle that took place in 1695 fought against Hussain Khan, an imperial general, resulted once more in a decisive victory for the Sikhs.

Period of Respite 1696-1699

Following the last rout of the Mughals, the Sikhs enjoyed a period of respite and Guru Gobind Singh was once more able to pay attention to the preparation needed to strengthen the faith against relentless persecution.

Foundation of the Khalsa Panth 1699

The long deliberations of Guru Gobind Singh were to lead to the conclusion that the Sikh faith needed a dramatic change of strategy from a still pacific spiritual entity to a dynamic force that would ensure survival of the faith. The result was the foundation of the Khalsa Panth in 1699.

Battles: Post Khalsa period 1699-1707

Anandpur Sahib 1700-1704

Meanwhile Emperor Aurangzeb was surrounded by unrest within his kingdom. Prince Muazzam, his eldest son and heir, had already fled his post as viceroy of Lahore, fearing his father's wrath. Aurangzeb perceived threats everywhere. The Hill Rajas had a ready ear in him when they complained again against Guru Gobind Singh. They petitioned him for help. In concert with contingents sent under imperial orders by the new governor of Lahore and those of the army commander of the state of Sirhind, they marched upon Anandpur and laid siege to the fort. The Sikh warrior army withstood six assaults and always sent away the attacking armies in retreat.

But Sikh resources were slowly being depleted. They had withstood the might of the Mughal Empire and the combined power of the Rajput rulers for over twenty years (1682-1704). The seventh and last battle at Anandpur Sahib, in 1704, resulted in a stalemate. Over the months, the Guru and his Sikhs firmly withstood successive enemy assaults despite insufficient food and equipment resulting from the prolonged blockade. While the besieged Sikhs were reduced to desperate straits, the besiegers too were exhausted because of the refusal of the Sikhs to surrender.

At this stage, the besiegers offered, to save their own face, on oath of the Qur'an, safe exit to the Sikhs if they were to quit Anandpur Sahib. It was during this time that forty of the Sikh warriors accepted the Mughal offer, against Guruji's advice, giving written letters of disclaimer to be the Guru's soldiers, and left the fort. The Guru knew it was a trap; he had no alternative but also to find a way out of his fort. Guruji, faced with privation and without resources but not trusting the Mughal peace offer, decided to make a dash for freedom at night.

As the Guru and his Sikhs came out, the hill monarchs and their Mughal allies set upon them in full fury. In the ensuing confusion, many Sikhs were killed and all of the Guru's baggage train of arms and food was lost. It was only through the bravery of Guru Gobind Singh and his Sikh warriors, drawing upon their last ounce of strength, that they were able to escape from the battlefield. It is said that just forty Sikh warriors were left to accompany Guru Gobind Singh and his two older teenage sons in his departure.

Chamkaur and Khidrana (Muktsar) 1704-1705
The imperial forces had not yet abandoned their attempt to engage Guru Gobind Singh in battle as the enemy seeing their advantage continued to pursue Guruji. The Guru was to engage in one more battle with the Mughals at Chamkaur Sahib, sixty miles southwest of Anandpur Sahib.

At the battle of Chamkaur, the Mughal army once again surrounded Sikhs in a mud fort. In a short, bloody encounter, Guruji lost his two elder sons, Ajit Singh (born 1687) and Jujhar Singh (born 1691) and all but ten of the Sikhs fell in the action that took place in December 1704.

Guru Gobind Singh and five of his warriors managed to make their way out of the fort. The remaining five warriors, who had stayed back in the mud fort, continued the battle to allow Guru Gobind Singh to make his exit from the battlefield. They too lost their lives in the final skirmishes.

The remnants of the imperial army, acting on their own, following closely on the heels of the Guru, caught up with him at Khidrana. It is here that one of the greatly commemorated events in Sikh history took place. The Guru saw from a hill that the forty Sikhs, deserters from Anandpur Sahib, had returned in remorse and just in time to intervene with the enemy, fighting gallantly against all odds, to perish on the battlefield. Once more, in spite of their overwhelming numbers, the Mughal troops failed to capture the Guru and were too demoralised to continue the chase. This event took place on 29 December 1705.

The forty Sikhs had fallen in the battlefield but had stopped the enemy's advance towards the Guru's position. Their leader, suffering from fatal wounds, managed to reach Guru Gobind Singh. He begged for forgiveness and asked him to tear up the letter of disclaimer which he and his followers had written. He requested the Guru to accept them all back in his fold. Guruji hugged him and said,

'You are my dear and brave Sikhs, you are not my followers, and it is I who am your devotee'.

The Guru blessed the forty dead as forty Mukte, the saved ones. A sacred shrine now marks the site and the town is called Muktsar, the place of liberation. The battle is remembered in Sikh Ardas.

Guru Gobind Singh's two youngest sons, Zorawar Singh (born 1696), Fateh Singh (born 1699), and their grandmother, Mata Gujri Ji, who had also evacuated Anandpur, were betrayed by their escort to the governor of Sirhind, the bitter enemy of the Sikhs. The Governor ordered the children to be converted to Islam. When they resisted, he had the young ones walled up alive on 13 December 1704, soon after the battle of Chamkaur Sahib. Their grandmother could not bear the grief and perished the same day.

Post battle period

Damdama Sahib 1705-1707
Guru Gobind Singh sought refuge in a place which was later named Damdama Sahib, place to breathe, on 20 January 1706 and stayed there for nine months. He recuperated his strength and established a Sikh settlement there. He began to lead a life as much as it was possible to do so in those tumultuous times, bereft in the loss of his sons, mother and his beloved Sikhs. It is here that Guruji added the compositions of his father, Guru Tegh Bahadur, to Guru Granth. This second and final recension of Guru Granth was named after the place, the Damdama Bir. This version is now accepted as the scriptures of the Sikhs.

It is also in Damdama Sahib that Guru Gobind Singh composed his Zafarnamah, the Epistle of Victory, in Persian verse, addressed to Emperor Aurangzeb. The letter stated his determination to preserve the Sikh faith. He reprimanded the Emperor who he accused of being a cruel ruler without regard for his subjects and for betraying promises he had made to the Sikhs. Guru Gobind Singh said in the Zafarnamah,

'When all other means have failed, it is but lawful to take to the sword'.

Post Aurangzeb period 1707-1708

Meeting with Bahadur Shah, the seventh Mughal Emperor of India
Following the death of Emperor Aurangzeb at Ahmadnagar on 20 February 1707, his sons contested succession. Prince Muazzam, the oldest son and the rightful claimant to the throne, was victorious in battles with his brothers and ascended the throne in June 1707 with the title of Bahadur Shah. The new emperor, in a deceitful act of reconciliation, invited Guru Gobind Singh to his court. The Guru first met the emperor at Agra in August 1707. The Guru then accompanied him on his campaign journey south for a time but then stopped at Nanded, on the banks of the river Godavri, in

Maharashtra, towards the end of August 1708. He met here Madho Das, a holy man, whom he initiated into his faith, naming him Gurbakhsh Singh, later popularly called Banda Bahadur, the bravest of men.

Abchal Nagar, Place of Departure (Nanded) August-October 1708
Guru Gobind Singh gave Banda Bahadur five arrows from his own quiver and an escort of five of his chosen Sikhs and directed him to go to Punjab to continue the campaign against Mughal tyranny he had begun two decades earlier.

Banda Bahadur, with a small Sikh army, was to seek revenge from the enemies of the Sikhs. Sikhs consider him the military, but not the spiritual, successor to Guru Gobind Singh. He fought many brave battles but was eventually captured and put to the sword in Delhi.

Bahadur Shah, the emperor, meanwhile, had secretly planned to assassinate Guru Gobind Singh, as the Guru had refused to succumb to his machinations when in Agra. He ordered Wazir Khan, governor of Sirhind, to carry out the deed. The governor despatched two of his trusted men to murder the Guru. These two Pathans presented themselves as Sikh pilgrims in Nanded. One of them stabbed Guruji on the left side below the heart as he lay one evening in his chamber resting after the evening prayer.

Before he could deal another blow, Guru Gobind Singh struck him down with his sabre, while his fleeing companion fell under the swords of Sikhs who had rushed in on hearing the skirmish. The deep wound failed to heal and Guruji passed away on 21 October 1708. The place where Guru Gobind Singh is cremated in Nanded is called Takht Sri Hazur Sahib and Sikhs call the town Abchal Nagar, place of holy departure.

Before passing away, Guru Gobind Singh vested the Guruship of the Sikhs in the Granth and named the Khalsa Panth guardian of his faith.

The year 2008 marks the tercentenary of the anointment of the Granth as Guru of the Sikhs.

CHAPTER 15
Guru Granth Sahib

Introduction

Guru Granth Sahib is the spiritual authority of the Sikh faith. It is an anthology of compositions of six of the ten Gurus, seventeen Bhagats, holy men, who lived before the time of Guru Nanak, one brother of Guru Arjan Dev, and eleven Bhatts, poet-musicians, who lived during the times of the third, fourth and fifth Gurus.

Guru Granth is divinely inspired. It is the word of God. It is inimitable. Its literary perfection is such that no other mortal being could hope to copy it. Guru Granth has an ascendant literary status in the Sikh faith. It is beautiful and fluent. It describes the majesty and attributes of God in sublime language.

The Granth describes spiritual and moral dilemmas facing us before proposing just and equable solutions. It condemns no one and its chastisement is gentle. The Gurus were of the people they lived with. They observed the world, its foibles and needs. The Gurus laid stress on living an honest life and sharing with others one's wealth. The Granth is positive about the future of humanity despite the cruel times the Gurus lived in. It gives us a perspective for the future; it is a tract of moral defiance and hopeful outcome.

The Granth describes the eternal truth, proclaims God as One and shows the way of his realisation. Sikh faith rejects idol worship. Guru Granth is not worshipped as an idol, but for the word of God within. The Gurus referred to themselves as ordinary people but Bani, their compositions, were divinely inspired as the word of God. We are told,

'Shabad Bani, Bani Guru, [Shabad is Guru, the Guru Shabad]'.

Guru Granth draws upon, first, pre-Hindu Vedantic times, when men walked the earth with gods, fought heroic wars and lived a true life. Vedic hymns are the beginning of religious stirrings in India. The Vedas, 4,000 years old, are the repositories of ancient wisdom and recording of the earliest meditation of the human mind. Our pre-history established the identity of its people and laid down the moral and philosophical foundation for them. As we emerge from pre-history, we find an established order which has endured for thousands of years.

The Granth next describes a nation very much in the grip of Muslim rulers. It reveals a demoralised people, afraid of their very shadow and unable to practise the faith of their ancestors. The period is from the twelfth to the seventeenth century, during the latter part of which the Gurus lived, mostly in Punjab. The Granth thus gives us a perspective of our most ancient and then the contemporary account of its mediaeval times to describe how faiths had evolved, changed and progressed to the times of the Gurus. The Granth accepts the validity of world faiths but is critical of human errors introduced in their practice.

We learn little of events that took place during the times of the first nine Gurus in the Granth. It is not a historical record. The Granth does occasionally provide us with a glimpse of the events to anchor its revelations. We could not, however, construct a biography of the contributors to the Granth or the history of the times from information gleaned from it.

Babar Bani is an example of narration of the invasion of India by Babar, the Mughal tyrant, in 1524. It is a vivid eyewitness account of the atrocities committed by the Mughal hordes upon the people of Punjab. It relates the moral desperation of the times rather than providing us with a chronicle of events. These are placed in the larger social and historical perspective of the times. The moral stricture and poetical eloquence of the pain and suffering of people during Mughal times in mediaeval India are evident from the Bani. Guru Nanak says,

'Bringing the marriage party of sin,

Babar has invaded from Kabul
Demanding our land as his wedding gift'.

A gentle remonstration with God, perhaps, though later Guru Nanak explains the purpose of such sufferings,

'[God] sends the Mughal as the messenger of death
When there was such suffering, killing, such shrieking
Did you not, O God, feel pain?'

Even then, there is no indictment of Babar. Guru Nanak wishes to draw a lesson from his eyewitness account. The lure of power divides men and violence, unresisted, tends to flourish. It cannot be wished away. Yet a corrupt and inhumane rule always ends in dissolution.

Compilation and Installation

Guru Arjan Dev, the fifth Guru, compiled the Granth. Bhai Gurdas, a devout and learned Sikh, was its scribe. The task took three years to complete. The Granth was installed in Harmandir Sahib, Amritsar, in August 1604. Baba Buddha, a companion of four Gurus, was appointed its first Granthi, custodian and reader of the Granth.

Authorship

The Granth that Guru Arjan Dev compiled contains the complete writings of the first five Gurus. The compositions of seventeen Bhagats – Hindu and Muslim holy people who believed in the unity of God and preached a moral and spiritual way of living, free of superstition and falsehood – are also included in the Granth. The first Guru had gathered the Bani of the Bhagats, who all pre-deceased him. Guru Arjan Dev also added the compositions of eleven Bhatts, bards, who lived during the times of the early Gurus. There is only one additional composition, of Baba Sundar, brother of Guru Arjan Dev, who composed Sadd, call, a dirge, after the death of their father the fourth Guru.

Guru Gobind Singh later added the compositions of his father, Guru Tegh Bahadur, the ninth Guru, to the Granth. The sixth, seventh and eighth Gurus did not compose Bani. Purported compositions by Guru Gobind Singh and Bhai Mardana in the Granth are now accepted to be the writings of other Gurus. There are no anonymous contributions, except Raag Mala, as the concluding page. Its inclusion in the Granth is controversial as it was added after the times of the Gurus.

Fate of historic Granths

The Granth that Guru Arjan Dev compiled was handwritten on single folio paper. It was then bound together with a hard cover embellished with gold. Granths were handwritten for 250 years until 1864 when the first stone block print was produced in the Punjab. Many handwritten Granths survive and are displayed in museums and Sikh shrines.

Once the original Granth was installed in Harmandir Sahib, there were no opportunities to transcribe from it. Guru Arjan Dev had arranged for another Granth, or Bir, to be simultaneously produced under the supervision of Bhai Banno, a disciple, from the original Bani folios as they were written or from the same manuscript collection. Bhai Banno employed a number of scribes to carry out this task. It is believed that at least two more, possibly three, Granths were further transcribed from the Bhai Banno Bir during the time of Guru Arjan Dev. Indeed, the source of all subsequent Granths is one of the original Bhai Banno Bir.

The original Granth, still extant today, had a chequered history. Dhir Mal, the eldest grandson of the sixth Guru, Hargobind Sahib, angered at not being offered Gurtagaddi, Guruship, of which he thought he was the rightful heir as the first-born son, took possession of it in 1634. It remained with his family for about a hundred years when Maharaja Ranjit Singh, the Sikh ruler of Punjab, forcibly acquired it and installed it in Lahore, his capital. On the collapse of the Sikh empire, the British rulers returned the Bir to the 'owners' who lived in Kartarpur, a town founded by the sixth Guru in Punjab. The

Granth is known as the Kartarpur Bir. The Sodhi clan, descendants of Guru Hargobind, have preserved the Kartarpur Bir with its original gold stand and display it once a month for worship.

Unauthorised additions were made to one or more transcripts of the Bhai Banno Bir, most probably after the times of the Gurus. These were the source of production of other adulterated handwritten Granths during the eighteenth or early nineteenth century. A Bhai Banno Bir with its false additions is in the possession of his descendants. One or perhaps two transcriptions of the Bhai Banno Bir made during the time of Guru Arjan Dev survive which do not have the unauthorised additions.

Guru Arjan Dev had invented a security system of numbers, which ensures the authenticity of authorship and verse numbers and prevents later interpolations of spurious verses. These are easily detected if carried out as has happened with adulterated Bir in the past.

Gurtagaddi bestowed on the Granth Sahib

Guru Gobind Singh, during the respite after his last battle at Chamkaur Sahib, spent about nine months in Damdama Sahib in 1705. Guruji instructed Bhai Mani Singh, a scholar, to produce a second recension of the Granth from an authentic Bhai Banno Bir, with added Bani of his father, Guru Tegh Bahadur, the ninth Guru. This recompilation is now accepted as the true Granth of the Sikh faith. The Granth, known as the Damdama Sahib Bir, was first installed in Nanded, Central India, the place of last abode of Guru Gobind Singh.

Guru Gobind Singh ended the line of personal Guruship by investing the Granth Sahib with the status of eternal Guru and his successor in 1708. Poet Bhai Nandlal, one of Guru Gobind Singh's disciples, recorded the Guru's words,

'He who would wish to see the Guru
Let him come and see the Granth

He who would wish to speak to him
Let him read and reflect upon what it says
He who would wish to hear his word
He should with all his heart read the Granth.'

The Damdama Bir stayed in Nanded until 1732 under the care of Baba Dip Singh Shahid, a trusted companion of the tenth Guru. He had four transcriptions made from the Damdama Bir during 1726. Mata Sundri, the widow of Guru Gobind Singh, instructed Bhai Mani Singh, the scribe of the original second recension, to install it in Harmandir Sahib and appointed him the Granthi for its safekeeping. This Bir was lost to the Sikhs during the first, 'Great' Sikh holocaust in 1762 in which the Harmandir Sahib was desecrated, the Damdama Sahib Bir traduced and thousands of Sikhs lost their lives. One of the Damdama Sahib Bir transcribed under Baba Dip Singh was then installed in place of the Bir transcribed by Bhai Mani Singh.

Language

Guru Nanak received education in Sanskrit and Persian. Even during his childhood, Guruji sought the company of Bhagats who lived in nearby forests and he discoursed with them in Sant Bhasha, a form of stylised Indian holy language, with much of its vocabulary rooted in Sanskrit. Sant Bhasha had its own grammar and textual structure. The format of Guru Granth is Sant Bhasha, based mostly on Punjabi dialects. The influence of other Indian languages is also readily discernible. There is considerable variation in its language depending on the part of the Punjab the authors lived in. Moreover, languages change with time. Bhagat Bani were recorded from the twelfth century to the fifteenth century and Guru Bani from the fifteenth to the seventeenth century. The thirty-five authors whose compositions are recorded in the Granth each also have their own style of writing.

During his twenty-five years of travel, Guru Nanak visited Hindu shrines in India, Buddhist ones in Sri Lanka, Nepal and Tibet and Muslim ones in India and the Middle East in Arabia, Iraq, Iran and Afghanistan. Guruji developed a vast repertoire of philosophical thought of these three regions of the East. The erudition of Guru Nanak's expression and thought is elegantly displayed in his compositions. Apart from some Bani recorded in Sahskriti (Guru Nanak), Gatha (Guru Arjan Dev) and Dakhni (Guru Arjan Dev) dialects, now defunct, the compositions in the Granth are recorded in Sant Bhasha, using versions of Punjabi dialects.

Collation

Guru Nanak recorded his thoughts and compositions in Pothis, notebooks. He would, as poets do, record his thoughts as jottings in verse form. These are called Saloks, two-line verse formats. Saloks are the foundation stones of the Bani. Saloks were then used to produce longer compositions or later added by Guru Arjan Dev to other compositions. The other Gurus also made recordings of their thoughts in Saloks. The fact that the Gurus recorded their thoughts explains why   Guru Granth contains all their writings.

In many artefacts, Guru Nanak is depicted with a satchel on one shoulder. This appears to be his only worldly possession. The importance he gave his Bani is shown in that when he installed Angad Dev as the second Guru it was the handing over of the Pothis that established the change in Guruship. The successor Gurus were to hand over the collective compositions, including their own writings, to the next Guru until Guru Arjan Dev, with these and the collection of his own, was to compile the Granth. The Sikh faith claims that the Gurus were one spirit in ten bodies. The transfer of the Pothis marked the spirit. Gurus after Guru Nanak were successive custodians of the Gurbani, first in the form of Pothis and then Guru Granth. It is the reason why the name of no Guru except Guru Nanak is mentioned as the author of the Guru Bani.

Guru Nanak introduced a new script to write his Bani. The Patti, alphabet, a composition of Guru Nanak recorded in the Granth, uses each letter of his alphabet to compose a verse. This shows it was Guru Nanak who was the father of the alphabet of Bani script. Guru Angad then systematically developed the script and called it Gurmukhi. Gurbani is recorded in Gurmukhi script. Guru Nanak, who had gathered the Bhagat Bani during his travels, made no changes to the actual compositions. As most Bhagats had either lived in Punjab or travelled through it in earlier centuries, their compositions reflect different styles of Punjabi dialects and include the language influence of their places of origin.

The Punjabi we speak today is very different to the multiplicity of Punjabi dialects spoken in the times of the Gurus. Sant Bhasha was rooted in mediaeval Punjabi. The fact that Sant Bhasha is dated and no longer a spoken or written language should make it difficult for a Sikh to understand Bani even if it was written in Gurmukhi. It was bound to become difficult to understand and interpret as knowledge of old languages and their grammar would be essential to understand the Gurbani today.

Yet the constant recitation, use, explanation and interpretation of the Gurbani makes Sikhs easily familiar with the language of the Bani. Sikhs may not be able to speak or write Sant Bhasha, but familiarity with the Granth is second nature to Sikhs. If one asks Sikhs what language they understand they will mention Punjabi and English but not Sant Bhasha, as the latter has become part of their Punjabi repertoire.

This is important. Guru Granth is a compendium of Punjabi literature and poetry. It contains compositions by Sheikh Farid, the father of Punjabi poetry. Punjabi was a rustic language until the publication of Guru Granth. The Granth vastly increased the vocabulary and depth of Punjabi. It introduced systems of Indian philosophy and the writing of poetry in many formats. There was little Punjabi literature written before the times of the Sikh Gurus. Moreover, Punjabi was regarded as a language of the vulgar by the Muslim rulers, who refused to speak it, and aristocratic and Brahmin sections of Hindu society never paid attention to it. Scholars claim that we have only skimmed the surface of the Gurbani, their further deeper understanding awaits elucidation.

Verse structure

Raag is the Indian structure of musical melody. It is an evolving musical tradition combining ancient Vedanta culture and folk musical genre.

The thematic nature of the Gurbani, apart from Raag, is also cast in the mould of Punjabi folk music. In folk Bani, the title indicates the theme, besides the Raag in which the Shabad is to be sung. Shabads in the folk mould sing of the divine presence in the world, using seasons, times of day, months or years as allegories. Life events are metaphors to describe the glory of God, derived from ancient Indian religious traditions.

The oral Raag traditions contrast with the written format of Western music. The oral framework is used to compose or improvise melody. Melodies in a certain Raag are recognisable yet allow endless variation. Variations occur between styles and performers or by the same performer at different times. Hours of the day, morning, afternoon, evening or night, each have their specific Raag. There is no absolute pitch. Each performance simply picks a ground note, and the other scales follow relative to this note. The compositions are recorded in various metres and rhythms and are organised accordingly. Within each Raag, there is a division, first by number of verses and then by the Ghar, musical clef, in which the composition is to be sung.

Shabad Formation

Salok
A Tuk is a line of text of Gurbani:

Two Tuks make a Salok. A variable number of Saloks make up a Shabad, and together Shabads form a Gurbani Raag. There are thirty-one Raags in the Granth. Together the thirty-one Raags constitute the 1430 pages of the Granth.

Saloks were initially jottings by the Gurus, later developed into Shabads. Guru Arjan Dev inserted the miscellany of unused Saloks in Nit-nem and Vaars, where they enhance, support or explain the Bani they are coupled with. Inserted Saloks are usually by the same author. If Saloks of other authors are interpolated, this is mentioned within the context of the composition. Finally, Saloks which were surplus to the need of Nit-nem and Vaars are so titled, in the case of the first five Gurus and as Bhog Bani, epilogue, for Guru Tegh Bahadur. These are inserted in the third and final part of Guru Granth. The third part also contains Bhagat Saloks, again surplus to their use in their Bani compositions.

Shabads

The use of the word Shabad is ubiquitous. Literarily, it means a Padd, word, or string of words. In Gurbani, its widest generic use is to describe all compositions, in full or part, as Shabads. More specifically, it means a short composition in Raag of one to sixteen stanzas. The commonest verse form is Chaupad, four-verse form (1255 compositions in the Granth). Chaupad precedes all other formats in classification under each Raag. Once Chaupad are listed, the subsequent order of listing is in ascending order from two-verse (Dupade), three-verse (Tripde), five-verse (Panchpade), six-verse (Cheeped), eight-verse (Ashtpadiyan) and the least common, sixteen-verse (Sohilas). The next most common format to Chaupad is Dupade (608 compositions) and then Ashtpadis (311 compositions). The Ashtpadis are the ancient foundation of Vedic Raag verse formation.

Bani

Bani or Gurbani is the collective word for the totality of compositions in the Granth, used in singular or plural sense. Shabads are compositions which are short and have no specific subject headings. Bani with a subject heading are usually much longer than Shabads, though also in Raag, either pure or in folk melody.

Ghar and Taal

Ghar is a musical sign used in the title of a Shabad. It binds music and poetry in their metrical form. Ghar instructs musicians the musical clef (beat) in which to sing the Shabad. There are seventeen Ghars mentioned in the Granth. There is some uncertainty on the precise link between the traditional Indian Taal and Ghar, as both deal with beats. The consensus is that Ghar is sub-Taal. There are over twenty different Taals – beat patterns. Musicians tend to use only the most popular three or four Taals. The most common is Theen Taal, a cycle of sixteen beats divided into four sectors. These beat patterns can also be played at different speeds. The main instruments for keeping rhythm are the tabla, dhol or mridang.

Pauri

A Pauri, step or ladder, is a paragraph of verse in Nit-nem Bani, daily prayers, and Vaars. They generally consist of a stanza of six to eight lines. Pauri is equivalent to a Shabad but it may not have the latter's verse uniformity. Pauris, as the name suggests, often link different themes into a cohesive pattern, as in Vaars, or one Pauri leads to the next one in developing the same theme in increasing complexity, as in Nit-nem Bani. Pauris are also used in question and answer formats as in Japji, the Nit-nem composition of Guru Nanak.

Vaars

Vaars, ballads, are an ancient form of poetry narrating exploits of heroism and chivalry. There are twenty-two Vaars in Raag in Guru Granth, composed by the first, third, fourth and fifth Gurus. Asa Ki Vaar, a composition by Guru Nanak, is the best known Vaar, sung in the morning service in Gurdwara. Guru Arjan Dev later added Saloks by both Guru Nanak and Guru Angad to this Vaar. A Salok precedes each Pauri of the Vaar to enhance the thought contained in the Pauri. The Pauris of a Vaar are by the same writer but Saloks may be by the same or another author. Asa Ki Vaar contains Saloks by Guru Nanak and Guru Angad.

Both the Gurus and Bhagats composed Vaars. There is one added Vaar composed by Bhai Satta and Bhai Balwand, musicians in the service of Guru Arjan Dev. The Vaars, composed in Raag in folk tunes, have the battlefield as their motif, but use the analogy of a spiritual battlefield where good and evil fight each other to gain supremacy.

Chhants

These are compositions in praise of God. A stanza of a Chhant contains four to six verses. In Asa Ki Vaar, it is customary to include Chhants composed by Guru Amar Das when musicians are singing it, though this arrangement is not included in the Granth. Chhants follow Pauris in Asa Ki Vaar, when it is being sung.

Swayyae

These are compositions in praise of the Gurus in their quest for unity with God. Swayyae use long and short syllables in unique arrangements as their distinguishing feature at the end or within a verse. There are 122 Swayyae in the Gurbani, composed by Guru Arjan Dev, in praise of God, and by Bhatts in praise of the first five Gurus as devotees of God. Bhatts served as poet-musicians to the third, fourth and the fifth Gurus.

Bhagat Bani

Compositions by seventeen Bhagats are recorded in Gurbani. They lived from the twelfth to the fifteenth century. The lives in brief of four Bhagats whose Bani constitute eighty-five per cent of Bhagat Bani are as follows:

Bhagat Kabir (1308-1395) was born to an unmarried Brahmin mother near Varanashi. A Muslim weaver family adopted the abandoned baby. Kabir was married and had several children. Kabir challenged Hindu beliefs based on superstition and ignorance. Kabir is the best known Bhagat in the Indian religious pantheon. There are 541 compositions by Kabir, recorded in seventeen Raags and numerous Saloks in Guru Granth.

Sheikh Farid (1173-1265) A Sufi Muslim who was born in the Punjab. He is the first recorded poet of the Punjabi language. There are 134 compositions of Bhagat Farid in two Raags and 112 Saloks in Guru Granth. These deal with love, forbearance and good actions. Death, he pronounced, was most often a wasted life, due to indifference to God and righteousness.

Bhagat Namdev (1270-1350) Born in Maharashtra to a caste Hindu family, Bhagat Namdev was married and had five children. He lived in the Punjab for twenty years. Sixty of his compositions are recorded in the Granth in eighteen Raags. They show the influence of the Marathi, Hindi and Persian languages. Namdev rejected caste and advocated the worship of one God.

Bhagat Ravidas (14th century) Ravidas was born near Varanashi to a low caste Hindu family. He is believed to have been a contemporary of Kabir. He travelled extensively in the Punjab. Forty of his compositions in six Raags are recorded in Gurbani. Ravidas emphasised God's omnipresence and omnipotence.

Named Bani

Named Bani show the interest of the Gurus in nature, the changing seasons, social issues, past history and Indian languages. The Gurus used folk music in Raag to express their thoughts in popular language. Gurus used their compositions as metaphors for the need for spirituality, the path to knowledge and self-realisation.

Their wide interests are reflected in their compositions on the four divisions of the day, seven days of the week, twenty-eight lunar days of the month, four seasons and twelve months of the solar year.

Verse experimentation is shown in Phuney, repetition. The word 'Harihan' is repeated in the fourth verse of each stanza in Phuney Bani. Chaubole, four speakers, a popular song format, is a discourse between Guru Arjan Dev and four Bhatts – Somoan, Moos, Jan and Patting.

Patti is a composition by Guru Nanak, in which each letter of the Gurmukhi alphabet is represented by a verse. Guru Amar Das, in his Patti, has used some other alphabet of the period. Two more similar compositions are named Bawankhris, fifty-two letters. The first is by Guru Arjan Dev. The second is by Bhagat Kabir but it has only thirty-six letters.

Sahskriti, Gatha and Dakhni are dialects from South India in which some compositions were recorded. These dialects are now extinct. The named Banis in the Granth are as follows:

Subject	Author and Raag
Time	
Pahrei, quarters of the day	Gurus Nanak Dev, Ram Das and Arjan Dev
Barah Maha, 12 months, seasons	Gurus Nanak Dev (Raag Tukhari), Arjan Dev (Raag Majh)
Din Rayni, day and night	Guru Arjan Dev (Raag Majh)
Thittin, lunar calendar days	Gurus Nanak Dev (Raag Bilaval), Arjan Dev and Bhagat Kabir (Raag Gauri)
Vaar Sat, seven days of the week	Guru Amar Das (Raag Bilaval), Bhagats Kabir and Namdev (Raag Gauri)
Alphabet	
Patti, alphabet	Guru Nanak Dev (Raag Asa)
Bawan Akhri, acrostic	Guru Arjan Dev and Bhagat Kabir (Raag Gauri)
Nit-nem Bani	
Sukhmani Sahib	Guru Arjan Dev (Raag Gauri)
Anand Sahib	Guru Amar Das (Raag Ramkali)

Japji Sahib	Guru Nanak (verse, not in Raag)
Reheras Sahib	Composite Shabads in various Raags of Gurus Nanak Dev, Ram Das and Arjan Dev compiled by Guru Arjan Dev
Kirtan Sohila	Composite Shabads in various Raags by Gurus Nanak Dev, Ram Das and Arjan Dev compiled by Guru Arjan Dev
Asa Ki Vaar	Guru Nanak Dev (Raag Asa). Guru Arjan Dev added Saloks by Guru Nanak and Guru Angad.

Miscellany

Vanjara, the merchant	Guru Ram Das (Sir Raag)
Ghorian ('mares'), wedding songs	Guru Ram Das (Raag Vadhans)
Alahnian, dirges	Guru Nanak Dev (Raag Vadhans)
Kuchji, ill-natured woman	Guru Nanak (Raag Suhi)
Gunvanti, good-natured woman	Guru Arjan Dev (Raag Suhi)
Sadd, the call	Baba Sundar (Raag Ramkali)
Sidh Gosh, dialogue with Sants	Guru Nanak Dev (Raag Ramkali)
Anjuliyan, supplication	Guru Arjan Dev (Raag Maru)
Phuney Saloks	Guru Arjan Dev (Raag Jaijawanti)
Chaubole Saloks	Guru Arjan Dev (Raag Jai)

Dialect	
Dakhni Onkar Saloks	Guru Nanak Dev (Raag Ramkali)
Dakhni Saloks	Guru Arjan Dev, Bhagats Kabir, Namdev and Jaidev (Raag Maru)
Sahskriti Saloks	Gurus Nanak Dev and Arjan Dev (Raag Jaijawanti)
Gatha Saloks	Guru Arjan Dev (Raag Jaijawanti)

Structure of Guru Granth

The standard edition of Guru Granth contains 1,430 pages. The Granth always consists of the same number of verses in the same order on the same page. The Granth is available in large, medium and small size. Large and medium formats are accommodated by changing the type size. The Shiromani Gurdwara Parbandhak Committee (SGPC), Amritsar, is responsible for its publication. There are also a limited number of private publishers who print the Granth under the aegis of the SGPC.

Divisions
The Granth divides itself into three sections. These are arbitrary divisions and do not appear in the Granth.

Part One (Pages 1-13)
This opens with Mool Mantar, the Sikh proclamation of faith. It then records the three Banis of Nit-nem. The first, Japji, composed by Guru Nanak, is the morning prayer. Japji is exceptional in its composition in being set in a non-Raag verse measure.

Next, Reheras, the evening prayer, consists of nine Shabads by Guru Nanak, Guru Ram Das and Guru Arjan Dev. The last composition is Kirtan Sohila, night prayer, with Shabad compositions of Guru Nanak, Guru Ram Das and Guru Arjan Dev. Reheras and Kirtan

Sohila are composite Shabads drawn from within Guru Granth and compiled by Guru Arjan Dev. Some Shabads thus will appear more than once in the Granth.

Part Two (Pages 14-1353)
This is the body of the Granth and is recorded in thirty-one chapters in thirty-one Raags. Each Raag is self-contained and consists of all the Bani composed by Gurus and Bhagats in that Raag. Of the thirty-one Raags, Jaijawanti is the shortest and it concludes the section with one composition by Tegh Bahadur, the ninth Guru. Only Guru and Bhagat Bani are recorded in part two.

Each chapter (or Raag) is arranged firstly by authorship. The authorship is in ascending order from Guru Nanak Dev, followed by the Bhagats. The second level of organisation is the metre of the verse and the third the Ghar, musical clef. The Ghars are numbered 1-18.

All the Guru Bani conclude in the name of Guru Nanak. The authorship is recognised with Mahala 1, for Guru Nanak, Mahala 2, Guru Angad, Mahala 3, Guru Amar Das and so on, inserted in the title. The Bhagat Bani then follow the conclusion of the Guru Bani.

Raag Asa

I have chosen Raag Asa, of the thirty-one Raags, as an example of a Raag chapter in part Two. It is the most familiar and popular Raag with Sikhs as it records Asa Ki Vaar. A study of this Raag in detail illustrates the division of Gurbani within a Raag. The divisions stated are not included in the Granth but are chosen to explain the order of the compositions.

Shabad title	**Comment**
Guru Bani	
Mahala 1, Chaupad, Ghar 1, page 347	The chapter begins with Chaupad, with Guru compositions in ascending order. Within the latter Ghar is accommodated also in ascending order. Other verse formats follow in Chaupad
Mahala 3, Chaupad, Ghar 1, page 348	
Mahala 1, Chaupad, Ghar 2-5, pages 348-360	
Mahala 3, Chaupad, Ghar 2, pages 360-364	
Mahala 3, Panchpade, pages 364-365	
Mahala 3, Kafi sub-measure, Ghar 8, page 365	
Mahala 4, Chaupad, Ghar 2, pages 365-368	
Mahala 4, Kafi sub-measure, Ghar 8, pages 369-370	
Mahala 5, Chaupad, Ghar 2, pages 370-396	
Mahala 5, Kafi sub-measure, Ghar 8, pages 396-409	
Mahala 5, Asavari sub-measure, Ghar 17, pages 409-411	
Mahala 9, Chaupad, page 411	

Mahala 1, Ashtpadiyan, pages 411-418 Mahala 1, Ashtpadiyan, in Kafi, pages 418-422 Mahala 3, Ashtpadiyan, pages 422-424 Mahala 3, Ashtpadiyan, in Kafi, pages 424-430 Mahala 5, Ashtpadiyan, pages 430-432	Ashtpadiyan, octet, eight-verse stanzas, the third most common verse format, follow at this point. Ashtpadiyan is in the ancient Vedic tradition of writing poetry
Mahala 1, Patti (Acrostic), pages 432-434 Mahala 3, Patti (Acrostic), pages 434-435	Ashtpadiyan are followed by thematic, named longer compositions. In this, instance Patti, alphabet, in which each letter of the Gurmukhi alphabet is represented by a verse (Guru Nanak Dev) and in an extinct dialect (Guru Amar Das)
Mahala 1, Chhant, pages 435-439 Mahala 3, Chhant, pages 439-442 Mahala 4, Chhant, pages 442-452 Mahala 5, Chhant, pages 452-462	The next compositions are Chhants, lyrics in four- to six-verse format in one or two stanzas. They recite praise of God

Asa Ki Vaar, pages 462-475

Of the 22 Vaars in Guru Granth, Asa Ki Vaar is the best known. It is a composition by Guru Nanak. Guru Arjan Dev added Saloks by Guru Nanak and Guru Angad to it. Asa Ki Vaar is sung in Asa Todi Asraaja, most commonly in the morning service. In its musical rendition, Chhants by Guru Ram Das are added to the repertoire. The order of singing is Salok, Chhant and then a Pauri

Bhagat Bani
Bhagat Kabir, pages 474-485
Bhagat Namdev, pages 485-486
Bhagat Ravidas, pages 486-487
Bhagat Dhanna, pages 487-488
Sheikh Farid, page 488

The Bhagat Bani follow the same order as the Guru compositions. Bhagat Bani in Raag Asa is in Chaupad. Bhagat Chhants, Vaars and Ashtpadiyan are not found in this Raag. The composition of Bhai Dhanna will be familiar to Sikh readers as it is sung in Arti after the conclusion of the complete reading of the Granth

Part Three (Pages 1353-1430)
The third part of Guru Granth begins at the end of the Raag Shabad section. It consists of a miscellany of Saloks combined in common themes or simply inserted in Guru and then Bhagat order respectively.

Mahala 1, Saloks in Sahskriti, pages 1353-1360	Sahskriti and Gatha are two dialects that are now extinct
Mahala 5, Saloks in Gatha, pages 1360-1361	
Mahala 5, Phuney, pages 1361-1363	These are two compositions by Guru Arjan Dev. Phuney means repetition. In this Shabad, the word 'Harihan' is repeated in every fourth verse. Chaubole, four speakers, is an address by Guru Arjan Dev to four people
Mahala 5, Chaubole, pages 1363-1364	
Bhagat Kabir, pages 1364-1377	Bhagat Saloks are in the next section. The Bhagat Saloks include a commentary in Saloks by Guru Nanak and Guru Amar Das to expand on the Bhagat Saloks. In the commentary on Kabir, Guru Arjan Dev also comments on Bhagat Namdev and Bhagat Trilochan
Sheikh Farid, pages 1377-1385	

Mahala 5, Swayyae, in praise of God, pages 1385-1389 Bhatt Swayyae in praise of Guru Nanak, pages 1389-1390 Bhatt Swayyae in praise of Guru Angad pages 1391-1392 Bhatt Swayyae in praise of Guru Amar Das pages 1392-1396 Bhatt Swayyae in praise of Guru Ram Das 1396-1400 Bhatt Swayyae in praise of Guru Arjan Dev, pages 1400-1410	Guru Arjan Dev composition in praise of God. Then follow the Swayyae composed by Bhatts in praise of the first five Gurus as one spirit in search of unity with God. The compositions are sung in traditional folk tune
Mahala 1, Saloks, pages 1410-1412 Mahala 3, Saloks, pages 1412-1421 Mahala 4, Saloks, pages 1421-1424 Mahala 5, Saloks, pages 1424-1426	Saloks described as in excess of the need of the Vaars
Mahala 9, Saloks, pages 1426-1429	Bhog Bani, epilogue, begins at this point. The 57 Saloks of Guru Tegh Bahadur included in Guru Granth by Guru Gobind Singh are chanted. The Sangat joins in the refrains

Guru Arjan Dev, Mundawani and Salok, page 1429

Guru Arjan Dev concludes his compilation in Mundawani, the seal on the Granth. Mundawani reiterates the gist of the Granth. It says, 'Three things are there in this vessel: Truth, contentment and intellect. The name of God, our sustenance, is added to it. He who absorbs and enjoys it [God's name] shall be saved. One must not abandon this gift. It should ever remain dear to our heart. The dark ocean of the world can be crossed by clinging to his [God's] feet. O Nanak, it is He who is everywhere.'

End of Part Three and conclusion of Guru Granth compiled by Guru Arjan Dev and then by Guru Gobind Singh in its recompilation.

Raag Mala, String or Index of Raags, pages 1429-1430

The last page of the Granth, after Mundawani, contains a further composition called Raag Mala, string of Raags (index). It is of unknown authorship and was probably surreptitiously inserted in the eighteenth century. It provides a summary of eighty-four Raags, whereas only thirty-one Raags are described in the Granth. Its language and style are different from that of the Granth. There has been much debate about its inclusion in the Granth for the past hundred years. Many Sikhs believe that however much doubt about its authenticity, since it is present in the Granth it should stay there. There appears little likelihood that it will be deleted. Any attempt to remove it is likely to cause a permanent rift in the unity of the Sikh faith.

The Sikh Rahet Maryada has struck a compromise. It is against its deletion but it leaves to the discretion of the local Sangat or individuals about its recitation at the end of a complete reading of the Granth. This compromise has largely satisfied the Panth and the author has witnessed both its inclusion and deletion according to the wishes of the Sangat.

106

PART FOUR
The Sikh Way of Life:
Beliefs, Values and
Moral Conduct

CHAPTER 16
The Cosmos in Sikh Faith

Guru Nanak was a gifted child. He found learning easy. Guru Nanak was soon well versed in Persian and Sanskrit, the state and religious languages of the times. Whatever money he had, he gave it to the poor and others he brought home for his mother to feed and clothe. He spent his time with Sants who lived in the jungle near his village.

At the age of twenty-seven, he began his Udasis, odysseys of self-discovery. These lasted twenty-five years during the course of which he made three great journeys. He visited seats of learning of the Hindu, Buddhist and Muslim faiths in India, Assam, Sri Lanka, Nepal and Tibet. He travelled to the Muslim countries in the Middle East, Iran and Afghanistan; Guru Nanak spent more than a year in Baghdad, the centre of Islamic learning.

His quest was to seek knowledge and enlightenment. He was a polymath with a free ranging and formidable intellect. While we do not know much about his contemporaries, Guru Nanak has left his mark as the founder of a major new world faith, the only one in the last 1,500 years.

Global climate change

Great literature lives forever. For every generation, it reveals new insights. Global warming rings bells of alarm throughout the world. Japji is Guru Nanak's composition of his judgement over a lifetime of observing human behaviour. We perceive in Japji his voice, whose meaning becomes clearer as time and events reveal man's progress through the centuries. Guru Nanak urges us to preserve the earth's bounty and not forsake it for selfish ends. Guru Nanak says he cannot conceive of life unless it has a harmonious relation to nature. As a close observer of nature, he missed nothing. Man was but a grain of sand in the order of creation. Though the earth was blessed with such abundance, man should not treat its bounty with abandon. The creation was infinite but man's abode in it was finite. Guru Nanak made these observations 500 years ago, thoughts that are beginning to haunt us in the twenty-first century.

The creation of the universe

In ancient and mediaeval times, theology was used to explain nature and natural phenomena. Guru Nanak put his faith in a creative force that was within and outside its creation. He declined to accept that humans were in a position to explain its existence – past, present or future: we could only speculate.

In Japji, morning prayer, Guru Nanak presciently reflects on our universe. Guru Nanak says that the universe contains a countless number of celestial heavens with infinite stellar bodies. Only the Creator would know the real number. There are billions of galaxies and each galaxy is composed of uncountable stars, their planets with their own moons. Our sun, having nine planets revolving around it, is just one of the billions of stars of our galaxy, which we call the Milky Way.

What is remarkable about Guru Nanak's revelations is that, unlike all other religions, he admits not to comprehending the mysteries of our universe and tells us why.

Guru Nanak wrote his observations in Punjabi, the language of his people. He imparted to them the knowledge of natural philosophy, theology, science and logic. The advantage of illuminating complex thoughts in such basic prose is that it makes it readily understandable and brings it within the grasp of ordinary people.

Guru Nanak (1469-1539) laid the foundation of the Sikh faith during the period of Western renaissance (fourteenth to seventeenth centuries), when science was challenging the concepts of the doctrines of Christianity and the practices of the Church in Europe. For example, Roger Bacon, the thirteenth century Christian monk, spent the final fourteen years of his life in a dungeon for writing that in the quest for truth, observation and deduction are valid challenges to the uncritical acceptance of spiritual authority. During 1633, the Christian church imprisoned Galileo for challenging the concept that the earth was the centre of the universe and the sun revolved around it. The conflict between Christianity and science still goes on although perhaps less dramatically than in the past. Yet Guru Nanak had predicted the nature of creation even before the European renaissance had taken root.

Guru Nanak, in the east, was challenging the ancient philosophy, mythology and rituals to which the people of India, indeed the world, had been shackled for centuries. He promulgated a philosophy of universal humanism based on logic, consistent with modern science. Guru Nanak preached to liberate people from the clutches of priests and their craft, entrapped in the web of superstition, rituals and baseless beliefs.

Manifestation of the Creator

Guru Nanak in his Mool Mantar, Creed of the Sikh faith, explains the Creator as,

'One universal being, truth in name, personified in his own creation
Without fear, without hatred,
Beyond the cycle of birth and death
Self existent, in Grace'.

Guru Nanak says the Creator is Nirgun, without, and Sagun, within, his creation,

'[The Creator] in existence before the beginning
The past and the present
Will remain [in existence] for ever and ever.'

Origin, time and extent of the Universe

Guru Nanak in Japji reflects on the nature of our universe, part of the creation:

Origin of the universe
Guruji says that in the infinity, beyond time, there was a sound (we now call this the Big Bang), the elements began to coalesce and then expand. Thereafter appeared many visible things. What are those things? A number of galaxies each composed of a myriad of stars and suns with their own planets.

Time of origin
Guru Nanak says it is not possible to tell the time of creation, for he asks us to consider the imponderables:

'What was the time and what was the moment
What was the day and what was the date
What was the season and what was the month
When, then, was the universe created?'

In the opinion of Guru Nanak,

'The learned could not find the time,
Even if written in the Purana [Ancient Hindu texts]
Or known to the Mullah either
Even if written in the Qur'an
Neither the hour, the day, the month nor the seasons will be ever known'.

Guruji says the next question is, who knows this? Guru Nanak answers,

'Only the Creator, whose creation it is, knows [the time of creation]'.

Infiniteness of the universe
The universe is not at a standstill. It shrinks in some places but expands in the rest of it. The universe contains a countless number of celestial bodies. Only the Creator would know his creation. Guru Nanak explains the infiniteness of the universe as follows,

'It is not possible to count [celestial bodies]
As the person who counts
Reaches the end of his life during the count
His task remains unfinished'.

Our finite earth

Our earth, like all celestial bodies, is finite. It is a mere grain of sand, a speck, in the scheme of creation. However, this mere speck envelops the wondrous order of our world, its seasons, tides, days and nights. We are part of that order. The Creator infuses his creation with glory as we do ourselves. Guru Nanak says people are not helpless beings bound by fate without a will of their own.

Guru Nanak claims that for the good of their being people must be in harmony with creation, play their earthly role in obedience to the natural law and not be in conflict with it.

The Sikh way of life

Guru Nanak reminds us in Nit-nem, daily prayers,

'Think of the future, look not to the past
Make the present a worthy one to live in
For you will not be privileged to be born again'.

It is thus that Sikhs believe their faith is a way of life, a life like the one Guru Nanak led. It is indeed the dear wish of every Sikh to emulate that way to live.

CHAPTER 17
Guru Nanak Dev: Life Lived

The Sikh faith is a way of life, the life Guru Nanak lived. Six centuries later, in different times and a changed world, his devotees emulate his sacred life with undiminished belief. Guru Nanak is the role model of Sikh living. Guru Nanak devised a moral way of life, which allows its followers to be in harmony with the Creator who permeates his creation. There are no webs and complex patterns to negotiate for a Sikh to follow the life Guru Nanak led as he preached it.

The test Guru Nanak chose for his successor was not just piety but also a life of spiritual and moral conduct, as so beautifully recorded by Bhai Satta and Balwand in their Ramkali Ki Vaar, ballad of succession, recorded in Guru Granth. Guru Nanak wanted his successors to be exemplifiers of moral living, not demigods or ascetics remote from their world.

In his lifetime, Guru Nanak determined the direction of his faith and founded the institutions, which became the way of Sikh moral life. Guru Nanak declared that God ordained the affairs of man. This was his world we lived in. We gain or suffer for our deeds in this world. There was no other world to aspire to.

The daily chores of this world were part of life. Life was not a cipher to be abandoned for a garb of monastic life and giving oneself up to contemplation for future bliss. This was neglect of responsibility upon this earth. It could not be the life God had meant us to lead. Guru Nanak taught that asceticism or abandonment of the world was unnecessary, the hermit and the householder being equal in the eyes of God. Release from priestcraft, from the grossness of idolatry, meant, rather, to set aside evil conduct and to free people from these strangleholds.

Guru Nanak tells us that people who seek eternal life in their piety are in error. Grace is marked with the exercise of our free will and the beneficent use of our faculties. Grace is bestowed upon doers of good works and uprightness of conduct. Gurbani says,

[God will surely ask] 'What have you done to merit Grace?'

Guru Nanak has described these principles in Gurbani. He pronounces,

'I know there is no Hindu, there is no Muslim
God does not recognise caste, ritualism, idol worship
And the beliefs that have no spiritual content'.

The belief was his message and mission on this earth.

It is upon this message that later Guru Gobind Singh infused the minds of his Sikhs with a new order, and to give effect to the doctrine that the lowest is equal with the highest, in race as in creed, in human rights as in religious hopes.

During a lifetime of travel within India and to other countries lasting twenty-five years, Guru Nanak acquainted himself with the faiths of other people and the way they practised them. He discoursed with Buddhists, Hindus, Jains and Muslims in their holy places. Guru Nanak never asked others to change their faith but, within the context of their own religion, to meditate on God in a true way. He urged them to become better Hindus and better Muslims.

Guru Nanak imparted his message of meditation in the name of truth, honest living and care of the poor. Guru Nanak chose to live with poor people and people of the lowest castes. He practised what he preached,

'Oneness of man.'

The offerings he received were given to his hosts to feed the poor and his devotees so that all would sit and eat together without distinction of caste and status. The institution of Langar, sharing together of food, was a nucleus in introducing equality of people, and sharing with others who were less fortunate. His prescription for honest work and living, and condemnation of exploitation, has, from the very beginning, become a core moral tenet of the Sikh faith.

On the completion of his travels, Guru Nanak settled as a peasant farmer in Kartarpur village, on the banks of the river Ravi in Punjab. He spent the last eighteen years of his life there.

Bhai Gurdas, scribe of Guru Granth Sahib, writes that Guru Nanak told devotees not to shirk family life. Family was the fountain of religious worship. Life was not a burden but a privilege. Family life was the medium of moral training and living.

Devotees came to visit and even settle in Kartarpur to meditate in the company of Guru Nanak. Guru Nanak recited Gurbani from before daybreak until the sun was up. He then prepared Langar for devotees with his own hands. Guru Nanak worked in the fields to earn his daily bread. In the evening, it was again time for meditation and recitation of Gurbani.

Guruji told his devotees to return to their villages and preach his way of life. Guru Nanak said that the home of each Sikh was a Gurdwara, abode of God. All Sikhs were equal in the eye of God. Sikhs do not practise rituals or believe in superstition. There were no priests or hermits in his order.

That was Guru Nanak's way of life.

CHAPTER 18
Naam Simran: Meditation upon the Name of God

The Sikh faith is rooted in Naam Simran. Naam is an encompassing word for God and his creation. Simran is meditation in remembrance of Naam, God. God is revealed to a Sikh through Simran.

Guru Nanak instructs Sikhs to keep God in mind and meditate upon his name at all times. Naam Simran, contemplation of God, is achieved with repeated recitation of the word Waheguru, wondrous God. Gurbani uses tens of names for God. However, these are drawn from existing usage of the word. Waheguru is unique to Gurbani. It is not found in any other language or script. Sikhs meditate on the word Waheguru. A devotee may sit in a quiet place to utter Waheguru to himself or while going about life's business. There is no set time, place or mode to recite Waheguru. Any hour of the day or night is suitable for the purpose.

Simran in Sangat, gathering of devotees, has an additional virtue, as God is present in his Sangat. Naam Simran in Sangat cements the relationship between the Guru and his Sikhs. Gurbani says,

'Guru is the Sikh and the Sikh who practises the Guru's words is one with the Guru'.

God is Nirgun, ascendant, outside his creation, and Sagun, within his creation. Guru Nanak says the human body is the shrine in which God puts his light. Our soul is the spark of divine will. The spark will perfuse us with divine light when our self (ego) becomes one with Waheguru.

What separates us then from the Grace that is within us as God intended? What is it that holds us in bondage, not letting us be one with God? Gurbani says,

'It is haumai [ego]
That leads to spiritual blindness
Creates a wall around us
Ruled by passion and instincts
The soul becomes self-centred
Outside the Grace'.

How is haumai, ego, to be overcome? Gurbani says,

'With devotion to God'.

Guru Nanak prescribes no rites, austerities or penances. He rejects outward forms of piety – pilgrimages, fasts and ascetic practices. Devotion alone leads to Grace. Devotion is meditation by immersing oneself in the constant remembrance of Waheguru, the divine name. By devotion one gains control of one's mind. Moral and spiritual virtues spring from man's devotion to Naam. With Naam, man merges into the divine light. A Guru is a teacher, not a divine being. A Guru cannot intercede on our behalf. A devotee who turns to the Guru for instruction does so because of the Guru's wisdom and moral piety, because he is already one with God. The Guru has attained this status through Naam Simran.

The relationship is directly between man and his Creator. Nothing intervenes. Nanak ruled out division among men on grounds of birth, caste or country,

'All men are God's own creation
False is caste and false are worldly titles
One supreme Lord sustains all
Know men by their birth
Do not ask their caste
No one knows the hour or the day
The season or the month of its origin
Only the Creator who made the world
Knows when he made it.'

The creation is self-contained. Nothing divine is lost and nothing gained. The drama of the soul – salvation and transmigration – acts in the shrine within man himself. The spark of life cannot be extinguished. Guru Nanak did not accept existence of heaven or hell as separate entities outside oneself. These are states within us. Wandering souls, celestial flights, paradise or burning worlds are metaphors as real as one believes them to be. If God is within, and God is indestructible, then what need the soul to travel from its abode within man himself? Transmigration is within the sphere that all of us hold within. For Gurbani says,

'If a man loves to see Waheguru, what cares he for salvation or paradise?'

God reveals his creation to us in myriad ways. The will of God is not arbitrary. Man lives in harmony within his Grace. Man is thus his own master in his actions. This is why man has free will to act, with one proviso: Grace circumscribes free will. Man must achieve Grace first. For man is a creation of God, he must first obey his will.

Guru Nanak equates God with truth. Why should we attain truth and live within it? Guru Nanak tells us why,

'Truth is higher than everything else is
But, higher by far is the living of truth
Living of truth is wisdom, patience and obedience.'

How does one put truth into practice? With self-abnegation. Abode in Sach Khand, paradise, is being one with God. It is the object of Sikh devotion. Unity with Waheguru is his paradise. It is when Nirvan, cessation of self, is achieved that the soul blends with God, Grace within. Gurbani reflects,

'And then
Your soul seeks shelter in Naam
Employ all your thoughts on this
Grieve not, hemmed in the mortal frame
Gain in Nirvan is your final joy.'

Again,

'As water blends with water
Two streams their waves unite
Light of human life does blend
With God, celestial light'.

Immersed in meditation upon God, man achieves Nirvan. As Guru Nanak asks,

'What shall we offer him that we may behold his mansions
What shall we utter which will move him to give us his love?'

What is with God that we must meditate upon and how will that alone bring us within his Grace? Gurbani responds,

'Before there was creation
Waheguru was within himself, formless
As Waheguru made the creation, he became sagun,
Manifest within his own creation.'

Within every breath of the creation is Naam. Naam is love, the love we seek by remembering him. Waheguru is not a moral or immoral force but a power diffused within his creation. Guru Nanak tells us that God is not wilful. The will of God does not act as an arbitrary force provided we do not separate ourselves from it. This is the reason for our meditation upon his name. Gurbani says,

'Be one with Waheguru
There is only one way to seek his Grace
Meditate upon his Naam
Only Naam will bring us his love
Knowledge, rituals, meritorious service
Are of little use without his Grace'.

What is Guru Nanak's message? What is it about Naam that is Nanak's mission? What is his proclamation for the Sikhs? Gurbani says,

'Without pleasing Waheguru
All actions are worthless
Serve your Waheguru and remember him'.

Ego is the cause of disorder in our universe. We are mere grains of sand in the creation, yet man presumes to be master of the universe. Man claims to have a special relationship with God. God does not belong to one or other of the religions. Pride blinds us into anger, greed and selfishness. We commit the cruellest of deeds against each other, yet think we are pious and our causes worthy. The way to overcome pride is to consider oneself as a mere vassal of God and to meditate upon Naam. There is no other way. Meditation alone will bring peace upon humankind.

This is what Naam Simran is about.

CHAPTER 19

The Sikh Moral Code

The moral code is revealed to a Sikh in Hukam, divine order.

Hukam

The aim of the life of a Sikh is to seek union with God, so that we may live under his Nadar, Grace. In Sikh faith, Grace is achieved by worship and leading a principled, moral and spiritual life.

Hukam, divine order, guides the universe. Hukam is revealed in Gurbani. Hukam itself does not bestow Grace upon a Sikh. Hukam enables the Sikh to recognise the word of God. It is when a Sikh practises what the Gurbani tells him that Grace is bestowed.

Hukam enables the universe to function in the moral mode. God transmits to the universe, through his Hukam, an awareness of the manner in which to attain Grace.

Gurbani is the voice of God for a Sikh seeking to understand divine purpose. However, and this is crucial to Sikh faith, understanding the purpose is not enough to attain Grace. Mere meditation will not do. A Sikh must also display understanding of the moral purpose of life by living it. Only then is Grace bestowed upon a Sikh. A Sikh interprets Hukam as the moral and ethical governance of life on earth. The unlit divine spark is present in the being of all of us. The spark is lit and Grace bestowed when we recognise its presence and act in accordance with its will. This is Hukam.

For a Sikh, the act of worship consists of meditation upon the name of God and reflection upon the Gurbani to understand Hukam. A Sikh seeks to discover the presence of God in his daily act of worship. He expresses devotion to God by meditating upon Naam, and reciting Gurbani.

The moral and spiritual goals are achieved in three stages. These stages are Puja akal Ki, worship; Dharm Ki Kirt, honest labour; and Vand ke Chhakna, sharing with others.

Stage One: Puja akal Ki, worshipping God

God does not reside in the seventh or fourteenth heaven, or any other place far from the earth, over or under it. God lives within us. There is no place without Him. He expresses Himself through his creation. Sikhs do not worship the elements: fire, water, air, earth or other mythical forces. These elements or forces are themselves the creation of God. These cannot intercede with God on our behalf. It is the Creator not the creation that Sikhs worship.

i. *Naam Japna, reciting God's name*
Sikhs recite God's name in two ways: Naam Simran, meditation upon God, and reciting Gurbani.

A Sikh wakes up in the hours before dawn and begins his worship. He does so sitting in one place or as he embarks upon and goes about his daily chores. He never forgoes an opportunity to recite God's name during his waking hours.

A Sikh reflects upon his Grace. A Sikh meditates to inculcate the virtues of love, benevolence and kindness into his own character. The purpose is not just to carry out a ritual in a prescribed way, but also to feel affection and love for all humans in the fabric of his soul.

This state of bliss becomes stronger with meditation and a stage is reached when Grace is reflected in the demeanour and behaviour of a Sikh. It then gives him inner peace and he achieves oneness with the Creator. He feels the presence of God permeated within himself and his universe. In this state of Grace, instead of hate, serving others becomes life's purpose. A Sikh in Grace is incapable of doing harm as he sees God in every living object. This is why love of Naam, meditating upon God's name, is given the highest priority in Sikh faith.

ii. *Parcha Shabad ka, understanding Gurbani*

Gurbani teaches a Sikh God's virtues and how they are revealed to him. The disciple becomes aware of God in the words of the Gurbani. The daily recitation of Gurbani reminds a Sikh of the pitfalls such as egotism, lust, attachment and greed. Gurbani encourages a Sikh to develop a moral character as they remind him that its virtues will bring peace to him. A Sikh accepts the word of the Gurbani as his guide. He regards Guru Granth as his living Guru because he obtains daily the spiritual guidance he needs from it.

iii. *Didar Khalsa ka, obeying the Sikh Rahet*

A Sikh does not worship pictures, statutes or idols and neither does he honour any living person as his Guru. He obeys only the teachings in the Gurbani and the decisions of the Panth, collective Sikh entity. Guru Gobind Singh bestowed Guruship upon the Granth and the power directly to the Panth to conduct its affairs under its aegis.

iv. *Sarbat ka Bhala, wishing humanity well*

A Sikh wishes others well. In his Ardas, he asks God to give his blessings to all. Sikhs pray not only for themselves but also for the whole of humanity.

The belief in the oneness of humanity, and devoting one's life to working for the welfare of all people in a world torn by strife, is at the heart of Sikh moral and ethical philosophy. Sikhs treat all people, believers and non-believers alike, with respect. Sikhs have no ill will against any person, including even their enemies.

Stage Two: Dharm Ki Kirt, family living and honest labour

In the Hindu religion family living is an impediment to spiritual life, an entanglement to be avoided by seclusion, monasticism and celibacy. Guru Nanak said that meditation and righteous deeds alone were the path to spiritual progress. Man was free to choose between the good and the bad and shape his own destiny by adopting virtue and fighting evil.

Domestic life is a fundamental tenet of Sikh faith. It is laid down in Sikh faith that an ordinary family life, led honestly, alone is the basis of moral progress. The institutions to promote a moral family living which Guru Nanak founded came to be the chief concern of the later Gurus.

Sikhs must earn their livelihood by honest work. Others are not obliged to provide for them. This way they retain their self-respect. A person dependent on others because of obligations is influenced to act as his bread-giver expects. Such a person cannot lead and act an unselfish life. Dishonest living pollutes the mind in the same way that blood stains our clothes. Only honest living is like 'milk' and hence 'sweet'.

Stage Three: Vand ke Chhakna, sharing with others

Naam helps a person to realise that he is part of the shared humanity. Honest living enhances his faith. A Sikh helps those who need his assistance. He shares his earnings with those who have not been as lucky as he is in meeting all their needs.

This sharing is done out of a sense of responsibility, and not as an act of charity. A person can judge how near he is to God by how much he shares his bread with the needy. If he can do so without pride that he has done someone a favour, then he is on the right path. Such acts provide one with the feeling of peace and happiness. If people broadcast the fact that they feed the needy and feel proud of their image as benefactors, then this pride denies them the moral benefits obtained by a person who remains humble.

Guru Nanak identified the moral problems of his age to be caste and class divisions. Guru Nanak observed a greedy and corrupt priestly class. He deprecated the degrading practices of inequality. He repudiated religious rituals that sanctioned such practices.

In Guru Nanak's view, love of God was the criterion to judge whether a person was good or bad. As the caste system was not based on divine love, he condemned it. Nanak founded a casteless, equal society akin to the modern social governance in which all are equal and free of exploitation. The institutions he established to achieve equality are now the cornerstone of the Sikh Panth.

CHAPTER 20

The Core Values of the Sikh Faith

A Sikh is obliged to believe in these values:

1. All are equal before God
2. All creatures possess God's spirit
3. Every person has a right to life
4. Sikhs lead a domestic life
5. Sikhs share their wealth with others who are less fortunate
6. Sikhs respect people of all faiths
7. Sikhs believe in the trinity of Simran (meditation on the name of God), prayer and service
8. A good world is just and fair to all. Force is used as a last resort to uphold justice.

A Sikh is prohibited from these acts:

1. Withdrawing from the world or becoming an ascetic
2. Belief in priestcraft, rituals to propitiate God and superstitious acts
3 Pilgrimage, fasting, ritual bathing, worship of graves, idols or pictures
4 The wearing of the veil for women
5 Intoxicants including alcohol, drugs and tobacco
6 Discrimination on the basis of caste, race, class or gender.

PART FIVE
Sikh Liturgy

CHAPTER 21
Recitation of Gurbani

The Rahet Maryada commends Sikhs to install Guru Granth at home. It is auspicious that a Sikh family carries out regular recitation of Guru Granth and completes a full reading about every one or two months. The family undertakes the reading through its members, relatives and friends. The number of reciters is not prescribed. If unable to install the Granth at home, devotees should listen to recitation from Guru Granth in a Gurdwara at some time during a day.

Paath is the formal recitation of Gurbani. It is recited in various formats. The format described here is the recitation of Guru Granth in its entirety, by a family at home or in a Gurdwara. Five forms of complete Paath are recognised.

Akhand Paath

Akhand Paath is the uninterrupted, complete reading of Guru Granth, over a pre-determined period, usually of forty-eight hours. An Akhand Paath can be performed in a Gurdwara or at home.

The introduction of Akhand Paath in Sikh liturgy is assigned to Guru Gobind Singh who asked his disciples, on his deathbed, not to mourn his demise but take solace in reading Gurbani. It may also be true that Gurbani were recited after the demise of earlier Gurus. Akhand Paath became a common practice in the time of the persecution of the Sikhs following the passing away of Guru Gobind Singh and the sadness they felt at his premature death and the suffering of his family. It gave Sikhs great solace and brought the Sikh Panth closer together in times of such sadness.

As time passed, Akhand Paath came to mark both happy and sad occasions for Sikhs. An Akhand Paath is performed to mark specific occasions, for example a birth, a wedding, a death, an anniversary or other important religious and family events. Paath in Gurdwara marks important dates on the Sikh calendar. Gurdwara also perform Akhand Paath as part of the regular services to allow devotees to come at any time and listen to Gurbani. Akhand Paath for important dates in the Sikh calendar is most often performed at the Gurdwara, whereas those marking family events may also be performed at home.

Initiation of Akhand Paath
Before Akhand Paath begins, the preamble consists of reading the short Anand Sahib, followed by Ardas. After Ardas, Hukam is taken and a Paathi, reciter, ceremoniously begins reading from page one of Guru Granth. Karah Parsad, sacramental food, is distributed when the first five Pauris of Japji have been recited.

A number of Paathis perform Akhand Paath in an unbroken manner. The reading is usually divided into two-hour segments. As one Paathi completes his or her session, the next Paathi continues from the word that the previous Paathi was reciting. A Paathi must be an Amritdhari Sikh. They have a bath and a change of clothes before reciting Paath. Talking or other distractions are not permitted during a recitation and the Paathis must concentrate solely on the reciting of Guru Granth throughout their slot. The recitation must be clear and correct, due care being taken with pronunciation and diction. Reading too fast, so that the person listening to it cannot follow the contents, amounts to irreverence to the Granth. The person reciting Gurbani chants in a melodious voice so that the Naad, the sound current, brings out the poetic quality of Gurbani and their power so grips the listener as well as the reciter that virag, emotion, for the love of the divine overwhelms them both. In Gurdwara, it is a common practice for Japji to be recited simultaneously alongside the Akhand Paath for the same duration.

Variants of Akhand Paath

Any occasion, whether of joy or sorrow, wish fulfilment or trial, associated with life events, anniversaries, commemorations and other occasions would prompt a Sikh household to perform a Paath of the

Granth at home or in the Gurdwara. The form the Paath usually takes at home is known as Sahaj Paath.

Sahaj Paath (Sadharan Paath, Khulla Paath)
This is similar to the Akhand Paath, but there is no time limit to the recitation and completion. The Rahet Maryada suggests one to two months. It is the most common way of complete reading of Guru Granth at home. Sahaj Paath is recited as a religious duty or in anticipation of a family event, a birthday or in memory of a family member who has passed away. For such a recitation, although no time limit applies the family does aim to finish on the day it is being undertaken to commemorate. The commencement and Bhog, end ceremony, are the same as Akhand Paath. The Bhog portion (the last five pages beginning on page 1,426) is either recited at home in the presence of family, relatives and friends or in a Gurdwara even if the previous recitation was conducted at home. The Bhog ceremony is similar in all recitations of the Granth. After the Bhog, Ardas is said, a Hukam taken and Karah Parsad distributed.

The following three variations are occasionally performed in some Gurdwara but are not included in the Sikh Rahet Maryada.

Saptahaik Paath
Saptah means seven and a Saptahaik Paath is an Akhand Paath performed over the duration of a week. It is performed with convenient breaks between the readings. The Saptahaik Paath is begun and finished in the same way as an Akhand Paath.

Sampat Paath
The Sampat Paath is also, like Akhand Paath, performed through an unbroken reading. A certain Gurbani verse is chosen, known as the Sampat, and read after each Shabad in the Granth, hence increasing the duration of the reading, usually to a week. On rare occasions, the Sampat may be recited after each verse and this can increase the duration to around a month. The time is determined beforehand. The Sampat (Bani verse chosen for repeated recitation) is decided by the occasion or purpose of the Paath. Repetition of the Mool Mantar, Sikh code of faith, is the most prevalent choice.

Ati Akhand Paath

One Paathi performs an Akhand Paath in its entirety without a break. The duration is not stated, but has been known to be accomplished within twenty-four hours. The author has not come across an instance of it or met anyone who has, but historical records reveal it was not an uncommon practice before engaging in battles with the enemy during the seventeenth century. The most famous occasion is when Baba Dip Singh Shahid, companion of Guru Gobind Singh and caretaker of the Nanded shrine (last resting place of the Guru), completed an Ati Paath and then went to Amritsar to avenge the sacrilege of Harmandir Sahib committed by the Muslim army.

Bhog, conclusion of Akhand Paath

The last five pages of the Granth are always recited in their entirety in a single session without a break. The Bhog Bani consists of fifty-seven Saloks, called Bhog Saloks, compositions of Guru Tegh Bahadur, and Mundawani Mahala 5 with its Salok, the seal to the Granth, composition of Guru Arjan Dev.

Raag Mala, the end piece on the last page, is then recited. Raag Mala is sometimes omitted according to local convention since there is a difference of opinion on its authenticity within the Panth. Some may wish to conclude Akhand Paath after the recitation of Mundawani and its Salok and not proceed to Raag Mala.

The Bhog Bani is read lyrically and the congregation joins in refrains. The initiation of reading of the Granth and its Bhog are considered auspicious and large gatherings can be expected to mark the occasions.

After Bhog Bani, the Japji is recited followed by Anand Sahib, without interruption. Granth Sahib is closed and Ardas is said, Hukam taken and Karah Parsad distributed. A family organising a Paath will give donations of draperies for Guru Granth Sahib, monetary contributions for the upkeep of the Gurdwara, various

Panthic causes and charitable organisations, and often a set of Pagri, garments and money for the Paathis.

The conclusion of the service is followed with a Langar for the Sangat whether at home or in a Gurdwara.

CHAPTER 22
Nit-nem

The compositions in Guru Granth are called Bani or Gurbani. Recitation of Gurbani from Guru Granth alone is permitted in Sikh liturgy with three exceptions. The first exception is Gurbani of Guru Gobind Singh not included in the Granth. The second is compositions of Bhai Gurdas, scribe of Guru Granth, and Bhai Nandlal, a poet companion of Guru Gobind Singh. The third exception is Ardas, which is partly Gurbani, partly consensus statements approved by the Sikh Panth.

Nit-nem is the name given to five Banis, in the Rahet Maryada, to be recited daily in the form of prayers. A Sikh may recite them alone, with family or in Sangat in a Gurdwara. It takes about two hours. There are other Banis which Sikhs recite on special occasions or on set days established by tradition or the Rahet Maryada. A devotee may also choose to recite these Banis daily as part of his Nit-nem.

There is no need to face in a certain direction, assume a certain pose or seek special surroundings. All places and occasions are suitable for Nit-nem. Nit-nem is recited while wholly devoted to the task, seated in the presence of Guru Granth, if possible, or when carrying out daily chores but concentrating on the Paath. A devotee may also attend a Gurdwara to listen to the recitation of Nit-nem.

Nit-nem Paath is recited three times a day. Ardas is said after each recitation. Three of the Banis – Japji, Reheras Sahib and Kirtan Sohila – are recited in the morning, evening and night respectively and are placed in that order at the beginning of Guru Granth. These were already part of Sikh daily prayers during the times of the Gurus. The other Nit-nem Banis are compositions of Guru Gobind Singh not included in Guru Granth but added by Panthic consensus later to Nit-nem. The convention has developed of reciting Bani either from the Gutka, a compendium of Nit-nem, or from memory, the more usual practice.

Morning Paath
Japji Sahib, Jaap Sahib and Tre-Parsad (10) Swayyae

Japji

At the beginning of Japji is Mool Mantar, the Sikh creed of faith. Japji Sahib consists of thirty-eight Pauris and a Salok at its conclusion. Japji appears at the very beginning of Guru Granth. It is the most revered Bani in Sikh faith, composed by Guru Nanak. The word 'Jap' means to recite. The suffixes Ji and Sahib indicate respect. Japji is the evolving thought of Guru Nanak over a lifetime. Angad, the second Guru, arranged the Pauris in Japji as ordered by Guru Nanak. Japji spans the first eight pages of the Granth. The composition is unique for the Granth since though in verse it is not assigned to Raag. Japji embodies Guru Nanak's vision of the reality of the universe and traces the path a seeker must adopt to realise spiritual enlightenment.

Jaap Sahib

Jaap also means recitation. It is the second of morning Paath. These Bani were composed by Guru Gobind Singh, most probably during his time in Paonta Sahib, a period which saw the flowering of the Sikh literary period. It is said that there were fifty-two poets at one time in the court of Guru Gobind Singh in Paonta Sahib. The contents of Jaap Sahib are divided into Chhants, rhymed couplets. Jaap Sahib has 199 couplets in ten different metres. The language of Jaap is partly Brij Bhasha, a Hindi dialect which freely draws upon the Punjabi, Sanskrit and Persian languages.

Jaap Sahib is an introduction to the understanding of the nature of the Creator. The glories sung by Guru Gobind Singh revolve around the manifest attributes of God. It is a paean to the divine, transcribing the multitude of names of the Creator drawn from different languages including Sanskrit, Persian and Arabic. Among the names of God in Jaap Sahib, there are seventy-five of the ninety-nine names of Allah known to Muslims. Jaap Sahib is a meditation upon the description of these names, illustrated by the opening verse,

'You have no form or feature, No caste or lineage
None can describe your appearance, colour, mark or garb'.

Jaap Sahib is inclusive of all faiths,

'You are the source of all light and the object of all praise
You are the supreme Lord of all and the moon of the universe
Perfect is your discernment, all turn to you for refuge
You are the great Companion, you are the assured Providence'.

Jaap Sahib states in its concluding verse,

'You enrich the universe, yourself self-existent
United with all, the embodiment of mercy
Deliverer from pangs of birth and death
You are man's constant Companion
Everlasting is your glory!'

Tre-Parsad Swayyae (quartets)
This is the third morning text to be recited. These Swayyae are culled from Akal Ustat, a longer composition of Guru Gobind Singh. It is praise of the manifestation of the Khalsa as a tribute to the glories of God.

Evening Paath

Reheras Sahib
The evening Paath is collectively called Reheras Sahib. It has the following component Banis:

Beginning with 'So-dar' is a miscellany of nine Shabads of Guru Nanak Dev, Guru Amar Das, Guru Ram Das and Guru Arjan Dev. It continues after the conclusion of Japji from page 8 to page 12 of the Granth.

Kabyo Bach Benti Chaupai (beginning *'Hamri karo hath dai rachha'* and ending with *'Dusht dokh te leho bachau'*).

One Swayyae
Dohira (couplet) beginning with the words *'Sagal duar kau chhad kai'*

Short Anand Sahib, first five and the last Pauri, composition of Guru Amar Das.

Mundawani Mahala 5 and its Salok, composition of Guru Arjan Dev, which is the seal upon the Granth at its conclusion.

So-dar, Short Anand Sahib and Mundawani Mahala 5 and its Salok Banis are recorded in the Granth. The Chaupai, Swayyae and the Dohira are compositions of Guru Gobind Singh recorded in the Dasam (tenth Guru's) Granth.

Reheras renews faith after a day spent in the chores of daily life. It consoles its reciter, applies balm to his bruised feelings. It concludes with optimism the day of a devotee, who accepts what has occurred as the will of God. The devotee thanks God for his blessings at the end of the day.

At night before repose

Kirtan Sohila
This is a miscellany of five Shabads. The first three are by Guru Nanak Dev, then one by Guru Ram Das and the concluding one by Guru Arjan Dev. It describes the pain of separation from God and celebrates the bliss of his Union. The Bani follows So-dar in Guru Granth on pages 12 and 13.

Recitation of Bani in addition to Nit-nem

Devotees also recited the following Banis as part of their Nit-nem before reforms of the Sikh liturgy in the early twentieth century. Conscious of time restraints and to achieve uniformity, and for no other reason, the Sikh Rahet Maryada introduced the set Nit-nem

Banis which all Sikhs could find time to recite rather than only those who had the inclination to recite all of the Banis daily.

Anand Sahib
Complete composition, rather than the shorter version.

Sukhmani Sahib
A lengthy composition by Guru Arjan Dev.

Shabad Hazare
A collection of seven Shabads from Granth Sahib compiled by unknown hands in either the seventeenth or eighteenth century. The first Shabad is by Guru Arjan Dev and then the remaining six by Guru Nanak. The word Hazare means separation. The word does not occur in the Granth itself. The theme of separation brings the Shabads together. The first Shabad by Guru Arjan Dev is in the form of four letters written from Lahore to his father Guru Ram Das, during his absence from the family. It was originally part of morning Nit-nem, but is not now recommended in the Rahet Maryada. Older devotees still recite it as part of their morning Nit-nem.

Patshahi 10 Kabeovach Benati Chaupai
Only a portion of it is recited in the evening Paath. Devotees may recite all the twenty-five couplets of which it is composed.

Paath for special occasions

Bani are also recited to mark specific occasions or purposes, stated in the Rahet Maryada or established by local Sikh Sangat or family tradition.

Asa Ki Vaar
Musicians in Gurdwara as part of the early morning service sing an ode in Raag Asa. Guru Nanak composed the twenty-four Pauris of Asa Ki Vaar. Guru Arjan Dev added fifty-nine Saloks, forty-five by Guru Nanak and fourteen by Guru Angad during his compilation of the Granth. The Saloks are interpolated between the Pauris. It is the Guru Granth Sahib version that is recited as part of morning Nit-nem

by some devotees. Just as the theme of the Vaar of Tunda Asraj is the victory of good over evil, in the same way the subject of Asa Ki Vaar is spiritual fulfilment. Hurdles in the path of Grace such as ego, hypocrisy and evil are conquered by following the path of truth and meditation. Instead of the clash of arms, we find in the Gurbani Vaars a clash between truth and ritual, piety and hypocrisy.

In singing, a more elaborate pattern is followed. The musicians include Chhants composed by Guru Ram Das, the fourth Guru, in Raag Asa, before each Pauri. These are collectively known as Chhakas – a verse of six lines – from the group of six quatrains, each counting as one unit. Musicians will also sing other Shabads in between the set Pauris if time permits. This is accepted in the Rahet Maryada. Asa Ki Vaar that is sung is available in the Kirtan Gutkas (music prayer books).

Anand Sahib

Anand Sahib, short version, is recited on all occasions at the end of a service at home or in Gurdwara. It is recited in full as part of the Nit-nem by some devotees and at the conclusion of the complete recitation of Guru Granth. Anand means bliss. A person who recites this Bani finds Grace and leads a contented life. The object of reciting the Anand as part of Reheras or at the conclusion of the Sangat gathering is to express joy and gratitude for communion with the Guru obtained after reciting his Bani.

Benati Chaupai

A Chaupai is a verse in Gurbani that uses a metre of four syllables. Benati Chaupai is a composition of Guru Gobind Singh, a prayer on behalf of his Sikhs in twenty-five couplets. Its full title is Kabyo Bach Benati Chaupai. Sikhs recite this Bani to gain solace from worries and afflictions, and to gain self-confidence and raise self-esteem. It gives devotees assurance of communion with God. Benati Chaupai used to be recited before and during skirmishes with the enemy. It is commonly recited in family and Sangat gatherings for strength and forbearance to cope with the daily stresses of life. The Chaupai opens with,

'Please guard us; all my heart's desires are fulfilled
My mind is focused on you; sustain us as your own
Destroy my enemies with your hands, protect me
In bliss remain my household, its members and all Sikhs.

O Creator. Give me your protection, restrain my adversaries
You have fulfilled my wishes; my thirst for your worship grows
If I leave you, may I never worship another
All my needs I get from you, you save my Sikh devotees
One by one you demolish my foes'.

Sukhmani Sahib
Sukh, peace, and Mani, mind or heart. Guru Arjan Dev composed
Sukhmani Sahib, song of Peace, in Raag Gauri. The recitation of
Sukhmani brings peace to the devotee. Sukhmani is the most popular
Bani to be recited outside of the Banis of Nit-nem. It is regularly
recited at home, in family gatherings and Gurdwara to thank God for
his bounty and blessings.

CHAPTER 23
Sikh Arti

Arti consists of Shabads in divine praise. It is recited either by the Granthi or sung by Raagis, to celebrate the Bhog, conclusion of reading of Guru Granth after Ardas and Hukam. Not all Gurdwara follow this practice. Some Sangats regard Arti as too ostentatious and not suited to the simplicity of Sikh liturgy.

The Sikh word Arti is derived from the Sanskrit Arati, a light waved before an idol in a clockwise direction in ritual Hindu worship, accompanied by the chanting of religious mantras to propitiate the deity. The light is from wicks soaked in ghee, purified butter, or camphor. The rite is descended from the rituals of fire worship in pre-historic India.

The Sikh faith rejects image worship and, as the Rahet Maryada states, 'It is considered superstitious to ring bells, burn incense, light ghee lamps and wave them in a platter before Guru Granth'. It is a matter of semantics, rather than its spirit, that many Gurdwara interpret this as allowing this ritual provided a platter contains only flower petals. The platter is not waved in front of the Granth in the form of worship, but the scented petals are gently sprinkled over Guru Granth and the Sangat. In some Gurdwara, Arti Shabads are sung without the spraying of petals.

Not surprisingly, the Rahet Maryada is silent on the performance of Sikh Arti, as it is on other rituals on which difference of opinion has not been resolved. The Sikh reformists of the Singh Sabha School as well as those of the more austere Akali School discouraged the Arti rituals even in their modified pleasing versions. They claim that loving devotion shorn of formal ostentatious practices is the path of true worship in the Sikh faith.

It is recounted that during his travels in India, Guru Nanak Dev stopped at the temple of Vishnu, Lord of the earth, in Jagannath. The local priest visited Guru Nanak and invited him to join Arati, the evening service of lights, in the temple. The Guru readily offered to accompany him to the temple.

As dusk fell, the priests lighted the lamps for the sumptuous ritual to begin, which many devotees had gathered to witness. Twinkling lights fed by ghee were placed on a jewel-studded salver, amid flowers and incense, and worshipfully swung in front of the enshrined image to the accompaniment of the chanting of Hindu verses, blowing of conches and the ringing of bells.

Guru Nanak remained seated in his place and did not participate in the ceremony. The temple priests felt angry and accused Guru Nanak for failing to make adoration to the deity within the sacred enclosure. The Guru replied,

'The sky is the salver
and the sun and the moon, the lamps
The luminous stars on the heavens are the pearls
Scented air from the sandal-clad hills is the incense
The winds make the fan
And the vast forests wreath of flowers
The unstruck music of creation is the trumpet
Thus goes on the Arati [adoration] for you
O [God], dispeller of doubt and fear.'

Nevertheless, the practice of Arti is well-established in Gurdwara, especially at the Sikh shrines. In shrines associated with Guru Gobind Singh, such as Nanded Sahib and Kesgarh, a more elaborate ritual is performed. It is claimed that these traditional rites were in practice before the modern Rahet Maryada was established. In most Gurdwara which allow Arti, including Harmandir Sahib, only the Arti Shabads are sung, without any accompanying rites, though scented flower petals may be sprinkled over the Granth and the Sangat in some places of worship.

The Sikh Arti is composed of Shabads from Guru Granth which have the word 'Arti' mentioned in them. Guru Nanak's Shabad above is one of them. Others are compositions of Bhagats Ravidas, Sain, Kabir and Dhanna. Ravidas says,

'God, your name to me is the Arti, all else is the incense.'

Bhagat Sain opines,

'May I be a sacrifice unto God that for me is the performance [of Arti] with lamps of ghee.'

Bhagat Kabir, trenchant as he always is in his pronouncements, says,

'This is how God's Arti is made. Let divine essence be the oil, God's name the wick, and enlightened self the lamp. Lighting this lamp we invoke God.'

Bhagat Dhanna's Shabad on Arti is a prayer for the common needs of life. Appropriate verses from Gurbani composed by Guru Gobind Singh are added to the Arti performance.

Sikh Arti is performed to show adoration of God as the path of true worship. Gurbani Shabads are chosen to fulfil these requirements. Arti Shabads do indeed reject Hindu Arati rituals, which seek solace from deities and idols. Arti is a celebratory rite after the completion of the reading of Guru Granth, except in shrines where it is recited at a set time every day.

CHAPTER 24
Sangrand

Sangrand is the first day of each month in the Indian solar-lunar calendar. This is the time when the sun passes from one sign of the zodiac to the next. From ancient times the sun and its satellites, the planets, were objects endowed with a celestial mind, capable of influencing the destiny of human beings. They were the deities whose favourable intervention men sought in their affairs. The worship of Surya, the Sun God, was a feature of pre-Vedic and Vedic times, and it has continued in the Indian traditions. This is the day devotees of the sun observe ritual performances such as fasts, bathing at holy places and distribution to charity.

Sikhs do not recognise deities except the Creator. In Sikh metaphor, Guru is the sun that illuminates the mind of the disciple. Guru Nanak composed Barah Maha, in Raag Tukhari, devoting one Shabad to each month of the twelve solar months. Barah Maha starts with the month of Chet, spring, the month of ripening crops, joy and hope.

The first day of Chet marks the beginning of the New Year in the Sikh calendar.

Guru Arjan Dev also composed Barah Maha in Raag Majh. He follows the order of the compositions of Guru Nanak but the Shabads are shorter and are the ones usually recited in Gurdwara.

Guru Nanak in his compositions compares the natural landscape, with passing months, as the yearnings of a bride (devotee) for the beloved (God). In Shabads of Guru Arjan Dev, the mood of the devotee in each month is described in mystical poetry. Guru Nanak says that in the month of Chet nature blossoms, but man's mind will blossom, even at this time of the year, only with remembrance of God. Guru Arjan Dev, in his composition, reiterates that meditation alone in this month would bring the devotee bliss. Living without

Naam brings only suffering and pain. Each moment, hour and day of the month spent on meditation on the Naam brings blessings of God.

Sikhs celebrate Sangrand with special services in a Gurdwara as it provides an occasion for recitation of one of the Barah Maha Shabads. Guru Arjan Dev's Barah Maha is recited to the Sangat. Devotees turn up in large numbers bringing offerings of food to join in these celebrations. Other Gurdwara limit the occasion to recitation of the relevant monthly Shabad on either the day or the next opportune occasion during an ordinary service. The day has no religious significance to Sikhs. Gurbani prohibit Sikhs celebrating any day as auspicious as all days are the same in the divine order.

Sikhs no longer follow the Hindu calendar and now celebrate Sangrand on the first day of the month in the Sikh Nanakshahi calendar. The calendar matches its Western counterpart in the number of months in a year and days in a month. The dates of Sangrand are now fixed and do not change from year to year as in the past with the Hindu calendar.

Guru Nanak tells us of his delight with the splendour of nature in his compositions. He links his message of God to the changing seasons. In his devotion, Guru Nanak takes on the role of a bride longing for her beloved, just as he sought union with God. The sublime description of the poetry of love between man and woman is a metaphor, beautifully entwined with Guru Nanak's love of the creation.

Nowhere is this imagery of love made more vivid than in the Barah Maha. Just as we long for winter to be over and welcome the spring, so does a bride long for her absent bridegroom, and so does he, Guru Nanak tells us, he longs to be united with God.

The sensuous and lyrical compositions of Barah Maha, the pleasure it gave Guru Nanak in composing them, illustrates Guru Nanak's belief in the wondrous order of the creation. Seasons change but there is an order to them. The cycle of change marks divine order imposed on its creation. When things go wrong, for example an earthquake or a storm, normality is soon restored. Guru Nanak says such order, which we are certain will always be restored, can only be the work of an omnipresent Creator.

Since the divine spirit is within us, then we should not look for salvation outside it. There is no heaven and hell outside this world. Our universe is self-contained. Nothing is lost and nothing gained. Ultimately, we are responsible for our actions and the results arising out of those acts. This is why Guru Nanak preached meditation upon the name of God, honest living and sharing with others as the sole objectives of a Sikh's way of life. Barah Maha is unfettered paeans for love of the Creator and his creation and pays tribute to its order, which brings harmony to its universe.

Like Sangrand, Poornmaasi, Massiya and Panchmi celebrate the solar and lunar eclipses, events celebrated as auspicious days in Hindu religion. Sikhs may mark them as novel events but do not attribute to them religious significance.

CHAPTER 25
Sikh Ardas

Ardas is a Sikh prayer of supplication in rhythmic prose. Sikhs recite it at the conclusion of a Paath or service at home or in a Gurdwara. It is recited at the beginning if the Sangat is embarking upon a task and wishes to be blessed. In a wedding, for example, Ardas may be said several times as divine approval is sought for the task in hand. Ardas also signifies agreement of the Sangat if agreement is sought for some action. A Sikh with his family will say Ardas at home to mark family events.

Ardas bears witness to the most moving prose in Sikh faith. It is crystallisation of the history of the Panth and the sentiment of its faith. Sikhs remind themselves when offering Ardas that they are a part of the Khalsa Panth that has triumphed over adversity and suffering. They pray for their Gurus, the martyrs and Sants and wish the future of their faith well.

Ardas is offered standing in front of Guru Granth or, if the Granth is not installed, in any suitable place or direction. Ardas is not inscribed in the Granth. Its format has evolved over centuries of Sikh history from the times of Guru Nanak. Ardas became more formal as the faith developed. Familiar expressions became coalesced and finally the Sikh Rahet Maryada put a stamp on its present form.

The first part of the Ardas is unalterable, as it contains words of Guru Gobind Singh. It quotes the opening lines from Vaar Sri Bhagauti Ji ki Bani. It invokes the blessing of God, and then pays tribute to the first nine Gurus. Next is a Panthic invocation to Guru Gobind Singh and the Granth, the Guru body visible to Sikhs. (The legal definition of a Sikh includes the interpretation of this paragraph.)

The devotee may then offer the full text or a shorter version of Ardas to suit the occasion as accepted by convention. Flexibility in expression is allowed in phraseology developed locally or by a devotee, provided it is in praise of God, recites Sikh historical events, or matters of local or personal interest related to family and Sikh faith in acceptable terms.

Ardas next gives a recital of Sikhs' deeds of sacrifice and suffering during the times of Guru Gobind Singh. Mention is made of the first five Amritdhari Sikhs, Guru Gobind Singh's four sons who were martyred at a tender age and the forty Mukte, immortal martyrs, who sacrificed themselves in the last battle fought by Guru Gobind Singh. Mention is then made of men and women in Sikh history who met martyrdom and kept up the brave tradition of their faith, faced unspeakable horrors but kept their faith unsullied.

The Sangat then prays for the Sikh Panth, their Gurdwara, associations, Chaunki (historic choirs moving nightly round the Harmandir), battles, banners and shrines, which all remind Sikhs of their past glory. Ardas calls blessings upon them all. Then comes the mention of the genocides that followed the times of the Gurus. It recalls the success of the Gurdwara reform movement (1880-1925), blessing those who laid down their lives for the sake of their faith to free their shrines from the hands of apostate Sikhs. It prays for the return of shrines to Sikhs lost in the partition of India in 1947.

The framework provided in the Rahet Maryada allows for the insertion of words to suit the occasion of Ardas. It may be to bless the recitation of Nit-nem, conduct of a regular service, supplication of personal and family events or whatever the circumstances dictate to suit the moment.

The Ardas concludes with a heartfelt wish of the Sangat, on whose behalf the prayer of supplication is being recited, or for the individual or family, for the spread of the word of God and for the welfare and well-being of all humanity.

Text of Ardas

At the conclusion of a service with the recitation of short Anand
Sahib, the Sangat stands up with folded hands. It then sings in
unison a Shabad from Sukhmani Sahib,

'You are my Lord, I make this Ardas to You
My soul and body are all yours
You are mother and father, we are your children
In Your Grace lie many comforts
No one knows your limit
O Lord, You are the highest of the high
The entire creation is strung on your thread
Whatever happens is as per your Command
Your stature and extent is known to you alone
Nanak, a slave of yours, is ever a sacrifice unto you.'

The Granthi offering the Ardas then embarks upon the prayer:

'Ik Onkar [One God]
Sri Waheguruji Ki Fateh [Salutation]

Sri Bhagautiji sahai
Vaar Sri Bhagauti Ji ki Patshahi 10
Pritham Bhagauti simar kai.'
[Ode to the might of the Creator by the tenth Guru: To the God of
just victory, May the Almighty protect us.]

'Having first remembered the prowess of the Almighty, let us think of
Guru Nanak. Then of Guru Angad, Amar Das and Ram Das. May
their protection be ever with us. Remember, then, Arjan, Hargobind
and Har Rai. Meditate on revered Har Krishan on seeing whom all
suffering vanishes. Think then of Tegh Bahadur, remembrance of
whom brings all nine Gurus to mind. God comes to aid everywhere.'
[Words of Guru Gobind Singh.]

There then follow words composed by the Panth.

'Then revered Guru Gobind Singh, who comes to our rescue. The embodiment of the light of all ten Gurus in Guru Granth. Think of its Darshan and reciting of it, say, 'Waheguru'. [Response from congregation.]

Meditating on the achievement of the dear and truthful ones, the five beloved ones, the four sons of the tenth Guru, forty martyred ones, steadfast ones, constant repeaters of the divine name, those given to assiduous devotion, those who repeated the Naam, shared their life and fare with others, ran Langar, wielded the righteous sword and overlooked faults and shortcomings of others, say, 'Waheguru'. [Response from congregation.]

Meditating on the achievement of those women and men who laid down their lives in the cause of their faith and righteousness, had their bodies dismembered piece by piece, their skulls sawn off, mounted on spiked wheels and their bodies sawn, made sacrifices in the service of the Gurdwara, did not betray their faith, sustained their adherence to the Sikh faith with unshorn hair until their last breath, say 'Waheguru'. [Response from congregation.]

Thinking of the five thrones [of Sikh religious authority] *and Shrines, say, 'Waheguru'.* [Response from congregation.]

Now it is prayer of the Khalsa, May its conscience be informed by Waheguru, Waheguru, Waheguru, and, in consequence of such remembrance, may its well-being obtain. Wherever there is Khalsa, may there be divine protection, ascendance of its needs and of the sword of justice, protection of the tradition of truth, victory of the Panth, succour of the holy sword, and ascendance of the Khalsa. Say, O Khalsa, 'Waheguru'. [Response from congregation.]

To the Sikhs, the gift of the faith, the gift of untrimmed hair, the gift of discipline, gift of discrimination, gift of trust, gift of confidence, above all, the gift of meditation and holy cleansing in the Amrit Sarovar of the Harmandir. May the Chaunkis, sacred flags and the sacred rest places [historic shrines in the Harmandir] *abide forever.*

May righteousness reign supreme. Say, 'Waheguru'. [Response from congregation.]

May the Khalsa be imbued with humility and wisdom! May Waheguru guard its understanding!

O Immortal Being, eternal helper of the Panth, benevolent Guru, bestow on the Khalsa beneficence of unobstructed visit to Nankana Sahib and other shrines of the Guru [in Pakistan] *from which the Panth has been separated.*

O Guru, the honour of the humble, the strength of the weak, aid unto those who have none to rely on. True Father, Waheguru, we humbly render to you. Pardon our errors, omissions, and mistakes. Fulfil the purposes of all.

Grant us the association of those pious ones, on meeting whom one is reminded of your name. O Nanak, may the Naam be ever in ascendance! In your will, may the good of all prevail!'

The recitation of the Ardas is complete. The Sangat bows to the floor, and then upon rising, it proclaims

'Waheguruji ka Khalsa, Waheguruji di Fateh.' [The Khalsa belongs to the Lord to whom also belongs the Victory.]

The Sangat, still standing, sings together confirmation of the command of Guru Gobind Singh Sahib, which he gave to the Sikh Panth on 19 October 1708, the day of his demise,

'As per command of the Almighty, the Panth was launched
Sikhs must have faith in Granth Sahib, their Guru-Eternal
Guru Granth is the manifestation of the Guru
Whosoever wishes to have a Darshan [view] *of the Almighty*
Shall find Him in the Shabad.
Khalsa shall be sovereign and none shall oppose them
Those who stray from the path shall rejoin the faith
Those who have faith in Him shall be protected by Him.'

The Granthi then shouts

'Bole So Nihal' [He who responds will be fulfilled].

In response the entire Sangat shouts

'Sat Siri Akal' [True is the Timeless Lord].

Ardas is complete. The congregation bows and then sits down. Hukam follows, Karah Parsad is distributed and the service is complete. The Sangat then proceeds to Langar.

PART SIX
Shabad Kirtan

CHAPTER 26
Shabad Kirtan

Shabad Kirtan has an unbroken tradition from the times of Guru Nanak to modern times. Singing divine praise is the most basic form of devotion in Sikh faith. Kirtan is an essential feature of a Gurdwara service. The main function of the Sangat is Kirtan. Other names for Kirtan are Gurmat Sangeet, Gurbani Sangeet and Sikh devotional music.

We associate Harmandir Sahib, Amritsar, with Kirtan. There is Kirtan from dawn to midnight. It has been ever so. Sitting inside the Harmandir, on its balconies and recesses, in the corridors and in the Parikarma, the devotee hears Kirtan and is immersed in its sound. There are no priests, no commentators, no intermediary between the musicians and the listeners. Kirtan began with Guru Nanak in the sixteenth century. Other Sikh Gurus too composed Gurbani in music. Kirtan during the times of the Gurus in the sixteenth and seventeenth centuries comprised the then-prevalent classical and folk music styles, accompanied by string and percussion instruments.

The Sikh faith has a distinct musical repertoire linked to Sikh Sangat, its devotional setting. Shabad Kirtan is rooted in the religious experience of the Gurus. Music is integral to Sikh worship, holding sway over all life events, birth, Dastar Bandhi (the turban tying ceremony), Amrit Chakkna (baptism), Anand Karaj (marriage) and Antam Sanskar (funeral rites), at home or in Sangat, purchase of a house or business, and celebration of joyous or sad events.

Kirtan is the traditional style of singing Shabads. The two main accompanying instruments, harmonium and tabla, establish the framework of modern Shabad Kirtan.

Shabad Kirtan combines Gurbani with music. Gurbani is chiefly composed in Raag but elements of classical and folk music merge in Shabad Kirtan. The combined music traditions are specific to the

Sikhs and Shabad Kirtan is separate from all other music forms found in India.

Traditionally, the teacher teaches Shabad Kirtan orally to the disciple, rather than by the notation method used in the West. Taksals are the institutions where Sikh theology, scriptures and rituals including Kirtan are taught. Damdama Sahib Taksal, established in the times of Guru Gobind Singh, is the best known of the five Taksals.

The Gurus wrote Gurbani in metric form and then linked it with Raag. A combination of notes of a Raag offers countless tunes to play with. Gurbani and Raag are two sides of the same coin. They are independent yet complement each other. Raag provides melody and cadence to Gurbani. Raag is based on Swar, notes, and a combination of notes with Ghars, beats, produces distinct musical effects in Shabad Kirtan.

Word (Shabad) communicates a message. Raag conveys a feeling. The balance between mind and heart produces spirituality. When Gurbani complements Raag and is bound by its Swar, the effect on the mind is one of utter bliss.

CHAPTER 27
Guru Praise of Shabad Kirtan

In Guru tradition, Kirtan blends Shabad with melody. Kirtan links consciousness with divine presence. The Gurus commend Kirtan as the most effective way of attaining spiritual fulfilment. The Gurus appreciated the power of music over the mind and they conveyed their Gurbani in music. Gurbani says,

Divine music resounds in the Mandir [Gurdwara]'.

Bhai Gurdas reminds Sikhs of the value the Gurus placed on Kirtan,

'Read of God, write of God, repeat God's name and sing God's praise
The Lord shall safely take you across the troubled ocean of the world'.

Guru Ram Das says Kirtan bestows Grace upon us,

'When you sing Gurbani, divine music is heard
The generous Lord has given us this gift
Through it the human soul merges in the Supreme Light'.

Through Kirtan in Sangat, a Sikh shares the divine presence. The devotee shares the state of equipoise (Sahaj) induced by Kirtan. Guru Arjan Dev says,

'By the blessings of Sants, one utters the holy name
By the grace of Sants, one sings Kirtan'.

The Guru is manifest in Sangat because in Sikh faith God is present in Sangat. Bhai Gurdas says,

'The Sangat is the Mansarovar Lake [holy Himalayan lake]
The Sikhs are its swan

They digest the diamond-like words of the Guru through Kirtan'.

Guru Arjan explained Kirtan by comparing it to the recitation of Gurbani,

'Prayer is like irrigation by water from a well, which only benefits a few fields
Kirtan in Sangat is like rainfall, which covers the world and benefits many people'.

Gurbani says,

Of all meditations, the most important is meditation of One [God].
Of all sounds, the most pleasing is the Kirtan of God'.

It is so because,

'Guru is Shabad and the Shabad Guru'

Guru Arjan Dev said,

'Kirtan is like a diamond,
Full of bliss and deep in qualities
On whomsoever the Lord showers his grace
Kirtan becomes his sustenance'.

Music transcends barriers of country, language, race or religion. Guru Nanak travelled to many countries in his twenty-five years of travel. Kirtan was his mode of communication. Music unites us with each other but, even more, it unites us to God. Music, Gurbani say, is the language of the soul.

Guru Ram Das said,

'Whomsoever performs Kirtan or listens to God's praise is loved by the Lord himself
People consider my Shabads as songs but know that they are meditations on the divine'.

Music overcomes ego. It intensifies longing for God. The Gurus' way begins to enlighten us. A Sikh becomes blessed with Grace. Gurbani says,

'As my ego fades, I realise
God is Shabad encompassing the worlds'.

How does Kirtan bring solace to the devotee?

'The melody of Kirtan pleases our ear
The Shabads bond us with love of Guru'.

Our minds are freed of worldly worries, angry thoughts and vengeful ideas,

'Whoever chants or listens to Kirtan
Their dark thoughts vanish
All wishes are fulfilled
In addition, hope is strengthened'.

And,

'Removes sorrow, brings joy to devotees'.

Our minds then become receptive to Gurbani. Our souls become one with the Guru,

'When the self awakens to the melody of the Shabad
The body is detached from worldly pleasures
The mind is tuned to the name
Devotion to Guru brings bliss in the Shabad'.

The Kirtan merges our consciousness with the supreme will,

'From the melody comes meditation
The Sikh is divinely enlightened'.

Kirtan reveals the truth contained in Gurbani,

'Nanak, the minstrel, conveys the divine truth
Through pious songs'.

And,

'Nanak, the bard, says this
You are the sustainers of all life'.

CHAPTER 28
Genesis of Shabad Kirtan

Classification
i. Classical music (Shastrya Sangeet) is played according to the scheme of Raag melodies.

ii. Light classical music (Bhav Sangeet) is less rigid and does not require extensive knowledge of Raag. Bhajans, Shabads and Dholak Geet, which produce a blend of rhythm, tune and tempo, are sung in this style.

iii. Folk music (Desi Sangeet) is the popular regional music based on simple tunes, dharna or taraz. Jotiyan-de-Shabad, the Sangat singing in unison, is a popular form of Desi music in the Sikh faith.

Indian music versus Western music

Indian music, like its Western counterpart, is based on melody and rhythm, but it does not have a foundation of harmony and counterpoint so vital to the latter. The Indian system is horizontal. One note only is played at a time in a given order, while the European music is vertical, harmonic, in which a group of notes is played simultaneously. Another notable difference is in the place of 'composition' in both systems. In Western music, a composer first composes music and then puts it in notation. The players then play it under the guidance of a conductor.

In an Indian musical performance, while the grammar of melody and rhythm is fixed, the skill and ingenuity of the musician lie in his improvisation and creativity, especially in evocation of mood. In the West, we first construct solid blocks of music. After having carved them out geometrically, in large sections, like building stones, the degrees of the diatonic scale are then lined up and placed on top of each other according to ingeniously worked out architectural laws called counterpoint and harmony. In this way are erected splendid edifices in sound. In the East, instead, music is refined to a wire-thin thread. The musicians strive to stretch out the sound, to refine it to the point of extreme delicacy.

Use of Raag in Gurbani

The Raag version the Gurus followed was the ancient Dhrupad, a meditative style of music. Four basic elements are discernible in this system: Raag (melody), Taal (rhythm), Padd (text or Shabad) and Dhyaan (meditation upon Padd). In Dhrupad, the text is of prime importance and music plays a supportive role. Gurbani music is a true reflection upon ancient elements of Indian devotional music. Its emphasis is, however, on the latter two elements, Shabad and Dhyaan. These are key to Kirtan and distinguished it from other forms of Indian classical music.

The Gurus continued to develop the distinct melodic and percussive system of Raag introduced by Guru Nanak. An example is Partaal, a variant within the Dhrupad style, unique to Kirtan, introduced by Ram Das, the fourth Guru. Different verses are sung in different Taal, rhythm, and tempo. The rhythmic variation draws the listeners' attention, by the frequent change in emphasis in Shabad singing into the nuances of its meaning. Partaal is akin to folk music, a variation within Dhrupad style. Folk music tradition is adapted to record life events – Ghorian, sung at marriage, Alahnian, at death, Vaars to glorify warriors and Swayyae in praise of the Gurus for their devoutness.

Kirtan has seen rapid changes in the past fifty years. The mediaeval, staid classical style has been largely replaced by contemporary lively classical genres.

While Kirtan has retained the ancient devotional Dhrupad style, the main trend in North Indian classical music even before the times of the Gurus was towards the Khayaal style, developed later in the Mughal courts, in which music became of paramount importance at the cost of the text as in Dhrupad style. Khayaal, the predominant North Indian classical style, is music for its own sake. Musical artistry is the focus, and the text of little significance. The Khayaal style explores melodic articulation whereas Kirtan explores spiritual expression. The purpose of Shabad Kirtan is not the development of Raag, but the exposition of the Shabad in it. While maintaining the structural purity of the Raag, its details are employed to express the nuances in the text. Gurbani says,

'Sing Bilaval [a Raag], but only with divine words'.

And,

'Melody, music, and the word of the Shabad are beautiful, when in meditation'.

Shabad is the focus in Kirtan. A musical performance that compromises this focus undermines its devotional impact. Musical syllables (akaar, sargam) are not sung in Gurmat Sangeet as is so common in other types of Raag. Melodic and rhythmic improvisation is performed in a manner that retains textual clarity and deepens the text's emotional content and its understanding. The purpose of Kirtan is to go beyond sensual enjoyment toward divine consciousness. Gurbani says,

'Above the six chakras of the body dwells the detached mind
Awareness of the vibration of the Shabad is awakened deep within
Unstruck melody of the sound resonates within my mind
Through the Guru teachings, my faith is confirmed in the divine'.

It is true to say that Shabad Kirtan is in the ancient Raag traditions, while other styles of music have departed from their roots and no longer evoke the sense of our ancient past as the Sikh Kirtan does.

Why did Guru Nanak adopt Raag as the medium of his expression?

There are three essential aspects of Raag. First, Svar, medium of expression in Raag, is not just a musical note, it is the link to our unconscious self. In Svar, Raag is an inward journey. Gurbani Raag takes us deep within our soul where the divine dwells. Gurbani says,

'The enlightened svar thus reinforces the message [In what way?]
O my mind, you are the embodiment of the divine light – recognise your own origin'.

Second, Raag leads to Ras, emotional awareness. In Kirtan, a listener perceives the reality in Gurbani that was not available to him otherwise. Ras inculcates devotion.

Third, different feelings and emotions are experienced with different Raags, played at certain times of the day and in changing seasons. For example,

Happiness and joy	Raags Bilaval, Basant, Mali Gaura, Nat Narayan
Sadness of separation, detachment (longings for union with God)	Raags Bhairaagi, Gauri, Maajh, Tukhari, Jaijawanti, Gujri, Sarang, Vadhans, Malaar, Tilang, Bhairav
Meditation on name of God	Raags Sorath, Parbhati, Kaanra, Kalyan, Sarang, Bihagara
Joy on union with God	Raags Soohi, Gaund, Devgandhari
Love, calmness and beautification	Raags Ramkali, Tukhari, Kedara
Motivation, satisfaction and balance	Raags Sri, Gujri, Bihagara, Sorath, Dhanasari

Another aspect of Raag classification is time and seasonal. There are morning, afternoon and evening Raags. The mind undergoes mood change during a twenty-four hour time cycle. No Raag is indicated from the time of midnight to three in the morning, a time of repose for the body.

6am-9am	Bhairaagi, Devgandhari
9am-12pm	Sarang, Soohi, Bilaval, Gujri, Gaund, Todi
12pm-3pm	Vadhans, Maru, Dhanasari
3pm-6pm	Maajh, Gauri, Tilang, Tukhari
6pm-9pm	Sri, Basant, Mali Gaura, Jaitsree, Kedara, Kalyan
9am-12am	Bihagara, Nat Narayan, Sorath, Malaar, Kaanra, Jaijawanti
3am-6am	Asa, Ramkali, Bhairav, Parbhati

Raags also have seasons associated with them. Basant Raag is sung in Basant, spring, and is associated with Raags of happiness.

Structure of a Shabad

Shabads were composed with the spontaneous outflow of divine inspiration and not with prior choice of melody. The Shabads were then set in a given Raag, using the Salok (couplets, foundation stones of Gurbani Shabads) format to build Padd, Shabad. Within the Shabad itself, the most important component of a Dhrupad composition is Rahau.

Rahau, pause, forms the central thought of a Shabad. The burden of the Shabad lies in the Rahau Salok. Rahau may occur at any place in a Guru Shabad, though it is always the first line in Bhagat Bani.

The musicians always sing the Rahau Salok first, usually in chorus (Asthai). Antra, the remaining Shabad verses, are numbered, indicating the sequence in which they must be sung. The Rahau verse is repeated after every recitation of an antra line. The Antra elaborate upon the Rahau theme. This flow, pause, and repetition of the Rahau verse in refrain helps its message to be drummed into the listener's mind. It is the essence of the Dhrupad foundation of ancient Raag.

Trends in Shabad Kirtan

Shabad Kirtan has evolved since the times of the Gurus but retains its traditional flavour. The Kirtan we see in Gurdwara today began from the time of Guru Arjan Dev. Kirtan Jathas, group of musicians, would sing Gurbani to Raag. There were two traditions of Kirtan Jathas. One played the rabab and the others non-rabab string instruments. Rabab players were mostly non-Sikhs, usually Muslims. Since the partition of India in 1947 the rabab school of music has died out in India.

The tradition of non-string instruments has also given way to the use of the harmonium and tabla. The harmonium was introduced to India towards the end of the nineteenth century. The harmonium liberated Kirtan. It is easy to learn. A novice learns to play and sing basic tunes with just a little training. In fact, that is the most common level of achievement in amateur players. However, it does take years of learning and practice to become proficient at it.

While the harmonium is of European origin, the tabla has evolved from the Indian barrel drum. Its introduction to Kirtan is no earlier than the introduction of the harmonium in the late nineteenthth century. The harmonium and tabla have almost exclusively replaced all other instruments in the performance of Shabad Kirtan.

Kirtan in modern times

Gurbani acknowledges the ancient music traditions of Indian music. Yet scholars claim that Shabad Kirtan has a style of its own. Modern times have seen the flowering of the tradition of the performance of Shabad Kirtan. A better understanding of Gurbani, higher standards of education and training, and advances in technology have led to immense popularisation of Shabad Kirtan. There cannot be some gold standard of Shabad Kirtan, past or present, which a musician must follow. Music, like all art forms, is not set in stone. Shabad Kirtan has kept with the times and has not lost its allure for Sikhs. Gurbani is now sung within a broad remit of a lighter interpretation of Indian musical tradition. It speaks not to its denigration but respect and understanding of Gurbani as the Gurus surely intended it to be.

Purists complain that traditional forms are dying out with radio, television and the internet introducing modern styled Kirtan. An example is the performance of Shabads with string band music producing a fresh and resonant melody. These innovations enrich the repertoire of Sikh sacred music. The 'internationalisation' of Kirtan and its performance in Indian and Western styles – though distinct at present – may result in the course of time in an amalgam of the two types. Just as the harmonium and tabla replaced traditional string instruments, which were difficult to play and limited in their scope, without anyone mourning their loss, so can we look forward to innovation and variety in Shabad Kirtan in the future.

Guru Granth specifies the Raag that the Shabads are to be sung in. However, the exact specification is of concern more to music theorists than performers. The art of performance is more attractive and sensual than adhering strictly to the Raag itself.

As the basic notes of two or more Raags may be the same, countless musical variations can be accommodated within the same Raag, as we have discussed above. That is the strength of Indian Raag. The same applies to the universality of Gurmat Raag.

It is a misconception that Raags are something highly 'classical', that is esoteric, difficult to learn and beyond the realm of the common person's understanding. However, in Guru Granth, the Gurus have gone into depths of poetry, music and metrical forms to lay the framework that is best suited to convey the feeling and message of the Shabad simultaneously to the mind and heart without a compromise to the ancient traditions of Indian music.

Link to the Past

The oral tradition of Indian music means we have little knowledge of how Kirtan was performed in the past. Similarly, we lack appreciation of the type and quality of stringed instruments used in the times of the Gurus. It is difficult to discuss specific Raags in the mediaeval context, as more than 500 years have elapsed since Guru Nanak's time, and Raags have undergone profound evolution during the period. The old forms of folk tunes are also matters of conjecture now and some forms are no longer performed. However, some formats do survive and give us a clue to the musical systems of the past.

Raags Maajh, Asa and Malaar form the basis of Vaars. Guru Nanak composed three Vaars using these Raags. In his Tunda As Raja Ki Vaar, we can compare the dhuni, tune, of the Vaar with the Raag, which the Guru has adapted elsewhere in his Bani. The similarities between the Raag of Guru Nanak's Bani and folk musical forms allow us an insight into how Gurbani was sung during the times of the Gurus.

Tunda As Raja Ki Vaar is set to Raag Asa, which was developed from the folk tune Asa Des. Rababis and Dhadhis have preserved this tune in an authentic form to the present day. The tunes of the Vaars and the folk ballads have an intricate interrelationship. Because of the intact way these have passed through centuries, Tunda As Raja Ki Vaar is described as a valuable marker for us to study the originality of music in the times of the Gurus. The recitation of Guru Nanak's Vaars in Raag Asa has been performed every day in Harmandir Sahib for the past three centuries.

The Tale of King As Raja

As was a son of Raja Sarang. His stepmother, the king's second wife, fell in love with him. As refused her advances. The queen, frustrated, falsely accused him of advances towards her. Raja Sarang ordered the execution of As at the insistence of the queen. The executioner took As to a jungle and cut off one of his hands as a "proof" of his death and abandoned As to his fate. A passing party of traders heard the cries of As. They took him to a neighbouring village and sold him to a waterman. He called As, Tunda, a cripple (Tunda-As).

The king of the town died suddenly without leaving an heir. The ministers decided that the man who passed through the city gates first the next morning would be crowned king. As usual Tunda-As, who went out in the early morning with his washing to the river, happened to be the first man to pass through the city gate. He was crowned and called Tunda As Raja (King As, the cripple).

Soon thereafter, the crops failed because of drought. As Raja bought grain to feed his people. Raja Sarang, father of As Raja, also sent his ministers to buy grain from the neighbouring country. A minister came to As Raja's town in his search and recognised As. Raja Sarang came to know of his wife's trickery. He offered As his crown as the rightful heir to his throne. His other sons waged war to gain the throne. As Raja won. The court poet composed a Vaar to be sung in a dhuni (tune) in praise of As Raja, symbol of the victory of virtue over vice. Guru Arjan Dev found a great resemblance between the Pauris of Guru Nanak's Asa Ki Vaar and the Vaar of Tunda As Raja and prescribed the tune of the latter for the singing of Guru Nanak's Vaar.

CHAPTER 29
Shabad Kirtan in Gurdwara

Shabad is a composition in praise of God. Shabad Kirtan is Shabad singing. Shabad Kirtan conveys the message of the Guru in music.

A Raagi is a Sikh musician, man or woman, who combines training and ability in Raag music with an understanding of Gurbani. Raagi Jatha is the set of musicians, usually three in number, who combine playing music and singing Shabads.

Instruments

String musical instruments were used in Kirtan during the times of the Gurus. Guru Arjan Dev says,

'Rabab, pakhawaj, and rhythmic ankle-bells play
The Unstruck (celestial) music.'

There are two types of musical instrument:

'Note' instruments, for example, sitar, sarod, bansari and harmonium, and rhythm instruments, for example tabla, mridanga, pakhawaj and cymbals.

There are two types each of note and rhythm-producing Indian musical instruments.

Note producing instruments: String instruments and wind instruments
Rhythm producing instruments: Percussion instruments and idiophones

String instruments
When the strings of the instrument are touched or played upon, they vibrate and produce different notes. String instruments are played

with fingers, for example tanpura, veena, sitar, rabab, been and saroj, or with a plectrum, for example sarangi, dilruba, taoos, and asraj.

The tanpura/tamboora (four strings) is an old and popular instrument used for accompaniment of vocal music. The sitar (seven strings) is the best known of the Indian string instruments, played usually to produce music only, unaccompanied by singing. The components of a sitar are similar to those of the tanpura.

The veena is the oldest known string instrument, attributed to seventh century India. The instrument was the favourite of Saraswati, goddess of learning. The veena has seven strings of brass. It is played in a horizontal position as it rests on the lap of the player.

The sarangi is a popular thirteenth century north Indian string instrument. The body is of teak wood and the lower part is covered with a skin. The upper part containing the pegs is joined to the lower part. There are, usually, three strings made of catgut, held in a vertical position and played with a bow which is different from that used for a violin.

The rabab was the string instrument Guru Nanak chose to accompany his Shabad recitation. His companion, Bhai Mardana, played it. It is similar to the Persian rebec. A rabab has a piece of hollow wood at the top and a circular wooden belly covered with a sheepskin at the bottom. There are two bridges, one in the middle and the other at the tip. The two bridges support six gut strings. The rabab is played with a triangular wooden plectrum. Its sound resembles the human voice. The effect of the drum-sound produced by it is very pleasing. It is eminently suitable for devotional music.

The sarinda closely resembles the sarangi and was invented by Guru Arjan. It is about two feet (60 cm) long, its bottom is oval and it has three catgut strings. It is played with a bow. Sometimes small bells, gungroos, are attached to the bow to produce a rhythmic jingle along with the notes.

Wind instruments
In wind instruments, air columns produce notes. The air is blown in with the mouth, as in bansari, clarinet, shenai and flute, or through bellows as in a harmonium.

The flute, an old and commonly used wind instrument, is found all over the world. In India, the flute is made of wood, though flutes made of ivory, brass and silver are also common. Bansari and murali are other common names for it. The Indian flute is about a foot (30 cm) long and has a mouthpiece and a variable number of holes. The length of the flute and the number of holes differ from region to region.

Shehnai is a relatively later instrument of the wind family. The oboe-like double reed instrument is considered auspicious and is played at life events such as weddings and birthday parties. It is not used in Shabad Kirtan.

The harmonium is the mainstay of Shabad Kirtan. The word harmonium is derived from the Greek word harmony. The harmonium, a reed-blown instrument, is similar to a large harmonica with mechanical bellows and a keyboard. The bellows are worked by a player's hand to force air into a wind-chest and then through channels opened or closed by means of a keyboard. The notes are produced by reeds made of steel. When the keys are touched and the bellows are inflated by hand, the air passes through the inner reeds and produces twelve notes (seven shudh, four komal and one teevar). The harmonium has either single or double reeds. It is easy to handle and is the most commonly played note-producing musical instrument in India. The harmonium has fixed notes and its tones cannot be changed. It is very suited as an accompaniment to a vocalist in Kirtan, as the singer and the music player are the same person.

Percussion instruments
These instruments produce sounds when a dried animal skin, tightened by leather braces or cotton straps, is struck with the fingers or palms of the hand, or wooden or metal sticks. These instruments

are used to produce taal, rhythm. Mridanga, tabla, pakhawaj, dhol, nagara, dhadh and damru are well-known percussion instruments.

A tabla consists of two drums. The drum with the black paste is called siyahi, inky. It is played with the right hand and is the real tabla, with its octave tone range. The drum played with the left hand is the bass or the drone counterpart and is called dugga, duggi or bayan, left. A tabla player keeps the two drums in front of him, the real tabla on his right and duggi on his left. The tabla is the instrument of choice in producing taal in Shabad Kirtan. It is a difficult instrument to master and is physically demanding.

The mridanga and pakhawaj are ancient instruments. The mridanga was formerly a clay drum but is now made of wood. The pakhawaj resembles a tabla, with the difference that the latter consists of two drums, while the pakhawaj is one long barrel-shaped drum with skin covers on both its unequal ends. The left side is smaller than its right side.

Dhol is another popular drum instrument. It is similar to the mridanga, but its two sides are equal in size. It is about two feet long and a foot in diameter (60 cm by 30 cm). It can be played with hands or with sticks. It is used for Kirtan in folk tunes. It is popularly seen at weddings when a solo player precedes a marriage couple.

The dhadh is a small two-sided wooden drum, about 10 to 12 inches (25 to 30 cm) in length with a narrow waist in the middle. Cotton straps hold the parchments, its cover. It is held in the left hand and played with the right hand. It is associated with Dhadh Kirtan, introduced by Guru Hargobind.

Idiophones are self sound producing instruments which combine the properties of a vibrator and resonator, being struck together as cymbals or shaken as rattles. These instruments are made of wood, metal or both combined. There are earthen pots like matkes, pitchers, which serve the same purpose. Idiophones are the mainstay of Sangat singing or where the traditional harmonium and tabla are not used for Kirtan. It is used for women's Kirtan or at home and informal gatherings, especially in folk song singing before a marriage. Chimpta, tongs, with bells and a dhol are the most popular combinations for musical playing in social gatherings.

Kirtan in the times of the Gurus

Arjan Dev, the fifth Guru, introduced the string instrument sarinda and developed the jori, a two-headed drum derived from the pakhawaj. The jori is distinct from the tabla in its form and rhythmic pattern. The Dhadhis in their singing of Vaars use the daadh saranga (similar to the sarangi) and dhadh, a small handheld drum.

Musical instruments in common use during the times of the Gurus were the rabab, mridanga, pakhawaj, sarinda, sarangi, taoos, cymbals, khartal, dhol and dhadh.

Guru Nanak composed and sang his own verses from an early age. Bhai Mardana, a Muslim from the Mirasi clan of traditional musicians, was his companion musician during his travels. Shabad singing accompanied by Bhai Mardana on the rabab was Guru Nanak's way of giving the divine message to his listeners. Guru Nanak visited over twenty countries during his twenty-five years of travel. He stopped at places of Hindu, Muslim and Buddhist pilgrimage. He would stay at each place for several months, learn the local language and absorb the way of their life. Guruji would discourse about religion with the learned men at those places. He also learnt the intricate skills of Raag music that he so effortlessly displays in his compositions. Guru Nanak believed Shabad Kirtan superior to all methods of preaching the message of God. He would sing his compositions and then explain the message in the language of the listeners.

Guru Nanak mastered not only Sanskrit, Persian and Arabic but also dozens of local dialects on his journeys. His mastery of language and music is evident in his compositions such as Japji, Asa Ki Vaar, Barah Maha, Patti, Pahrei, Gosht and Alahaniya.

After settling down at Kartarpur in 1521, Guru Nanak would recite Gurbani and perform Kirtan in both the mornings and evenings. Mardana would play on the rabab for a few minutes. Guru Nanak would then start singing his Shabads in that Raag. This form of worship has endured to present times.

Hargobind, the sixth Guru, established another class of Kirtan called Dhadhi music and introduced the dhadh (hand drum) and sarang to play it. Dhadhis, the players and singers, sang of heroic deeds of ancient warriors to inspire his disciples. Bhai Abdullah and Bhai Natha, devotees of the sixth Guru, sang Asa Ki Vaar in Dhadh style in the court of Guru Hargobind. They also sang other Gurbani Vaars after the conclusion of the evening prayers. The Dhadhi groups performed before the Sangat and accompanied Sikh warriors in their battles.

Guru Gobind Singh, the tenth Guru, was a patron of poets and musicians. He also composed Gurbani himself. Baddu and Saddu, Rababis, performed Asa Ki Vaar in his court. As a poet remarks, 'He gave us music, martial art and Shabad. In him, we find a Sant singing Shabads, a soldier giving martial music, a householder singing the virtues of a good life and an artist creating wonderful pictures in music'.

Kirtan Performers

There are three types of Sikh musicians – Rababis, Raagis and Dhadhis – established during the times of the Gurus.

Guru Nanak started the rababi tradition by engaging Bhai Mardana as his accompanist-musician. Some of the notable Rababis who performed for the Gurus after Mardana were his son Shahjada, Balwand and Satta, Babak son of Satta, Chatra son of Babak, and Saddu and Baddu, well-known names in Sikh history, whose compositions are recorded as Swayyae in Guru Granth.

Generations of their descendants continued to perform Kirtan at Harmandir Sahib, Amritsar, until the partition of India in 1947 when the Rababis, who were mostly Muslims, migrated to Pakistan, and the tradition of rabab in Harmandir Sahib has since faded out with them.

Guru Arjan Dev introduced the Raagi tradition. The Raagis then used traditional Indian string and wind instruments to play Kirtan. Raagi tradition is now accepted as the main means of performing Kirtan, though the instrument of choice is the harmonium, rather than string instruments.

The earliest famous Raagis are Bhai Jassa Singh Ahluwalia, the great warrior, who performed Kirtan for Mata Sundri, widow of Guru Gobind Singh. Bhai Mansa Singh performed Kirtan at the Harmandir during the reign of Maharaja Ranjit Singh. Bhai Sham Singh Adanshabi sang Kirtan at Harmandir for more than seventy years. It is said that he never missed a day. In recent times, Raagis revered by the Sikh Panth include Sant Attar Singh, Bhai Sujan Singh and Bhai Randhir Singh who combined Kirtan with missionary work spreading the Sikh faith to the masses.

The Raagi Jatha, team, generally consists of three musicians. One plays the tabla, and the other two play the harmonium. The leader of the group sits in the middle and is the main singer. Raagi Jatha are employed by Gurdwara to perform Kirtan. Itinerant Raagi Jathas are popular and perform Kirtan in different parts of the world wherever there is a gathering of Sikhs. The most well-known Raagis prefer to travel rather than stay in one place. Historic shrines where Kirtan is performed around the clock employ a number of Raagi Jatha.

The third type of musicians, Dhadhis, though now less common, are still an important part of Sikh musical tradition. They tend to move from one place to another. The historic shrines no longer use their type of Kirtan. Modern Dhadhis usually sing their own Vaar compositions, in folk tunes, to remind Sikhs of the valour and heroism of their compatriots in the past. A Dhadhi group consists of three players, who perform standing up, one playing on the sarangi, another playing on the dhadh, and the third, the leader, discoursing on the contents of their compositions.

The tradition of Kirtan

The tradition of Kirtan performance since the times of the Gurus is as follows:

Shabads from the following sources only are permitted in Kirtan: Guru Granth, Guru Gobind Singh Gurbani and compositions of Bhai Gurdas and Bhai Nandlal.

The Kirtan Jatha sits on the right side of the Palki, seat, of Guru Granth. No special platform is provided for the singers in historic shrines, but the use of a platform or dais is permitted elsewhere, provided it is considerably lower than the Palki of Guru Granth.

Asa Ki Vaar is sung in the morning after the daily ceremonial installation of Guru Granth. The exception is at Harmandir Sahib and other shrines, where Asa Ki Vaar is begun and then interrupted to allow for the installation of Guru Granth. The interrupted performance then continues to its completion after the installation.

Appropriate compositions of Gurbani are sung to mark life events such as birth, marriage or a funeral. At the time of Anand Karaj, the marriage ceremony, Lavan, and at the time of a funeral, Kirtan Sohila, are appropriate Banis to be recited.

Shabads are sung in their appropriate Raag. If Dhuni is indicated in the title of the Shabad, that is used in preference to all other tunes.

Correct pronunciation and intonation of Gurbani is mandatory so that the Sangat understands the words and the meaning of the Shabad. The singer is not allowed to introduce any words of his own or make interpolations.

Raag technique and the sounds of instruments are subordinated to the singing of the Shabad. What are highlighted are Gurbani and its Ras, sweetness, and not the musical expertise of the players.

No Kirtan is permitted during Akhand Paath.

Music performance of Raag without accompanying vocal recitation is not permitted.

Divisions of Kirtan

Shabad Kirtan: The Shabad is all important. Raag is subordinated to the correct enunciation of the Shabad so that it is intelligible and the Raagi conveys its meaning to the Sangat.

Katha, discourse-oriented Kirtan: The Raagi gives, through commentary, prominence to the exposition of Shabad and the message of Shabad. More time is devoted to discourse than to singing. This type of Kirtan is only expected of highly qualified Raagi. Parallel Gurbani quotations, Parmans, to illustrate the theme are permitted during the Kirtan. Guru Arjan Dev said that Kirtan and Katha are both necessary for understanding the principles of Sikh faith.

Jotiyan-ke-Shabad: Sangat singing in chorus. This is the most direct way of worship and is considered the essence of Kirtan in Sikh faith.

Nagar Kirtan, Shabad Kirtan in ceremonial processions and prabhat-pheri, dawn rallies in shrines: The devotees sing Shabads to the accompaniment of indigenous instruments like the dhol, khartal or chimpta. A Raagi leads Sangat singing in several ways. The Raagi sings the Shabad line by line, alternate lines repeated by all, or the 'odd' lines and the congregation sing 'even' lines. The Raagi sings the line, and then the women, followed by the men, sing the same line in chorus. The Raagi sings the line and the congregation repeats the refrain.

Naam Simran: Rhythmic recitation of the word 'Waheguru', led by a Granthi or Raagi with the Sangat repeating the chant. In other formats, the word 'Waheguru' is combined with words or phrases describing God, but the emphasis in Naam Simran is recitation of 'Waheguru'. Naam Simran is recited with or without music.

Akhand/Nirban Kirtan: Uninterrupted Shabad Kirtan lasting a whole day or night.

Anand Sahib: the Raagi and the Sangat sing the short Anand Sahib in unison at the end of the service. Ardas, Hukam and distribution of Karah Parsad follow it.

A traditional Kirtan session

A Kirtan session, according to the Kirtan Maryada is a Chaunki, an ensemble of four musicians. However, the modern practice is for three musicians, two on the harmonium and one with a tabla. Occasionally, an additional string player is added to the Jatha.

The musicians play allap, a tune, on the instruments as a prelude to Kirtan for a few minutes. This is followed by Mangla-charan, invocation, which is traditionally a Shabad beginning with *'Dandot bandna anak baar, sarab kala samarath'*.

Kirtan then follows in Raag, most commonly in Dhrupad style. The latter is sung in four parts with its appropriate taal on the tabla. A composition in Partaal may follow the Shabad in Dhrupad. A Shabad in Khayaal style completes the main performance. The Kirtan sessions ends with a Pauri in Raag Bilaval, or Raag Kaanra.

PART SEVEN
Gurdwara and Sikh Governance

CHAPTER 30
Historic Evolution

In the face of momentous persecution of the Sikhs in the dying days of Mughal rule and then invasion by marauders from central Asia, Gurdwara became a refuge and rallying cry for Sikhs to fight for their survival. Gurdwara became a symbol of hope, courage and faith. It is not surprising that today they are more than merely a place of worship; Gurdwara are at the heart of Sikh faith.

It is difficult to imagine Sikhs without their Gurdwara. Gurdwara are the meeting place of the Sangat, the centre of their religious, political, social and cultural life. It is not the building but the gathering of the Sikhs in the presence of Guru Granth which is of the essence.

The origin of Gurdwara lies in the times of Guru Nanak, when a devotional space was set aside to recite prayers and sing Shabads composed by the Guru. The succeeding Gurus continued the practice. The place of worship was then called a Dharamsala, place of faith.

The earliest centres of worship were established at places sanctified by the visits of the Gurus. Other Gurdwara were then established in memory of Sikh Sants and martyrs. The installation of handwritten Guru Granth was at first confined to only a few of the shrines. Guru Granth later became the focus of worship in the late nineteenth century when printing made it possible to produce the Granth in large numbers. As the installation of Guru Granth became common practice, Dharamsala came to be known as Gurdwara, abode of the Guru.

The first organisation to manage the Gurdwara was the Manji, diocese system established by the third Guru, Amar Das. Manji leaders established Dharamsala, organised missionary work in their respective regions, collected tithes and arranged travel for devotees to pay homage to their Gurus or historic shrines. To make the missionary work more effective and comprehensive, Ram Das, the fourth Guru, reinforced the existing system. Manji leaders were appointed Masands, leaders, representatives of the Gurus in their regions.

The system worked well but with time, because of poor communication, hazards of travel, and increasingly oppressive measures adopted by the Mughal rulers against Sikhs, it became difficult to maintain links with Gurus and each other. The Masand system degenerated, local fiefdoms were established and Masands began to exercise autocratic authority without reference to either the Gurus or their Sangat.

Guru Gobind Singh disbanded the Masands after he had established the Khalsa Panth in 1699. He handed over the responsibility of Gurdwara to the Panth itself. The local leadership was vested in the Panj Pyarae, five Amritdhari Sikhs nominated by the Sangat for their devoutness, leadership qualities and character.

The premature demise of Guru Gobind Singh took place before the new arrangements could be put in place. Coupled with this was the intense persecution from the Mughal rulers who embarked upon genocide of the Sikhs. Sikhs could no longer practise their faith in the open. They had to seek refuge in jungles and deserts. This state was to last for almost eight decades.

Care of Gurdwara passed into the hands of those who professed Sikh faith but were not Amritdhari and in appearance looked no different from people of other religions. These Sikhs were predominantly the Udasis and Nirmalas.

The Udasis were the followers of Sri Chand, eldest son of Guru Nanak, who on being denied Gurtagaddi had set up his own sect. Udasis were very devout, with belief in Guru Nanak but not the other Gurus. Because of their pious nature, it naturally fell to the Udasis to care for the Gurdwara in these difficult times. Nirmalas were also devout Sikhs who worshipped the Gurus but retained their Hindu beliefs. Again, they looked no different from other people. Nirmalas tended to be ascetic and highly educated and the upkeep of the Gurdwara fell into their hands.

Udasis and Nirmalas served the faith well in its difficult time by maintaining the tradition of Gurdwara but gradually, without overall authority, Udasis and Nirmalas increasingly began to obliterate the difference between the Sikh faith and Hinduism. The devout Sikhs had no alternative but to tolerate this unsatisfactory arrangement.

These non-Amritdhari Sikh adherents believed the Sikh faith to be part of Hindu religion (one of the reasons for their non-initiation to the Khalsa Panth) and began to introduce into Gurdwara the very practices from which Guru Nanak had dissociated his faith. The non-Amritdhari keepers of the Gurdwara began to call themselves Mahants, a Hindu term for a priest. Mahants became the bane of the Sikh faith and it would take the Khalsa Panth nearly a century to dislodge them from ownership of historic Sikh shrines.

The Mahants began to accrue power and became a law unto themselves. Gurdwara became simply a place from which to make money for themselves and their families. They introduced Hindu worship in Gurdwara to increase their revenue. The Mahants kept the Gurdwara, however much corrupted by then, open during the eighteenth century, the most difficult period for the Sikhs, but in reality Gurdwara were Sikh institutions in name only.

With the decline of Mughal power, Sikhs began to organise themselves and establish their own fiefdoms where they were safe to lead their Panthic lives. The Sikhs established Misls, clans, in Punjab during the last quarter of the eighteenth century. The Sikhs had forgotten what their faith was intended for and took Mahants at their face value. In this mistaken belief, they allowed the Mahants to practise their version of Sikh faith. Moreover the Mahants were, unfortunately, so powerful that not even the Sikh chiefs could dare dislodge them from their seats in the Gurdwara. The Sikh chiefs made gifts of land and money to the Gurdwara, unwittingly further strengthening the already powerful Mahants. Increasing wealth led to further corruption and degradation of personal character. The

Mahants openly flouted the tenets of Khalsa Panth without fear of retribution. This practice continued during the rule of Maharaja Ranjit Singh whose mistaken support of the Mahant system with huge gifts of money and land made them as powerful as the Maharaja himself, if not more so.

This was the dire situation when the British took over Punjab from the Sikhs in 1849. They passed the Religious Endowments Act 1863, which enshrined in law that the British rulers would not interfere with religious practice in India, especially with religious endowments in Indian shrines. The British rulers saw no reason to change the system which they had inherited from Sikh rulers. The hereditary Mahants became de facto owners of the Gurdwara and the properties attached to them. They ignored Sangat participation in Gurdwara affairs and, continuing their profane habits, reverted to open Hindu religious practices of idol worship in Gurdwara. The law unwittingly immensely strengthened the wealth and power of the Mahants whom the British saw as the legitimate overseer of shrines and a stabilising force in the community. The Mahants transferred the Gurdwara land to their own names to become the de jure owners as well.

Sikhs felt betrayed, first by their Sikh rulers and now by the British government. The increasingly vocal Sikh reform movement made them suspect in the eyes of the British, who saw them as agitators to the rule of law. The British imperialists had come from a culture where religious practice was separate from the civil rule of law.

The policy of non-interference in the management of religious institutions, the conflict between the powerful vested conservative Sikhs (Sanatani Sikhs) and the far less powerful, reform-minded Sikhs without a voice (Tat, True, Khalsa) was to cause immense delay in the transfer of Gurdwara to the legitimate authority of the Sikhs. An official communiqué from the British Governor General in Delhi issued the warning to his subordinates in the Punjab: 'It would be politically unwise to allow the arrangement of Sikh Gurdwara to fall into the hands of committees emancipated from government control. I trust your Excellency [Governor of Punjab] will assist to pass such orders in the case as well enable to continue the system which has worked out successfully for more than thirty years' (sic).

The Government used the Sikh shrines as a channel for indirect control of the Sikhs. As the agitation for reforms continued, the Government took direct control of the important Sikh shrines including those in Amritsar, Nankana Sahib and Tarn Taran. A government appointed sarbrah (headman) managed Harmandir Sahib. The official patronage further emboldened the priests and managers of Gurdwara to flout Sikh tenets and to deny the Sikh Sangat legitimate access to the shrines.

On 12 October 1920, the reformers took Amritdhari Yatris, pilgrims of low caste origin, to the Harmandir. The priests refused to accept their offerings and indeed took steps to excommunicate the reform-minded Sikh leaders from their faith for associating with low class Sikhs.

The Gurdwara reform movement had awakened the Sikh masses to remove corrupt practices and persons in authority. The foundation of the reform movement was laid in 1879. The reformers issued an order summoning the Sarbat Khalsa, an assembly of Sikhs, on 15 November 1920 to take charge of Harmandir Sahib and other shrines. This assembly established the Shiromani Gurdwara Parbandhak Committee (SGPC). The SGPC pioneered the struggle for Gurdwara reform. It registered itself as a corporate body on 30 April 1921.

Shiromani Akali Dal (SAD), the political wing of the SGPC, was established at the same time as the SGPC. Both organisations, SGPC and SAD, acted in unison in the struggle for the reform of Sikh shrines. Most Mahants surrendered control of Gurdwara voluntarily but those of some of the more important ones resisted, leading to violent confrontation. The Sikhs under the Gurdwara Reform Movement liberated Gurdwara Tarn Taran from Mahants with the sacrifice of two lives in a non-violent protest. The Mahants, entrenched in control of Gurdwara Nankana Sahib (birthplace of Guru Nanak Dev, now in Pakistan), the richest of all the Sikh shrines, mercilessly butchered and burnt alive a Jatha of 150 Sikhs who had peacefully entered the shrine in the early hours of the morning of 20 February 1921. The incident spread revulsion and anger not only amongst Sikhs but also throughout India and the world. Twenty-two thousand Sikhs then marched to liberate the Gurdwara, forcing the Government to intervene and eventually hand over the shrine to the Sikhs.

The movement was to be crowned with complete success in 1925, when the Sikh Gurdwara Act (Management of Gurdwara) was passed removing the authority from the perverted and corrupt keepers of the Sikh shrines and into the hands of the Khalsa Panth. The Act established the principle that the Sikh Panth alone was responsible for the care of its Gurdwara.

The Sikh Gurdwara Act, 1925 enshrined in law the Shiromani Gurdwara Parbandhak Committee, elected by a Sikh franchise, to be in legal control of Sikh shrines. Gurdwara not under the management of the SGPC were to elect local committees to manage them. These democratic arrangements have become a permanent feature of Sikh Gurdwara in India and abroad.

Sikh power today emanates from Gurdwara. They are a symbol of everything a Sikh stands for. Sikhs sacrificed their lives in their hundreds and thousands for their preservation. The history of the Gurdwara is the history of the growth and development of the Sikh faith. However, as illustrated above, it was not always so.

CHAPTER 31
A Guide for Visitors

The Gurdwara is the Sikh place of worship. A family or even a few people living together will create a space for collective worship. Worship in Gurdwara is obligatory for Sikhs. The Sikhs are ordained to visit Gurdwara daily or as often as possible to listen to the recitations from Guru Granth and the Shabad Kirtan. Bhai Gurdas, a Sikh savant, testifies,

'Wherever my Satguru goes and sits, that place is beautiful
The devotee seeks that place, takes and applies its dust to his forehead.'

A Gurdwara is visible from afar because of a tall flagpole, fully draped in yellow or saffron cloth with a flag imprinted with Sikh emblems flying from its top. Gurdwara have no sacrificial symbolism, and have neither idols nor altars. There are no sacraments and no priestly orders. Sevadars, Gurdwara workers, are volunteers or paid functionaries. The latter are employed and paid to assist in the conduct of services and, though respected, hold no additional authority above that of unpaid Sevadars. Indeed, paid functionaries are disenfranchised from taking part in the democratic decision making of the local Sangat in a Gurdwara.

The essential feature of a Gurdwara is the presiding presence in it of Guru Granth. It reigns supreme over Sikh places of worship. Every Sikh place of worship – at home, a purpose built structure or temporary shelter such as a Sikh army camp – which houses the Granth is a Gurdwara.

Gurdwara provide Sikhs with a meeting place for worship. This consists of listening to Gurbani, Shabad Kirtan and Katha, exposition of Gurbani. The Gurdwara serves as a community centre, a school, a guesthouse and a base for local Sikh charitable activities. Apart from regular services, usually held in the morning or evenings, Gurdwara hold special services to mark religious anniversaries on the Sikh calendar. The aspect of Sikh faith most closely associated with Gurdwara, other than worship, is the institution of Langar, free communal kitchen.

Order of diwan, service

The Sikh Rahet Maryada, rules of conduct, dictates that Guru Granth be ceremoniously installed early in the morning (Parkash) and then put to repose at night in Sukh Niwas (a space or room specially designated for the purpose).

Nit-nem, the daily prayer, is recited at the appropriate time of the day. Japji, composition of Guru Nanak, followed by two compositions of Guru Gobind Singh, Jaap Sahib and Daas (10) Swayyae, are the morning prayers. The latter two compositions are not recorded in Guru Granth. Reheras Sahib, a miscellany of nine Shabads in Guru Granth, Benati Chaupai, a Swayyae and a Dohira, compositions of Guru Gobind Singh, followed by the first five and the last stanza of the short Anand Sahib, composition of Guru Amardas, constitute the evening prayer.

Kirtan Sohila is recited prior to formal closure of Guru Granth at night. These prayers are recited either from memory or from a Gutka, Nit-nem prayer book. Ardas is offered at the end of each of these prayers. Hukam is taken at the end of prayers followed by distribution of Karah Parsad. All Gurdwara must conduct these prayers daily without fail.

Once the morning prayers are concluded, then the non-obligatory general diwan may commence either daily or, as is the practice in smaller Gurdwara, once a week, usually on a Sunday morning. Shabad Kirtan is the mainstay of a diwan. Asa Ki Vaar, Gurbani composition, is sung first, followed by a medley of Shabads. Other items of service may include Katha, lectures and a women's or children's Kirtan programme. A service is always concluded by the recitation of the short Anand Sahib, followed by Ardas, Hukam and distribution of Karah Parsad. The Sangat will then adjourn to the Langar hall.

A diwan may also be held in the evening after prayers followed by Shabad Kirtan and Katha and the usual conclusion. It is the practice in Britain to offer Langar at the end of each diwan.

If Akhand Paath is in progress, then no other diwan is permitted. Family events such as marriage ceremonies are fitted in within this framework or held in a separate diwan hall in the Gurdwara set aside for such purposes.

Gurdwara buildings do not have to conform to any set architectural design. The only requirement is a designated space for the installation of Guru Granth. Most Gurdwara in Britain are located in converted church halls and schools.

Purpose-built Gurdwara, increasingly in fashion, tend to imitate the Harmandir, a fusion of Indo-Persian architecture. They have a hall, often square in shape, with entrances on all four sides. They have square or octagonal domed sanctums on the fringes and middle of the roof. A popular model for the dome is the ribbed inverted lotus topped by an ornamental pinnacle. Arched copings, kiosks and solid domelets are built for exterior decoration. The interior of a Gurdwara is of plain design without decoration. In this they differ from the interior of the historic shrines, which are richly embellished.

There is no restriction on the entry of non-Sikhs into the Gurdwara. All are welcome irrespective of race, caste, sex and faith.

Rules for visitors to a Gurdwara

Visitors must not smell of or be under the influence of alcohol or other intoxicating substances. Smoking or carrying tobacco products within a Gurdwara premises is prohibited. Visitors must remove their shoes before entering the diwan hall. A shoe rack or space for footwear to be deposited is provided in the entry hall to the

Gurdwara. Hands are washed after removing shoes. Hand washing facilities are provided next to the shoe racks.

A suitable dress code for attending the Gurdwara is loose clothing which covers most of the body, leaving face, hands and feet bare. In Western countries, clean socks or stockings are permitted. The head must be covered with a scarf or shawl. Soft, non-leather, non-protruding hats are also suitable wear. Most Gurdwara place scarves to be worn by those who need one in the entry hall next to the shoe depository.

Diwans vary in their formalities. When Guru Granth is being recited silence is mandatory, while during a wedding ceremony a bit of levity is tolerated. Children are most welcome during diwans. Gurdwara provide entrance facilities for the disabled but the provision within may be patchy. However, help is always at hand, and visitors only need ask.

To respect the sanctity of the diwan hall, and to permit the Sangat to meditate, pray and listen, visitors should observe silence or converse in whispers if it is necessary to do so. Mobile telephones must be switched off. Observance of the code of conduct is self-imposed. There are no Sevadars to supervise the Sangat. Visitors must always ask for assistance when in doubt. This may be done from any member of the Sangat. Photographs may be taken but it is best to ask first to comply with the sanctity of the Gurdwara and civil laws of privacy.

Diwan hall

After suitable preparation in the reception area, the visitors proceed to enter the diwan hall. They will notice, first, facing them, a raised dais on which is placed the Granth, draped in colourful silk cloth. Guru Granth is protected with an ornate canopy with four posts supporting it. Seated behind the Granth is a Granthi.

The Granthi, a respected volunteer member of the community or a paid functionary, may be reciting Gurbani from the Granth, which is open in front of him. Otherwise, the musicians are singing, the Granthi sitting silently with the Granth opened but covered with silk drapes. The Granthi will be waving a Chawri, a ceremonial fan, over the Granth. When Guru Granth is uncovered for recitation, another devout Sikh will stand behind the Granthi and ceremoniously wave the Chawri over the Granth. This shows the reverence in which Sikhs hold Guru Granth. The Chawri traditionally consists of strands of yak hair set into a silver handle.

The visitors will then observe the Sangat sitting, in reverence and silence, cross-legged facing the Granth on either side of the central aisle. The visitors will join the devotees as they proceed along the aisle to the front of the dais as they enter the diwan hall. They will then, with folded hands, genuflect to the Granth, bow their head until their brows touch the ground. They will then raise their heads, deposit a donation, get up, retrace their steps while still facing the Granth, turn slowly towards the side and sit in the Sangat.

The donation is usually from a copper to a pound coin or even a larger sum. It is invariably the practice, though it is not compulsory to place a donation. Visitors will notice parents encouraging their children to put their donation in the box. Visitors will also notice families bring uncooked food in bags and place it on the side in front.

Visitors may if they so wish only bow their heads and deposit a donation. Visitors may also simply bow their head when they enter the diwan hall or when they are half way through and then proceed to sit among the Sangat. They may decide to comply with the full Sikh ritual. The Sangat appreciates such an act of devotion.

The diwan hall is carpeted but there is no other furniture. The carpeted floor is covered with white sheets. Men sit on one side, women on the other, in a cross-legged or lotus position. Visitors can tuck their legs underneath their lower limbs, if they find the cross-legged position awkward. Whatever position is adopted, the feet should never point towards the front. It is disrespectful to do so. Female visitors will readily find a place among the women, but may choose to sit down with their spouses, provided sufficient space is available and their bodies are not in too close proximity with other male devotees. Children may sit with either parent. There is no place of merit or special assignment in a Gurdwara. On a busy day, devotees and visitors just have to find a place to sit wherever they can find a space.

Visitors will usually find themselves in the middle of a diwan. It may be recitation of the Granth, Shabad Kirtan or Katha. Both men and women can lead the Sangat in prayer or Shabad Kirtan. Visitors would notice a lower stage for musicians with a harmonium and tabla, the two musical instruments most commonly used in Sikh worship. No clapping or show of appreciation is permitted within the diwan hall.

At the conclusion of a diwan, the devotees stand up for Ardas and then bow down to the ground at the end of it, but stand up again to sing the refrain. Visitors may keep standing throughout the Ardas and then sit down at the end together with the Sangat. Someone near them will most probably guide them through the appropriate responses. It is not acceptable to be seated during an Ardas.

The Granthi then reads the Hukam, an excerpt from the Granth chosen at random, and ceremoniously cover the Granth again. The Hukam is the message of the day for Sikhs to reflect and act upon in their daily life. Karah Parsad, sacramental food, is distributed. The visitors may indicate with their fingers bunched together that they only desire a small portion. It is not permitted to refuse Karah Parsad.

Gurdwara diwan tend to be extended. The devotees do not necessarily wait for the end of it. They may enter or depart any time they desire. There are, however, certain acts of worship where attendance is timed for the beginning and end of the prayer. Devotees who are Sevadars, who serve in the upkeep of the Gurdwara or Langar hall, usually leave for their individual tasks after paying their respects in the diwan hall. There is indeed a considerable movement of people entering and leaving the diwan hall.

If Akhand Paath, recitation of the Granth, which lasts forty-eight hours, is in progress, there will be no other diwan. The devotees listen to the recitation for as long as they wish and then depart. Karah Parsad during Akhand Paath is distributed at all times and not just towards the end of the service.

Langar hall

After leaving diwan hall, visitors proceed to the Langar hall. Gurdwara will always have a Langar area where food is prepared and served. It is part of Sikh diwan service. The Langar is offered free to all Sikhs and visitors. It is a simple vegetarian meal of chapatti, lentils, vegetables and a sweet preparation. The Langar may be paid for from Gurdwara funds or a family may sponsor a particular Langar and cook and pay for the food. Devotees will also bring provisions for the preparation of the food. Visitors are welcome to bring food items for this purpose. Sugar, butter, fruit or milk are suitable items. Large Gurdwara serve thousands of meals a day and are open at all hours of the day and night.

The work involved in preparing food, serving it and clearing up afterwards is called Seva, voluntary service. It is always performed by volunteers. Paid functionaries do not take part in Langar Seva. Langar affords an opportunity for Sikhs for Seva. Any Sikh may take part in food preparation, serving, washing up or cleaning in a Langar kitchen or hall. Sikhs will usually ask a supervisor for an appropriate task to perform or simply join the other Sevadars in performing a task they desire. They may leave whenever they wish; others will readily take their place. Seva is considered to be of the highest merit in Sikh faith. There is never a shortage of Sevadars. Visitors wishing to take part in this meritorious service may do so. They may take on the task of serving water!

Langar is taken sitting cross-legged in rows on a matted or carpeted area. The head must be covered. If meals are served seated on the floor, visitors must remove their shoes before entering the Langar hall. It is becoming a common practice to provide tables for the Sangat to have their Langar standing up or sitting down if chairs are available. If tables are provided, there is no need to remove shoes. Visitors should ask about the need to remain barefooted or put on their shoes before moving to the Langar hall for a meal. Spoons are provided to eat food. Custom varies as to the removal of the plate to a washing area or leaving it in place after the meal is finished. Visitors should observe what others are doing. Visitors leave as soon as the meal is finished. Visitors should not thank or express appreciation of the meal they have consumed.

CHAPTER 32
Gurdwara in Britain

Gurdwara are the Sikhs' premier faith institutions and the resource for nurturing and developing Sikhs in Britain. Gurdwara are not just part of the Sikh Panth as in Punjab but are enshrined at the very heart of their religious, social and political fabric in Britain. The modern Sikh identity is inseparable from its Gurdwara.

Gurdwara are expanding to meet the growing needs of Sikhs. New Gurdwara are purpose built, though in the past churches, schools, warehouses and residential buildings were bought and renovated for Sikh worship. Even earlier than that, worship was mainly conducted in private homes.

Diwan, services, are held daily in large Gurdwara. It is more usual to have main worship on Sundays, as it is a convenient day for Sangat to gather in Britain. Gurdwara, even the large ones, maintain the tradition of voluntary service. It has increasingly become customary to employ functionaries to conduct devotional services and look after the needs of the Sangat and the upkeep of the buildings. In Sikh tradition, employed functionaries carry out set devotional tasks but do not have an ecclesiastical status within the faith. Paid Granthi are sometimes not even allowed to preach sermons or interpret the holy words of the Gurbani. They have no say in the management of the Gurdwara or the conduct of the diwan. That is entirely the responsibility of persons carrying out the task either voluntarily or elected or nominated by the Sangat. This system prevents paid clergy from becoming a dominant force in the faith.

The Gurdwara in Britain is the focus of Sikh communal life. There is hustle and bustle, a lively environment for their social and cultural life. The social network to care for the community, schools to teach Punjabi, religious music and Gurbani is an essential function of the British Gurdwara. Gurdwara provide facilities for Sikhs to hold social and religious ceremonies unlike in previous decades when they had to hire school halls, clubs and hotels for this purpose.

Gurdwara have rapidly grown in number. From a handful a few decades ago there are now over 250 of them in Britain, one for every 1,500 Sikhs. Most are located in urban centres, where Sikhs are concentrated. Attendances are high, forty to fifty percent attend once a week and most will come and pray on special days. There is felt a greater need to seek the shelter of the faith in an increasingly uncertain social climate in Britain. Interest in the faith is growing among Sikhs and the establishment of Gurdwara allows them a cohesive voice for themselves and their Panth. Community development and leadership among Sikhs emerges from within the institution of Gurdwara.

Sikhs are fond of imagining themselves a unified lump, a perception common also to outsiders. Any perceived difference is regarded as contrary to the interest of Panth. In reality, Sikhs share one faith and a remarkably cohesive one at that, but there is a built-in complex social diversity which often defies categorisation.

Fifty years ago, the Punjab was largely a rural economy. Villagers were barely literate and led a simple rural existence. The smaller urban population was a world of difference away from its rural counterpart. The village elite differed in outlook from the urban one. Caste providing Sikh sub-identity was well-established, harshly differentiated by poverty, education and basic human rights. There was little to join them with each other except their faith. Sharing their life in villages, towns and cities were the 'untouchable' Sikhs, outside the pale of the Panth. There was then a hierarchy of an elite, village and town, division by caste, high and low, leavened by lower classes and untouchables, the latter on the margins of Sikh society.

The earliest migrants to Britain, before World War Two, were low caste Sikhs, mostly Bhatras, who worked as labourers at the periphery of the British economy. They were then joined by other low caste Sikhs who were mostly itinerant street traders supplying goods and services in small villages and markets. Though Bhatras, arising from towns in the Punjab, maintained their Khalsa traditions, the later arrivals were mostly rural Sikhs, lacklustre in following the Sikh dress code or the appropriate way of Sikh life.

Sikhs were mostly invisible until their influx from East Africa in the 1960s and '70s. This is especially true of the Ramgarhia Biradri, whose arrival brought a revival of Sikh faith in Britain. Subsequent waves of migration in the '70s and '80s from the Punjab included a more diverse mixture of landed gentry and urban, educated classes, driven by land hunger and unemployment. These were added to the more orthodox Sikhs displaced following catastrophic events in the Punjab once the British left India in 1947.

This is, admittedly, a simplified picture, but it illustrates a diverse community. When the number of Sikhs was small, worship was practised in private residences, hired public places and then Gurdwara in converted public buildings. As the number of Sikhs grew in Britain, due to increased migration and Sikh births, Gurdwara began to diversify too, taking on the colour of the community they served.

Different castes, sects and groups with geographical loyalty in the Punjab were mirrored in Gurdwara. These reflected the changing presence of these communities in Britain. Sikh faith forbids caste acceptance but social stratification of the Sikhs cannot be apprehended without accepting the divisions based on these factors. Sikhs will claim that these differences are social and have no religious implications.

Caste oriented Gurdwara tend to be more prominent in Britain than in Punjab itself, though there is less class-consciousness among Sikhs abroad than in the land of their ancestors. Low caste and untouchable Sikhs are economically well off in Britain and are able to assert themselves within the Sikh Panth. The separate institutions owe more to regional, social or caste differences than faith orientation. It is more often communal convenience than projected doctrinal difference. These differences should not be exaggerated, as Sikhs of whatever persuasion are able to attend any Gurdwara, and do so, and will not find a difference in practice in Sikh liturgy from one Gurdwara to another. Gurdwara are occasionally set up because of conflict between factions in managing them. It is rare for such conflicts to be doctrinal.

Gurdwara are now less keen on exerting personal prejudices and such occurrences tend to be less frequent as the Panth gains confidence in itself and looks more assertively to the outside world and is less absorbed with internal squabbles. Besides, British born or educated Sikhs outnumber their immigrant forbears. They have less interest in Punjabi politics and are more comfortable with Western democratic ways and better able to tolerate and absorb the differences inherent in a free society. Such differences arise in all free societies.

Does social diversity reflect differences in the practice of Sikh faith?

Of the 250 Gurdwara, eighty percent follow the Sikh Rahet Maryada. The other twenty percent tend not to call their place of worship a Gurdwara and accept a mixture of the Rahet Maryada and their own separately developed liturgy.

Two-thirds of the Gurdwara are in the mainstream of the community. Most of the Sikhs in Britain, as in the Punjab, are Jats and therefore form the representative Gurdwara, not strictly caste oriented but Jat in orientation. These identify strongly with Khalsa traditions. They tend to be much more closely aligned with Sikh national institutions in the Punjab, also dominated by Jats. Sikh urban non-Jat castes, especially those originating from the undivided part of the former British India now partly in Pakistan, find the Jat-dominated but caste-plural Gurdwara much more to their liking, as they are free to take part in the management of such Gurdwara. In some areas of London, they dominate Gurdwara management.

Other Gurdwara are communal but under the patronage of a Sant, a devout Sikh. The Sant tradition of Sikh revivalism has a strong hold in Britain. The Sants provide a personal dimension to the faith, which has strong appeal to Sikhs living in an alien land. The Sant organisations provide an integrated support that embraces the whole family, marriage and social network. They provide a more personalised service for the spiritual needs of devotees than the mainstream Gurdwara. The Guru Nanak Nishkam Sewak Jatha is the most prominent Sant institution in Britain with strong emphasis on spirituality and social cohesion. It is a model of good practice of corporate Sikh living in modern times.

Sant-managed Gurdwara provide an overarching influence over Sikh institutions but no description of the changing role of Gurdwara would be complete without giving space to the role of the Ramgarhia Biradri in Britain. It provides the second largest number of Gurdwara after the mainstream institutions. The term mainstream is not descriptive of the practice of Sikh liturgy, as that description would then also apply to the Ramgarhia Gurdwara. Ramgarhia draw upon their caste heritage to emphasise their unique social identity in Britain. Once that is recognised, then it must be accepted that Ramgarhia Gurdwara are open to all Sikhs and their services are freely available to the Sikh Panth and in this respect are no different from their mainstream counterparts.

The Ramgarhia Biradri is one of the most upwardly mobile and progressive of the new commonwealth immigrants to Britain. Most Ramgarhia are second-generation migrants from East Africa and therefore have little affinity with Punjabi national institutions or politics, which has spared them many internecine problems. East African Ramgarhia are more committed Sikhs and their advent to Britain has been mainly instrumental in the promotion of Sikh faith in the country.

Along with Ramgarhia, the Bhatra – earliest Sikh settlers – have also established their own institutions. Bhatra tend to confine themselves apart from other Sikhs, but like the Ramgarhia maintain the Khalsa traditions in their religious practice.

The twenty percent of Gurdwara which do not wholly conform to the Sikh Rahet Maryada are conveniently divided into two groups.

Of the first group, the most prominent is the Namdhari sect, who believe in a living Guru. The Namdhari arose as a protest group against corrupt Sikh faith practices in the nineteenth century and then coupled it with opposition to the introduction of British rule in Punjab. The sect gradually parted from traditional practice of Sikh faith and established its own liturgy. Namdhari, however, tend to identify themselves with the main Sikh traditions and live amicably within the Sikh Panth.

Nirankari, a similar reform minded community to Namdhari, established in the nineteenth century, also believe in a living Guru. However, with time, though often maintaining an outward Sikh dress appearance, Nirankari have so moved away from the Rahet Maryada that their practices are found offensive by other Sikhs and are shunned by the Panth and treated as outside the pale of faith.

The second group with their own distinct institutions are low caste and untouchable communities – Ravidasi, Valmiki and Rhadasoami – at the boundaries of Sikh faith. While Ravidasi may be nominally described as Sikhs, this could hardly be a true calling for the other two sects. Yet, they all outwardly retain a superficial adherence to Sikh ritual. Their position as Sikhs in a social, religious and even legal context remains ambiguous. They identified themselves as Sikhs during British rule but have also taken advantage of special privileges accorded to non-Sikh untouchable classes in India. They partake of Sikh social provision in Punjab and abroad when it suits them.

The basic organising unit of Sikh faith is Gurdwara. In Birmingham for example the twelve Gurdwara provide a Sikh network with their support congregations. The local Sangat with their Gurdwara own it and look after its upkeep. The Sangat is very jealous of the autonomy of their Gurdwara.

There is no central faith hierarchy among Sikhs in Britain. The Sikh Rahet Maryada provides the necessary guidance to conduct their religious, social and communal affairs. Only when the Panth is faced with external threat does it consider acting together with each other. Sikhs confronted such threats together in the eighteenth century when the Muslim rulers were intent on genocide of the Sikhs. Even then, as noted by Western observers, Sikhs would accept only nominal authority and that with great reluctance. Such cooperation would evaporate the moment the threat became manageable.

Other occasions when it was necessary to present a cohesive front was, first, when the British occupied the Punjab and the Sikh faith found itself reverting to Hinduism, and secondly, to retrieve its historic shrines from the clutches of non-Sikhs. It took Sikhs fifty years of working together, first under the leadership of the Singh Sabha reform movement and then the Gurdwara Parbandhak Committee, to put the Panth back on its pedestal as we see it today. It was also an opportune moment, when Sikhs were uniquely united, to formulate the Rahet Maryada, the Sikh code of liturgical worship. While these pioneering institutions are now a mere shadow of their former glory of a united Panth, the Rahet Maryada has survived as the guide to Sikh faith. The Sikh Rahet Maryada has withstood the challenges of modern times. There is little evidence of discord among Sikhs over liturgy despite immense changes wrought over several decades.

Sikh faith provides every Sikh an equal right to express his or her views in Sangat. The will of the Sangat is supreme. Within Sikh faith, there is no established class of clergy and this is again related to the concept of equality of Sikhs within the faith. Devotees offer themselves to occupy administrative responsibilities within the Gurdwara or are invited to do so because they possess certain skills or knowledge. Gurdwara are autonomous entities maintained entirely by the local Sangat and owe no allegiance to any third party interest. Gurdwara are registered as charities and managed under charity laws. Trustees are appointed along with management committees under legally approved constitutions. However, the traditional overarching religious authority of the Sangat often comes in conflict with lawful requirements. The voice of the Sangat may be general public discontent or by opposition parties under its guise. Decisions taken by elected representatives are often reversed or rescinded by the Sangat.

Sikhs are required to conduct themselves in accordance with the Sikh Rahet Maryada. Differences that arise are communal and not doctrinal. Many such conflicts become entrenched and are not resolved for years because of the contradiction between the power of the Sangat or a part of it and formal constitutional requirements. The resolution of such cases, if not accomplished by arbitration, results in prolonged, expensive court battles or intervention by the Charities Commission. Many well-endowed Gurdwara have faced severe financial difficulties and disruption in such cases. Such conflicts, which have plagued Gurdwara in the past, are becoming less common as the younger generations increasingly assume responsibility for Gurdwara and better understand modern governance.

The main source of income of a Gurdwara is from its devotees. Golak is the offering Sikhs make when they visit the Gurdwara. It can vary from a few pence to several pounds. Fees and donations for officiating at birth, death and marriage ceremonies, hire of halls for religious ceremonies or functions add to this income. Akhand Paath requested by a family will similarly attract contributions. Gurdwara usually have a running account for their building funds. A recent source of additional income is local, national and European development funds provided for educational and social services or for community development in deprived areas.

Gurdwara face a challenge to meet the changing needs of British Sikhs, especially those born and bred or educated in Britain – the majority. We have noted that a distinctive British Gurdwara movement has developed in response to the social milieu faced by the Sikhs and promoted by the state in Britain.

How successful have Gurdwara been or are set to be to meet the changing needs of the Sikhs?

There is no doubt that Gurdwara have successfully transmitted Sikh values and norms to successive generations. The growth of Gurdwara corresponds with the growth of the Sikh Panth and reflects diversity with its associated political and social organisations.

Inherent Sikh pluralism is reflected in the autonomous Gurdwara management. Sikhs function optimally at Gurdwara level. The network of 250 Gurdwara provides a faith space for Sikhs to live in Britain. The network is similar to mini-states that exist autonomously but cooperate when the need arises. The pluralism creates a pragmatic approach. No one single institution dare exceed its authority. A consensus is the outcome. The Sikh mode of operation produces a moderate leadership. Local decision making allows competition and choice. Extremism soon fades away. It may take time to do so, but that is always the outcome. The more radical groups are marginalised and are unable to sustain a foothold within the pragmatic Sikh faith.

Diversity is a source of strength rather than weakness. We must celebrate diversity. We become stronger the more we recognise our diversity and build on it. However, it is not the purpose of Gurdwara to clash on political objectives, or to support or oppose some group or other.

The absence of a national structured leadership has the potential for a multivocal response to issues of doctrine or policy between leaders, individuals and Gurdwara. The lack of a formal national Sikh presence should presumably result in the failure to present Sikh interests at the State level. This, however, has not happened as Sikhs are governed by a strict Sikh code of conduct – the Rahet Maryada – that precludes differences in the Sikh way of thinking. They are, in modern parlance, joined at the hip, though the heads may wave in different directions.

It would appear appropriate to create a hierarchical structure, but Sikhs at Gurdwara level are unwilling to give authority to others. It would be wrong to assume that this failure to establish national institutions or a hierarchy is a kind of failure. The Western model of institutional governance does not necessarily fit all. This issue has blighted Sikh thinking, and instead of following their natural instincts and looking at the successes they have scored with their decentralised, self-governing mode of governance, Sikhs bemoan perceived lack of interest in national institution building.

Sikhs do come together when need arises. It is their way of resolving issues by presenting a united front, but they disband again when the crisis is resolved. It would not be the Sikh faith if it adapted artificial constructs to please others or Westernised Sikhs influenced by Western culture and frustrated by their inability to penetrate the Gurdwara movement. Its autonomous, federated structure allows the Sikh faith to rapidly shed notions and fads that come into fashion from time to time. It always reverts to its central ethos of Sikh worship. It is obvious that there is little likelihood of adopting a Western mode of Sikh organisation. Gurdwara wish to protect their autonomy. They are certainly wise not to get involved in matters irrelevant to the practice of the faith and well-being of their Sangat.

We must turn our attention to non-Gurdwara Sikh institutions to achieve an overall understanding of Sikh organisations in Britain.

The number of Sikh umbrella organisations, registered or unregistered, exceeds the number of Gurdwara in the country. The organisations outside the Gurdwara legitimise their action on promoting spiritual and temporal issues on behalf of British Sikhs, a role in which they have been remarkably successful. These institutions with their formal or informal networks have become an effective community voice to be partners in local regeneration, development and delivery – management of schools, hospitals and other public service institutions. This has greatly assisted in Sikh institution building and transmission of Sikh values and norms to successive generations. Several Sikh institutions provide a vehicle by which all expressions of Sikh faith are collated and presented to social policy makers and open up access to opportunities to participate in and influence decisions affecting their lives. Such organisations also work with other faith partners in advancing the role of not only Sikhs but also of other sections of the community through integrated cross-community action. This has helped build the capacity of the Sikh Panth as an integral part of the wider community.

The role of these organisations in ensuring the preservation of Sikh human rights, especially their dress code, has achieved remarkable results. The sentiment to preserve Sikh values generates spontaneous mass movement, bringing Sikhs together. In the 1960s, '70s and '80s Sikhs campaigned tenaciously for the right to maintain the Sikh dress code, especially the Pagri. Sikhs have never hesitated to assert their rights. It is important to recognise the role of non-Gurdwara Sikh institutions as adjuncts to the Gurdwara in these struggles. The State recognises this and is content to deal with Gurdwara and the Sikh civic organisations at an individual level.

It is, nevertheless, important for Gurdwara to keep their distance from day-to-day political issues. Gurdwara are places of worship, a haven of peace and quiet and not agitation. The umbrella organisations must accept this situation and not challenge the autonomy and supremacy of Gurdwara in Sikh affairs.

If the Gurdwara have organisationally responded well in keeping with times, then we must consider the issues facing the younger generations, born, bred and educated today in Britain. While Sikhs believe in their faith and wish to stay within its ambit, they do not all comply with the requirements of the Sikh Rahet Maryada. This is no different from what is taking place in other faiths but Sikhs owe their identity to their unique dress code, for which Sikhs for centuries have suffered and sacrificed. Their stay in Britain has been a struggle to uphold this identity. That is how the rest of the world judges them. If the dress code means little to some Sikhs, then what do they perceive to be their future identity? Every Sikh must answer this question.

For Sikhs born in Britain, the particular problem is lack of literacy in Punjabi as it is the only means of accessing the traditions of the faith. In some cases, it has proved a disincentive to following the Sikh ritual. An English version of the liturgy has little likelihood of acceptance by the present generation of Sikhs.

The British political parties, as part of their community cohesion agenda to mitigate the effects of ideological multiculturalism, vigorously promote the return of religion to communal life. The number of faith-based charities reflects the diversity of modern Britain. Charities often spring out of religious beliefs and remain the bedrock for building faith and social capital. They are important vehicles for bringing people together for the common good.

This change in thinking has suited the Sikhs, who were not only the pioneers of multiculturalism in Britain but are now prepared even more vigorously to welcome their faith taking the centre stage. The change in the national turn of events has breathed new life into Gurdwara. The Sikh professional and educated classes are returning to Gurdwara as these improve their image.

The Gurdwara have readily adapted to the changed national agenda. Gurdwara are increasingly geared to building their capacity to enable them to become effective community organisations. Gurdwara find themselves represented in the mainstream of local and national public voice.

Gurdwara provide advice, participate in learning and community development, and establish local welfare centres for the care of the elderly and physically and mentally disabled people. The faith has established one-stop shops for local agencies and competes with other professional and private organisations in this field. A range of funding is available through urban grants, lottery projects, EU support and voluntary aid agencies.

The concentration of services in Gurdwara places them at the heart of urban renewal programmes. Gurdwara have replaced family networks as their social role is displaced. An example is matchmaking. These services are indispensable to the Sikh way of life. No alternative is available. These are dramatic changes indeed in the modern role of Gurdwara. Gurdwara have extended their remit from the local to the international arena. Nishkam Sewak Jatha and Ramgarhia Biradri Gurdwara are examples. The ability of Gurdwara to negotiate their rights and have a say in national affairs has placed them in a pole position of authority and influence. The Sikh profile in Britain has risen at relevant decision-making forums.

The Gurdwara achievement belies the argument that its decentralised structure will limit its influence. Gurdwara protect their autonomy. Any supra-Gurdwara authority is unlikely to emerge in the near future. Sikh politics can only be understood by Sangat participation at Gurdwara level. The Gurdwara movement in Britain is a success story. The absence of hierarchy ensures that the Sangat rules for the good of the Sikh Panth, a faith for its times. The vibrancy of the Sikh Panth is a function of the Gurdwara. Gurdwara have played an important role in the life of Sikh immigrants as a source of cohesion and recognition of the moral symbolism of the faith. It is questionable if the Sikh faith could have survived, let alone thrived, without its Gurdwara.

Ramgarhia Biradri: Sikh Faith Personified

Eleven Sikh misls, confederacies, arose in Greater Punjab following the weakening of the Moghul rule in mid-eighteenth century India. Of these the Ramgarhia confederacy lay on both side of the river Beas, occupying territory in four out of the five Doabs – land between two rivers – and the Kangra Hill states.

The founder of the Ramgarhia misl was Maharaja Jassa Singh. Ramgarhia misl took its name from Ramgarh fort in the holy city of Amritsar. The fort under the supervision of Maharaja Jassa was the focus of Sikh resistance to Moghul forces during the eighteenth century.

Maharaja Jassa Singh gained a reputation as a soldier of daring and skill. The Maharaja fought many pitched battles against Ahmad Shah Durrani, the Afghan invader. Once the threat from the Afghan invaders receded, internecine conflicts saw the Maharaja pitched against the overwhelming forces of other misls. Not one to lose faith, the Maharaja raised a large cavalry and attacked Delhi, the Moghul capital, raiding its arsenal and capturing horses, guns and ammunition. He became the terror of central India, capturing and laying waste to many Moslem states.

He returned to Punjab in 1783 and once more recovered his lost possessions. The Maharaja died in 1803 at the age of eighty years. Though the Ramgarhia confederacy was to collapse under the rising power of Maharaja Ranjit Singh, the Ramgarhia Biradri was to survive intact and in great strength. Today it presents an influential united Sikh community in India and abroad.

The origin of the Ramgarhia lies in the artisan class. The word Ramgarhia was first applied to the direct descendants of Maharaja Jassa Singh. By the end of the first decade of the twentieth century the term began to be adopted by most of the Sikh artisans.

Devotion to Guru Gobind Singh's ideals of faith and community has always been a paramount feature of the Biradri. The whole Ramgarhia community stands in covenant with their Gurus and Guru Granth Sahib. The association of Sikh artisans to Sikh faith is routed from its very birth. No one is more revered as a disciple of Guru Nanak than by Bhai Lallo, a lowly artisan, whose life is held as an example to all Sikhs of devoutness, honesty and simple living. The library in the Ramgarhia Sikh temple in the jewellery quarter of Birmingham is named after him.

Bhai Subeg Singh, a prominent Ramgarhia Sikh, was offered governorship by the Muslim rulers in Punjab in the mid nineteenth century to placate Sikhs. Shahbaz Singh, his son, was to become

Moslem in return. This he refused to do. Both father and son were tried by the ordeal of the wheel and cruelly martyred.

The beginning of the twentieth century saw the flowering of the Ramgarhia Biradri with a steady increase in their economic status. Ramgarhias increasingly began to travel from their villages to Indian cities and then abroad as demand for their services as artisans and craftsmen grew with the increasing tempo of the development of the British Empire. The development of communication (for example railways) and industry required precisely those skills which the Ramgarhia were able to provide. It causes no surprise to learn that the largest section of East African Sikhs was that of the Ramgarhia. In Punjab, Ramgarhias became proficient in developing small scale industries which relate closely to the practice of their profession. Furniture making and agricultural machinery are two prominent examples

The role of the Ramgarhia in the political and social arena has been no less impressive. Giani Jail Singh, the first Sikh president of India, and Dilip Singh Saund, the first Indian member of the American House of Congress, were both Ramgarhia Sikhs. What makes Ramgarhia Sikhs outstanding is their corporate cohesiveness and engagement in enterprise which fosters advancements in the industrial age.

The secret of its success lies in the network of Ramgarhia Sabhas, associations, especially Gurdwara, to serve the community all over the world. The Ramgarhia Gurdwara in the jewellery quarter of Birmingham has provided the lead in directing the development of their community with great skill and not a little sacrifice to see their community flourish in Great Britain.

CHAPTER 33
Sikh Governance

Guru Nanak laid the foundation of the trinity of Sikh institutions of Guruship, Sangat and Gurdwara to serve the social, cultural and spiritual needs of Sikhs. The institutions regulate the relationship between Panth and Sangat and within the Sangat itself. The institutions left to the Panth by the Gurus have endured. Guru Nanak provided for his Sikhs a self-contained and self-governing structure which has withstood the momentous times for the Sikhs of the past five centuries.

The most important institution for Sikhs was the appointment of his successor by Guru Nanak. It marked the founding of Sikh faith to be guided by a Guru. The nomination of subsequent Gurus strengthened the foundations of the faith. Guruship emphasised the spirit of continuity. The spirit of Guruship was one, indivisible, but in many corporeal forms.

Guruship reconciled the position of Guru Nanak to the authority vested in his successors. The Guru was mortal, a trusted messenger of God. The Guru resided in the Sikh and Sikh in his Guru. This is the fundamental belief of Sikhs.

The Gurus' word is preserved in Gurbani. It is Gurbani that Sikhs worship. Gurbani is a Sikh's Guru. The Guru and his Bani are the embodiment of Sikh faith. Gobind Singh, the tenth Guru, invested the Gurbani with Gurtagaddi. Thus, the Granth is the Guru of the Sikhs.

Guru Nanak also laid the foundation of the Sangat. Gurdwara hold the Granth. They are the base for Sangat and the house of Guru Granth, the most revered of Gurus' gifts to their Sikhs.

The Sangat are devotees of the Gurus who pay homage to God in a Gurdwara. It is the organised fellowship of Sikhs, engaged in Naam

Simran and a moral and spiritual life. Five Sikhs or more constitute a Sangat. Sangat is divine as the Guru resides within it. Guru Gobind Singh invested the authority of the Sikh Panth in his Sangat with Guru Granth as its guide.

Sangat has a full sense of its sovereignty. No written constitution sits above its head. No canon law tells it what to do. Sangat is the supreme organ of the Sikhs. It will not surrender its prerogative to self-appointed leaders. It will not give up the right to sit in judgement on itself. The Sangat retains the right to dismiss those who disagree with it or who are perceived to have exceeded their authority or misbehaved. The Sangat will not allow scrutiny by tiny elites. The Sangat maintains the right to hold in contempt leaders who impose themselves upon it. It is not frightened to take responsibility. The Sangat regulates its own affairs. It has the confidence to be master in its own house. The Sangat demands honour and decency from its members.

The Sangat may act in unison or appoint five devotees, Panj Pyarae, to act on its behalf. Gurmata, the decision of the Sangat, is the will of the Guru. It is the religious duty of a Sikh to join the Sangat, share in the Sangat, and obey its Gurmata.

The Sikh Panth enforces the discipline necessary for a responsible society. Its members must live up to its expectation. That is the secret of its strength. Under the sway of its tolerance, it refuses to discard the values and standards of a decent society. It refuses to pander to personal ugliness, lawlessness and irresponsible behaviour, which are rapidly destroying the claim in the West to be a civilised society. The Panth will not allow the destruction of all that made it great. Sikhs live in a culture where social integration is declining. This contributes towards family breakdown and declining educational standards. Indeed a criminal culture is created.

Sikhs do not have a body of canon law. Instead, precedents drawn from the Granth and the words and cautions of the Gurus and their companions are accepted as governing Sikh behaviour. Such precedents are open to interpretation and change in light of changing times. Sikhs are ruled by compassion and tolerance. Divorce, adoption or homosexuality are subjects governed by no strict laws but self-governance, understanding and accommodation within the Sangat, thus further making redundant any need for canon law or Sikhs claiming to be expert on the faith or its interpretation.

Sangat is an essential feature of Sikh life. In the Sangat, no one acts in moral isolation. The Sangat aspires to live according to a model believing that people take after whom they serve and that ideal is their Guru. The Sangat is in miniature an ideal society. Leadership is invested in those living a conscientious life of spirituality, modesty, tolerance, service and benevolence. It is governed by acclamation or a method of selection, which may include an election. The strength of the Sangat lies in the unity and faith of the family that composes it.

To emphasise the purpose of Sangat, to create an equal society, Guru Nanak also laid the foundation of Langar, people sitting and eating together, without distinction of caste or class. From the time of Guru Nanak, Langar has become central to Sangat. Wherever there was Sangat there was also Langar.

Sangat is the source of Sikh cohesion and holds the key to Sikh governance. It provides a consensual, decentralised means of Sikh self-governance. From the smallest town to the largest city in Britain, its Gurdwara, a mosaic of independent institutions each with its Sangat, interdependent with each other, links the Sikh Panth living together in harmony in the country.

It is through their Sangat that the Panth comes together when the need arises. The great Singh Sabha movement, whose reforms lifted the Sikh masses out of their mediaeval torpor in the late nineteenth century, and the Gurdwara Parbandhak (Management) Committee, which brought Sikh shrines under the care of the Panth in the beginning of the twentieth century, were powerful organisations which owed their strength to Sangat and whose objectives were to strengthen the Gurdwara and their Sangat to let them rightfully serve the Panth.

Why do Sikhs then bemoan the absence of hierarchical structures within the Sikh Panth?

The Sikh Panth is the most progressive and successful of the immigrant communities in Great Britain. Sikhs have the ability to form ad hoc representation when the need arises to deal with matters that concern the Panth. Even what appears as a pyramidal structure within a Gurdwara is not so. The people whose opinion matters most are the Sevadars, the more lowly their positions – symbolic cleaning of shoes, washing utensils or sweeping the floor – the more respected a position they hold within the Sangat. The officers are merely tolerated. Sikh governance is more of an inverted pyramid when authority of the Sangat is considered. If a lowly Sikh holds such an exalted position in the Sangat, then there is little danger of demagogues or authoritarians arising in the Sikh Panth. When, unfortunately, they occasionally do occur, for never more than a short period, the Panth suffers, but soon rectifies the status quo to restore the authority of the Sangat.

It is the view of the author that to understand Sangat and its Gurdwara is to understand Sikh governance. Those who wish to promote Sikh faith do so through Sangat and the Gurdwara.

The place of the Sant-led Sangat in the Sikh Panth is unique. Sants have no formal elevated place in the pantheon of Sikh faith. All Sikhs are equal. Sants hold their positions due to the reverence of their devotees, the Sangat. Sant influence extends over Gurdwara maintained under their spiritual guidance. However, they are still Sangat institutions; they obey the guidance set out by Guru Nanak for the Sikh faith.

PART EIGHT
Stages in a Sikh's Life

CHAPTER 34
Naam Sanskar (Naming a Child ceremony)

Origin and fashion in Sikh names

Sikhs choose names for children with reference to their faith, culture, history and aesthetic qualities of beauty, bravery, generosity and grandeur. Among Sikhs, it is obligatory to use Singh (lion) as second names for males and Kaur (prince) for females.

There are several patterns of choosing names among Sikhs. The first tradition is that of the names of Sikh Gurus. This is an uncommon practice. Sikhs usually avoid the practice, as they do not like to equate themselves to their Gurus.

Bhai Gurdas has listed about a hundred names chosen by the first five Gurus for their families. Sikhs prefer not to choose names from this list because many of those names were in the Hindu tradition as they originated before the foundation of the Khalsa Panth.

The next source of names is from the period after 1699, for about two centuries, following the inauguration of the Khalsa Panth. These names are of those Sikhs who were companions of Guru Gobind Singh, struggled for the survival of their faith and eventually became martyrs for their beliefs. The list includes the names of the four sons of Guru Gobind Singh, the first five Amritdhari Sikhs and the forty Mukte from that time. The list also contains names of leaders of the Sikh armies in the seventeenth and eighteenth centuries. The common names were:

Ajab, Ajaib, Ajaypal, Ajit, Anik, Bachitar, Banda, Baz, Binok, Bota, Chitar, Desa, Dip, Fateh, Garja, Gurbakhsh, Hatthi, Jassa, Jujhar,

Kapur, Mahitab, Mani, Nand, Rai, Ratan Sukkha, Tara, Taru, Udey and Zorawar.

During and after the times of the Misls (ruling Sikh chieftains) and Maharaja Ranjit Singh (1748-1850), the Sikhs preferred to choose martial or religious names. Most prominent names of this period were:

Bir, Fauja, Gurmukh, Kharak, Nidhan, Ranjodh, Sant, Sher, Tegha and Teja.

Maharaja Ranjit Singh also gave the names of the conquered towns after his victories to his children:

Multana, Kashmira, Pishaura, Lahora and Ajmer.

During the Hindu Arya Samaj revival movement, in the second half of the nineteenth century, a period during which many Sikhs reverted to Hinduism, Hindu names became popular among Sikhs. The trend continued for half a century. When the more Hindu sounding names fell out of fashion, others were absorbed as Sikh names. Most prominent among these were:

Bhagat, Darshan, Dhanna, Gopal, Hanuman, Ishwar, Jaswant, Lachhman, Narain, Prehlad, Sawarn, Narayan, Prithipal, Radha, Satbir, Shiv and Tarlochan. Hanuman, Radha and Shiv are no longer used by Sikhs

With the beginning of the Singh Sabha movement in the late nineteenth century, Sikhs once again started choosing religious and martial names for their children. During this period, Bahadur and Kartar became very popular names.

Sikhs have chosen a few Islamic names such as Gujjar, Iqbal, Jahan, Jahangir, Khuda and Umrao.

Inder as a prefix or suffix
Until the beginning of the twentieth century, the name Inder, a Hindu God, hardly featured among Sikhs. Sikh rulers of Punjab states began to adopt it as a suffix for the names of the royal children. Examples are Davinder, Surinder and Narinder. Inder as both a prefix and suffix became very popular with Sikhs, so much so that some have described it as an epidemic of 'inders'(the author is a bearer of this suffix).

'A' as a suffix
Hindu names often end with an 'a'. The practice became popular among Sikhs during the times of Maharaja Ranjit Singh. The old Sikh ruling classes have continued the practice to this time. Anyone with an 'a' as a suffix probably belongs to an old royal family.

Bikrami Calendar
There was a short period, during the Hinduisation of names, when Sikhs also began selecting names from the Bikrami calendar after the names of the months and seasons. We find Chet, Visakha, Jetha, Harha, Sawan, Basant and Maghar as example.

Panthic names
Despite the 'inder' epidemic, Sikh parents have preferred to choose Panthic names for their children. The following are among the most favoured:

Ajit, Amar, Amrit, Avtar, Balwant, Changa, Channan, Darshan, Daya, Deep, Dit, Fateh, Gian, Gurcharan, Gurdial, Gurdit, Gurmit, Gurmukh, Gurnam, Gursagar, Harbans, Harcharan, Harjit, Hari, Harnam, Jagjit, Jagjiwan, Jagtar, Jang, Jassa, Jiwan, Jujhar, Kamal, Kamaljit, Kanwal, Kapur, Kartar, Kirpal, Kuldip, Kultar, Labh, Lakkhi, Lal, Manjit, Mohan, Partap, Pavitar, Piara, Prabhdial, Prabsharan, Punjab, Sahib, Santokh, Sardar, Sarup, Satnam, Sewa, Sukhdev and Zorawar.

Post-1984 Khalistan movement period
After 1984, parents for a short period began to give the names of the martyrs to their children:

Amrik, Manbir, Sukhdev, Sukkha, Subeg and Talwinder.

Names for women
Until the turn of the twentieth century, most Sikh women had Hindu names. It was uncommon for Sikh women to become Amritdhari until the Singh Sabha reform movement towards the end of the nineteenth century brought women to the forefront of Sikh emancipation. Then parents begin to give their daughters the same names as for their sons. Only by knowing the suffix, Singh or Kaur, is it possible to know whether the named person is a male or female in most cases.

Modern names
Sikhs no longer name their children with Hindu connotations. The suffix/prefix 'inder' is now uncommon. Much more pronounced is the practice of amalgamation in names. Deep, Pal, Preet and Raj are examples which can be used as either a prefix or suffix to create pleasing, extended names. The choice of names then becomes infinite. Common names are becoming rare. Parents take pride in creating unique names for their children. It is increasingly becoming a challenge for non-Sikhs to be able to pronounce such names, especially for schoolteachers! A changing trend is to use prefixes and suffixes in such a way that the sex becomes clear from the first name.

Meaning of names
All names have a meaning. Parents like to give names with a pleasing sound and inspiring meaning, hoping their child will live up to the name given to them. A list of a few names, starting with the first letter of the Gurmukhi alphabet illustrates the point:

Ujjal	Bright, clean
Ujalla	One who radiates light
Ujjalroop	A pure and beauteous person
Updesh	One who preaches
Upraj	Noble king
Uttam	Exalted person

Naam Sanskar (Naming a child ceremony)

Parents may indulge in flights of fancy in naming their children, but when it comes to seeking divine affirmation and Sangat blessing in Gurdwara, the ritual is simple, elegant and moving as the child is welcomed into the fold of the Sikh Panth. Only humbleness, Sikhs realise, is appropriate in the presence of Guru Granth.

After discharge from hospital, the mother and the newborn may visit a Gurdwara, if convenient, before going home, to seek Guru's blessing. Parents would say a short Ardas or ask a Granthi to do so. In some Gurdwara, a few drops of Amrit are given to the baby and mother to imbibe either on the first visit or at the naming ceremony. The Granthi may add the following passage in his Ardas,

'I present this infant to you
With your Grace
I administer him the Amrit
May the child be a true Sikh
Devote himself [herself] to service
Of his fellow beings
May he be inspired with devotion to you [God].'

As the birth of a newborn is an occasion of joy and a blessing, Sikhs are forbidden to observe the extensive Hindu cleansing rituals, which are linked to the belief that the mother is polluted because of the birth of a baby. Gurbani says,

'Birth and death are by His writ
All food and water are clean
At all times as he provides them.'

The ritual of naming a child is a simple affair. As soon as possible after the birth of a baby, when the mother and baby are able to, the family arranges for the naming of the baby in the Gurdwara. The family informs the Granthi that a baby is to be named. After the Ardas, when Hukam is taken, the Granthi instructs the parents to use the first letter of the first word of the Hukam Shabad as the initial letter of the name of the child to be chosen. If there is more than one baby to be named, consecutive letters are assigned.

Parents may give a name to the Granthi either then or at a later date. The name is announced to the Sangat for their approval. The child is then blessed with the good wishes of those who are present there and is presented with a ceremonial gift of a Roomala which has been used to drape the Granth.

The family will donate to the Gurdwara and any charity they wish to support. The family may also use the occasion to provide Langar for the Sangat and present them with boxes of sweets.

The parents may wish the ceremony to be more marked and arrange for the diwan for that day to be conducted in the name of their child. They may arrange for an Akhand Paath beforehand and the diwan used for its Bhog. It is an occasion to which the family will invite relatives and friends. The Granthi will announce the happy occasion in the Ardas, bless the child, and wish it prosperity and future happiness on behalf of the Sangat. The Raagis will sing joyful Shabads from Guru Granth to celebrate the birth and naming of the child. Three popular Shabads are,

I

'Almighty has given support
Suffering and sorrows are over
Men and women rejoice
God has been benevolent
There is peace
God's love has spread to us all.'

II

'Almighty has been benevolent
My longings are fulfilled
Sanctified with God's love
Obtained blessing, happiness and peace
Only God bestows truth
Remember God
Seek Grace day and night.'

III

'Son[daughter], mother's blessing
Fill your soul for ever with God
Meditate on the Almighty
To guide you
May God be your protector
May you love his devotees
May God robe you
With honour
And may you
For ever sing his praises.'

The ceremony concludes with Ardas, Hukam and Karah Parsad before the Sangat proceeds to the Langar hall.

CHAPTER 35
Dastar Bandi Sanskar (Pagri Tying Ceremony)

Dastar (Pagri, Pag, turban) in Sikh faith

Dastar Bandi is for a Sikh boy the first step in his being later initiated into the Khalsa Panth. He joins his older brothers, father and grandfathers to be a proud Sikh, to learn his Nit-nem and the history of the faith. His sisters, mother and grandmothers will from now onwards respect and love him to grow up into a fine and handsome young Sikh with a beautiful Pagri and a beard.

The Pagri is associated with Sikhs. Wearing a Pagri is mandatory for Sikh males. The Sikh Pagri is also called Dastar, a more respectful word for it. When a Sikh dons a Pagri, it ceases to be just a piece of cloth but becomes part of his Sikh dress code. It is the *raison d'être* of being a Sikh. The Pagri is an emblem of his identity and foundation of national cohesion for the Sikh Panth. Women need only cover their head with a dupatta, scarf, but some prefer to wear a Pagri too.

The Pagri and the five articles of Sikh faith, the five Ks, have spiritual and temporal significance. The Pagri is symbolic of sovereignty (at one time the Pagri was meant for royalty and ordinary people were forbidden to wear one), courage (people with Pagri were hunted as animals) and piety (all the Gurus and their companions and disciples wore a Pagri) but the reason Sikhs wear the Pagri is just one – out of love and obedience to the wishes of their ten Gurus.

If a Sikh desires to become one with the Gurus, he must look like a Guru (wear a Pagri). Guru Gobind Singh has said,

'Khalsa mero roop hai khaas
Khalsa me hau karo niwas.'
[Khalsa is in my true image
I dwell in my Khalsa].'

The Pagri provides Sikhs with a unique identity. It is commitment to faith. A Sikh who wears a Pagri stands up to be counted and stands out from the rest.

In mediaeval times, the Pagri was a sign of moral rectitude. People of other faiths, Hindus and Muslims, felt safe when there was a Sikh around them. Imran Khan, the famous Pakistani cricketer, in his book, 'Indus Journey', describes how his people, the Pathan, fearless warriors, found their match in Sikhs. Imran says even in his lifetime he has heard mothers say to their children, 'Behave, the Pagri man is coming'.

Though not strictly part of the five Ks, the Pagri is an integral part of Sikh dress code. It is its most visible symbol. Pagri has been an inseparable part of a being a Sikh from the time of Guru Nanak. The Gurus sought to end caste distinctions and opposed stratification of society. The Pagri, by providing a visible common dress, removed these distinctions.

The Pagri symbolises spirituality. When Guru Nanak handed over the responsibility of the faith to the second Guru, Angad Dev, he tied a Pagri on his head with his own hands. This custom was continued for all the Gurus who succeeded him.

A similar custom is Rasam Pagri, the Pagri ceremony. This ceremony takes place once a man passes away and his eldest son takes over the family responsibilities. It signifies that he is now head of the family.

Siropa, honour to the head, is the Sikh way of presenting a Pagri to Sikhs and non-Sikhs in recognition of service to the Sikh Panth.

A Sikh only takes off his Pagri in public to express deep sorrow, at the death of a grandparent or parent. At no other time may a Sikh remove his Pagri in public. It is said that a person, after taking a bath at the village well, forgot his Pagri there and came home bareheaded. When the women saw him at home without a Pagri, they thought that a parent had died and they started to cry. Deliberate disturbing or knocking of a Pagri is disrespectful and constitutes a grave offence to Sikhs.

Sikhs exchange Pagri, Pag vatauni, with close friends. A solemn pledge is taken to share their joys and sorrows. Exchanging Pagri is the glue that binds two individuals or families. Families present Pagri to each other to mark special occasions such as birthdays. In a marriage ceremony, the parents of the bride and bridegroom present Pagri to each other as symbolic of shared social esteem and dignity and to put a stamp on their relationship.

Sikhs had to struggle to gain the right to wear a Pagri as a symbol of their faith. During the seventeenth and eighteenth centuries, Sikhs were hunted like wild animals for wearing a Pagri. There was a bounty on the severed head of a Sikh with a Pagri.

The Sikh soldiers serving the British imperial forces refused to wear helmets during the two World Wars. They fought with Pagri on their heads. The valour and bravery of the Sikhs was recognised by awarding many Sikhs the Victoria Cross, the most prestigious gallantry award in the British army, which was proudly worn on their Pagri.

During the Indian freedom struggle, Sikhs refused to remove their Pagri even in prison. Bhai Randhir Singh, the most renowned Sikh imprisoned by the British for his beliefs in freedom to practice his faith, had to undergo torture and suffer from starvation to win his and other Sikhs' right to wear the Pagri anywhere at any time, in prison or outside it.

In several countries abroad Sikhs have had to fight to retain their rights to wear Pagri. The most famous confrontation was the Mandla case, in which a Sikh child in Birmingham, Britain, won the right in law to wear a Pagri to school or anywhere else in Britain. Sikhs had to fight to be allowed to wear the Pagri instead of a hard helmet while riding motor cycles or on construction sites. Sikhs have also obtained the right to wear Pagri as soldiers and police officers.

In Norway, Sikhs had to fight for their right to get a passport with a photograph in Pagri. In Europe, North America, Australia and New Zealand too, Sikhs have won the right to wear a Pagri as part of the uniform in public transport, the police force and the armed forces.

The Pagri is usually made of fine cotton muslin, about five yards (4.5 metres) in length. Other Pagri are made of voile – dense cotton cloth. The length varies but it would not be longer than six to seven yards (5.4-6.4 metres). Children will wear Pagri of the same cloth but of shorter length. The pattern of the Pagri has become established by tradition. It is remarkable how in this simple operation of winding between three and six yards of muslin so many different styles in fashion have emerged.

The Sikh Rahet Maryada lays down no rules about the colour and shape of a Pagri. By tradition, certain colours or styles have cultural and social significance and even denote a Sikh's geographical origin.

For the Nihangs, warrior Sikh class, a Pagri is spun around their heads in a conical shape. The Namdharis wear white in a flat, coif-like style. Peasants usually wrap them over their heads without any concern for their form. Elderly Sikhs will generally wear a white Pagri tied in a modest fashion.

Sikhs of East African origin are easily recognised by the modest, plain folded style of their Pagri in white colours, which occasionally gives way to black for convenience to cope with pollution and weather in Britain.

Elaborate, colourful Pagri styles suggest origin from the Punjab. A style popular with urban youth and young men is a Pagri wrapped sprucely like a boat, to a sharp, high frontal point, imparting to it a regal look, a particularly colourful style which goes by the sobriquet of Patiala style.

A soldier or police officer's Pagri, in India and abroad, matches his uniform. It marks another distinctive mode with its neatly arranged emphatic folds.

Pagri, its colour, as a symbol of defiance, has a place too in Sikh history. During the freedom struggle of India, black, orange and saffron coloured Pagri were seen as a challenge to British authority and Sikhs courted imprisonment for wearing these colours. Black and steel blue – the favourite colour of Guru Gobind Singh's warriors – is the accepted colour for Akali Dal, the party of Sikh political struggle. These colours also played an important role in the Sikh struggle to regain their shrines.

White is worn for mourning, pink at weddings and bright yellow at the Basant festival (in honour of the mustard flower, which is in blossom at the time). Orange and saffron coloured Pagri also signify religious devotion, as these are religious colours of the Sikhs. When Sikhs go to demonstrations or protest marches to stand for the rights of their faith, they usually wear a saffron coloured Pagri, which is a symbol of sacrifice and martyrdom. Sikhs carrying out religious duties also tend to wear saffron coloured Pagri.

Dastar Bandi Ceremony

As the child's hair grows, a mother will tie it in a knot at the top of the head. When there is enough hair, at about the age of four years, the knot is covered with a piece of white or black cloth (patka) for a boy. Later the whole head can be covered with a cloth, usually black, until the child is ready to support a Pagri.

Children, sportsmen and Sikhs at home often wear a patka (tight Pagri) for comfort and to prevent its toppling off in games and sports, but it is not a substitute for a Pagri.

A child wears a Pagri as soon as it is practicable to do so. The age of ten upwards is accepted as the right time. Sikh children often wish to wear a Pagri before they can tie it themselves. Parents will tie it for them until they are able to do it themselves. In schools where there are a significant number of Sikh pupils, a teacher will often help to tie a Pagri, if it comes off the head. The English headmistress of the primary school where my eldest son was the only Sikh child appointed herself the school Sikh Pagri tie-er. Sikh children will be expected to tie their own Pagri by the time they enter their teens.

The Dastar Bandi ceremony is an important mark in a Sikh boy's progress to the next step in life. The ceremony is similar to the one for naming a child. The family and friends gather in the Gurdwara. Shabads appropriate to the occasion are sung. There is a lovely Salok of Bhagat Namdev starting with,

'How handsome is your Pagri
How sweet is your speech.'

After Ardas and Hukam, the priest, a grandfather, uncle or a dignitary, at the request of the parents, sits the child in front of the Granth and ties his Pagri. The Sangat is asked to give recognition of the act. They do so with great joy. The Pagri tying ceremony precedes the Amrit ceremony by a few years. This ceremony designates the respect with which the Pagri is regarded. The child with a Pagri is a sign he is entering into his adulthood.

CHAPTER 36
Amrit Sanskar (Khalsa Initiation Ceremony)

Amrit Sanskar is the sacred ceremony for the initiation of Sikhs into the Khalsa Panth. Gobind Singh, the tenth Guru, inaugurated Amrit Sanskar on Vaisakhi day in 1699. Guru Gobind Singh defined his initiates, the Khalsa, thus,

'He who meditates on the Ever-radiant Light
Day and night rejects all else but the one Lord from his mind
He embraces himself with perfect love and faith
Believes not in fasts, tombs, fire and hermitage,
Radiant Light is a true and pure Khalsa.'

The age of initiation is not fixed. It requires initiates to be mature enough to practise the commitment required after initiation. By custom, a Sikh child should be about fourteen to fifteen years of age. The initiate may be a man or woman of any caste or previous religion.

The principles of Amrit Sanskar are outlined in the Sikh Rahet Maryada, code of discipline, promulgated by the Sikhs' supreme religious body, the Shiromani Gurdwara Parbandhak Committee. The ceremony is conducted in the presence of Guru Granth Sahib on set days or when there are enough Sikhs wishing to be initiated. Vaisakhi day or other Gurpurb days are popular dates. Generally, a person who seeks Amrit Sanskar must already have followed the Sikh way of life to be initiated into Khalsa Panth.

The initiates are required to wash their hair, cover their head with a Pagri or dupatta and wear clean clothes. All marks of another faith or ornaments must be removed. The initiates put on the five Ks and present themselves before Guru Granth Sahib at the required time.

The Panj Pyarae, five devout Amritdhari Sikhs, men or women, chosen by the Sangat, are present to conduct the ceremony. Another Amritdhari Sikh sits in the presence of Guru Granth Sahib to recite from it during the ceremony. All six are attired in the Khalsa uniform, the five Ks and orange or yellow robes and blue, dark or orange Pagri.

All the initiates stand in reverence in front of the Granth. The Jathedar, leader, explains the principles of Sikh faith, belief in the oneness of God and mediation upon his name, as the sole means of gaining spiritual strength. Sikhs are required to participate in Gurdwara diwans, render service to the Panth, Sangat and the destitute, promote the good of others and live within the Khalsa discipline.

The Jathedar then asks the initiates, 'Do you accept the tenets of Sikh faith?'

On an affirmative response, the Jathedar performs the Ardas for the preparation of the Amrit, holy nectar. The Granthi takes Hukam. The Amrit ceremony is now ready to begin.

Preparation of Amrit
The Panj Pyarae kneel around a steel bowl on a pedestal in Bir Asan, heroic posture, with the left knee up and right knee down on the ground. This is a half sitting position as if one is about to get up. This is symbolic of ever preparedness for a Sikh. It is also the position Sikhs adopt when after genuflection in front of the Granth, they prepare to bow to the Granth and then get up again.

The Panj Pyarae surround the bowl. Pure water and patasha, sugar wafers, are added to the urn as the five Nit-nem Bani are recited. Each Pyarae holds an edge of the bowl with the left hand, and stirs the bowl with a Khanda with the right hand and recites the Bani in turn. The recitation takes about two hours. When the recitation is complete, Amrit is ready.

Ardas is offered again. The Panj Pyarae then sit down as before. The initiates, who have been standing throughout the preparation of the Amrit, step forward one by one, kneel before the Panj Pyarae in Bir Asan with the right hand cupped into the left one. Amrit is poured into the hands five times, which the initiate imbibes.

At each pouring of the Amrit into the cupped hand, the Jathedar says, 'Say, Waheguruji Ka Khalsa Waheguruji ki Fateh'. The initiate imbibes the Amrit and repeats the chant. Then five handfuls of the nectar are sprinkled at the eyes and then hair of the initiate. The Jathedar asks the initiate to repeat the chant at every sprinkling of the Amrit.

The Panj Pyarae then together chant the Mool Mantar, Sikh declaration of faith, and the initiates repeat it after them.

The Jathedar instructs the initiates in the Sikh Rahet Maryada, the vows of Sikh disciplines, as follows,

'You have of your choice joined the Khalsa Panth. You are reborn. Your father is Guru Gobind Singh and your mother Mata Sahib Kaur [revered spouse of the Guru]. Your place of birth is Kesgarh Sahib [Guru Gobind Singh initiated the first five Sikhs here], and your home is Anandpur Sahib [Kesgarh is situated here]. You begin your life afresh as the Khalsa, purified ones, who believe in one God. You conduct yourself in the teachings of the ten Gurus and put your faith in none other than Guru Granth. You say your Nit-nem every day; pay your daswandh [dues] to your Gurdwara and Sangat. You wear the five Ks [articles of faith] at all times as the tenth Guru, Gobind Singh, has so ordained, as a mark of your spirituality and disciplined warrior of Khalsa Panth.'

The initiates are instructed in the four commandments, part of the Amrit Sanskar,

'Abstain from intoxicants, tobacco, drugs and alcohol
Wear unshorn hair
Not commit congress with a person outside wedlock

Eat wholesome food that is honestly acquired [Halal meat is specifically forbidden].'

Amrit Sanskar concludes with Ardas, Hukam and Karah Parsad. The initiated Khalsa are now Amritdhari Sikhs and part of the Khalsa Panth.

Note: Formerly, Amrit Sanskar was held in public, as Sikhs are forbidden to carry out Guru's instruction in private. This led to lively sessions, as the Sangat would object to any novice being initiated if they were felt to be undeserving of such an honour. The ceremony is now held in private in a Gurdwara open only to the initiates, Panj Pyarae, a Granthi and Gurdwara Sevadars.

CHAPTER 37
Anand Sanskar (Lavan – Marriage Ceremony)

A reference book describes weddings, a whole labyrinth of spectacular marriage custom and rite among Sikhs despite the Rahet Maryada injunctions against elaborate ritual and superstitious behaviour. Customs also vary enormously within caste, social and geographical differences. Sikhs observe in varying degrees ancient ritual sanctioned under Hindu customary law and practice but these find no place in a Gurdwara. It is true that most Sikhs have abandoned these rituals, retaining a few pleasing family customs to celebrate the girl and boy stepping into the next stage of their life. Adding Western customs to Sikh ones has instead taken place to replace ancient Indian ones.

The Rahet Maryada-prescribed marriage ritual, the Anand Karaj, is an expression of basic principles of the faith. Anand Karaj Sanskar is the Sikh marriage ceremony. Marriage is obligatory for Sikhs. Anand Karaj is a sacrament: not only is it a contract between two persons but also union of two souls to play their worldly role as ordained by the Creator, solemnly agreed in the presence of Guru Granth. For Gurbani says,

'They alone are called husband and wife
Who have one soul in two bodies.'

The marriage date is arranged according to the convenience of the families. It is forbidden for Sikhs to seek an auspicious day for the purpose. Prayers offered to God sanctify all acts and times. The marriage can take place anywhere the Granth is installed in a Gurdwara or a temporary site, such as a specially erected marquee temporarily designated a Gurdwara. A Sikh marriage ceremony is usually conducted in a Gurdwara in Britain. The bride's parents choose the place of marriage. The marriage ceremony must be performed in an assembly of Sikhs, which every Sikh is free to join as a member of the Sikh Panth. Secret marriages are forbidden.

A Sikh wedding is likely to be a combination of Indian traditions and faith rituals approved in the Sikh Rahet Maryada. There is a difference between Indian ostentation and Sikh simplicity in its faith rituals. Most marriages attempt to strike a balance. Gurdwara forbid excessive displays of gaudiness. However, as always, compromise is accepted. Decorative headgear for men, and finery in clothes for the woman, though frowned upon in the Rahet Maryada, pass for acceptable allowance for the occasion. However, the Gurdwara will ask that the man's face is not hidden behind a face garland and the woman's face is only modestly covered.

Among Sikh families, parents and relatives play a leading role in helping their children find suitable marriage partners. Marriage is regarded as an alliance between two families. The children may also suggest a likely partner to their parents. Even if the children choose each other without family assistance, parents do usually, after show of reluctance, enthusiastically take on the responsibility for the organisation of the wedding.

Family background, socio-economic status, educational qualifications as well as personality and social skills are factors that influence the choice of a spouse.

Child marriages are forbidden. Age is not specified in the Rahet Maryada but, by custom, the girl and the boy should be at least eighteen to twenty years of age before marriage. Polygamy, though not proscribed, is unacceptable in modern Sikh society. Although caste consideration is forbidden, and should not influence the choice of a partner, it still plays a role in most unions. The adherence to caste varies but, in practice, the boundaries of caste define the universe within which social relationships are constructed. Sikhs should only marry a Sikh or someone who does not believe in some other faith. Most Gurdwara will conduct intermarriages, now commonplace, as long as one partner is a Sikh.

The tenets of the faith deny asking for a dowry. However, it is an ancient custom that many Sikhs find difficult to ignore. Provided the dowry is given voluntarily, it is acceptable. The bridegroom's enlightened parents usually declare that they are not expecting a dowry apart from the traditional exchange of presents without financial hardship to the bride's parents, but would be critical if the dowry fell short of their unspoken expectation.

In Britain, as in many other countries, civil marriage is a legal requirement. In Britain, Gurdwara are usually registered for this purpose, no longer making it necessary to hold a civil ceremony outside it. In the eyes of Sikhs it is only the religious ceremony that matters; civil ceremonies if held before the wedding are low-key affairs. After a civil ceremony alone, the girl and boy return to their own homes and resume unmarried life.

Kurmai (sagu), engagement
The kurmai period is protracted and may last from weeks to months. If the need arises, it can be shortened to a few days. The Rahet Maryada, being conscious of this 'foot dragging', has pronounced kurmai unnecessary but, just to be on the safe side, recommends that if it is desired to have one, it should be in the presence of Guru Granth. Sikhs consider kurmai mandatory but it can take different forms. I give a few essential details.

The first ceremony is the rokna, hold. The girl's family take sweetmeats, dried and fresh fruit to the boy's home to mark the occasion. Rokna is an understanding rather than a firm commitment to marry but it is rare for events not to proceed further once rokna takes place.

Generally, kurmai, betrothal, takes place in a Gurdwara. The kurmai ceremony is simple and is organised by the boy's family. It is carried out in the absence of the intended betrothed. The bride's parents will present gifts – dried and fresh fruits, sweetmeats and nuts – to the boy. A gold ring, Pagri, a Kara and an amount of cash is presented to the intended bridegroom. The girl's father puts a dried date in the willing mouth of the boy to signify that the marriage proposal is made and accepted by his family. Ardas is offered to solemnise the kurmai. Hukam is taken and Karah Parsad distributed. The sacred ceremony is complete. The relatives and well-wishers invited to witness the ceremony congratulate the betrothed boy and his parents. Wedding arrangements can now go ahead with confidence. A formal letter of engagement is presented to the boy's parents, either then or nearer the wedding date, confirming the kurmai and the date and place of the wedding, which is arranged by the girl's family.

The chunni, dupatta, ceremony is the ritual that takes place after the formal engagement. The betrothed girl is sent clothes, a gold ring and an embroidered dupatta to her home by her prospective mother-in-law. This ceremony is confined to the girl's family and relatives at her home. Once the girl receives her gifts there is much rejoicing, singing and dancing in celebration.

A formal separate kurmai ceremony, described above, is now becoming uncommon in Britain. It is combined with the marriage ceremony, taking place immediately before the arrival of the bride inside the Gurdwara.

Pre-wedding rituals

Sikhs refrain from the intensity of Hindu rituals, which are loaded with symbolic and social significance usually lost on the boy and girl, a week before the wedding day. Purification is perhaps the most important. The girl (and often the boy) is ritually cleansed in the morning and evening by rubbing a scented mixture which includes among its ingredients flour, oils, henna and tamarind powders followed by a ritual bath. The ceremony is called maainye. The final cleansing is carried out on the morning of the wedding. Most parents avoid the purification every day of the week, only following the ritual the night before or in the morning on the day of the wedding. The groom usually escapes this regular ritual, but may like the girl have a symbolic one the night before or the morning of the wedding.

One evening is reserved for viewing the daaj, trousseau, consisting of clothes, jewellery, household linen and other items, which are gifts for the bride from her parents and family. This practice is now becoming uncommon.

The chura, bangle, ceremony is performed a day or two before the wedding day. The girl's maternal relatives weave twenty-one red and ivory coloured bangles on her two arms in addition to gifts of money. The idea is that it makes it difficult to carry out household chores and is a reminder to her soon to be in-laws that she is not to be given domestic work when she is just married. These bangles are worn for forty days after the wedding.

On the eve of the wedding day is Mehndi-ki-Raat (henna night), when the hands and feet of the girl are patterned with a potion, mainly of henna. Mehndi symbolises strength of love, the darker the potion the stronger the love.

The wedding day
On the wedding day, the marriage parties assemble in the forecourt of the Gurdwara. The bride's party welcomes the barat, the groom's party, for the ceremony of milni, meeting. Milni is the formal recognition of two families to be joined together by the holy matrimony of their respective son and daughter. First Ardas is offered to sanctify the occasion. Equivalent family male relations greet each other individually and the girl's relatives put garlands on the necks of the opposite member and present them with a gift. Men will usually receive Pagri, shirts or gold rings. The milni for women is a modern innovation, and is usually held later, after the wedding. However, it is increasingly combined with the milni for men.

After the milni, the bride's parents will treat the bridegroom's party with refreshments. The parties then proceed to enter and sit in the Gurdwara hall.

Anand Karaj, wedding ceremony

In the Gurdwara, the couple is seated in front of Guru Granth. The bridegroom sits on the bride's right. The seating arrangement is an ancient Indian custom and has no religious significance for Sikhs.

The Granthi, reader of the Granth, who will perform the ceremony, is already in place behind the Granth. The Raagis sing Shabads while people compose themselves for the ceremony. Once the bride and the bridegroom are in place, the Raagis sing,

> *Friends have come to my house**
> *We have been divinely enjoined*
> *The union is pleasing to God*
> *The seeds of tranquillity come*
>   *from the union of two hearts*
> *Heart's desire now is requited*
> *Mind content, house beautified*
> *Ringing with music, and silent joy. Friends have come to my house'.*

*In the past the milni and marriage were conducted at the bride's home. Most Raagis omit this Shabad

The assent of the bride and bridegroom and their parents to the marriage is then obtained. The Granthi who is to conduct the wedding asks the bride and the bridegroom, as well as their parents or guardians, to stand up. The Granthi then recites Ardas. The standing parties give consent by bowing before the Granth after Ardas is complete. Now the consent of the Sangat is required, so the Granthi calls out 'Bole so Nihal' (blessed is the one who replies). The congregation gives consent with shouts of 'Sat Siri Akal' (God is truth). Hukam is taken to put a seal upon the agreement.

Then the Raagis sing,

'God's grace must be sought
before all endeavours
Who [God] sits in the company
of Sants
And expounds the truth
That success is attained
It is with the True Teacher
That we taste the ambrosia

O! Destroyer of fear
And embodiment of mercy
Bestow your grace on your
servant
Nanak says, by praising God
We apprehend the infinite.'

The Granthi then explains the duties of husband and wife to the couple. The marriage is not just a social contract but aims at the fusion of two souls into one. The Lavan, wedding Shabads, state the four stages on the path of attainment of bliss in life. It is only by the faithful performance of duty to each other that a married couple fulfil their vows.

The bride's father picks up one edge of a palla, scarf, saffron or pink in colour, which is draped over the left shoulder of the groom and places it into the hands of his daughter, the bride. It symbolises the bride's father giving the bridegroom the responsibility of the care of his daughter. Then the Raagis sing,

'Praise and dispraise
I cease to relish
All other relationships
I find false
O Nanak! I seize the hem
Of your garment [God's]
With that I am attached.'

The Lavan
The Lavan, wedding ritual, is going round the Granth Sahib four times, while the Lavan Shabads are first recited from the Granth

and then sung by the Raagis. The Lavan constitutes the binding part of the ceremony, as required by the Rahet Maryada.

The couple circumambulate the palanquin on which the Granth Sahib is placed, four times in a clockwise direction, while Lavan, the four Shabads from the Granth are recited one at a time. Lavan Shabads describe the union of two persons with God. The four Lavan Shabads are the four stages of this union. The first is the stage of understanding the necessity of the union; the second stage is that of living in God's noble obedience; the third stage is of surrender and immersion of oneself in God, and, finally the fourth Lavan Shabad indicates the stage of union where the bride and bridegroom have become one soul in two bodies to strive together to live under the command of God.

Shabads relevant to marriage often appear to be addressed to the bride. Guru Nanak addressed God as his beloved in which he acted as the bride seeking union with God, the bridegroom. Only the Lavan Shabads are specific to marriage, other Shabads are brought into the ceremony because they suit the occasion. Even the Lavan Shabads use marriage as a metaphor for union with God. Guru Nanak showed great respect to women and he believed them equal to men. The Shabads during the wedding are in that spirit and not as some people suggest that the Gurus felt it necessary to place the whole responsibility of the marriage on the bride.

The Granthi opens Guru Granth and reads the first Lav Shabad. When he finishes the recitation, the Raagis then sing it to music. As they begin to do so, the pair bow to Guru Granth, stand up and walk slowly round the palanquin on which the Granth Sahib is placed. The Raagis time the end of the singing for the moment the pair return to the front of Guru Granth. The couple then bow to the Granth and sit down again.

The Granthi reads the second Lav, and the pair go round again as musicians take up the refrain in the same way. This is repeated four times until all the four Shabads have been recited and sung. During the fourth Lav, the couple may be showered with flower petals as they complete the round but this practice has now become uncommon.

Lavan (marriage vows) composed by Ram Das, the fourth Guru.

'1

*In the first nuptial round
God ordains
The performance of daily duty
The voice of God and his words
Declare the path to follow
And the way to avoid sin
Disciplined in the performance of duty
Repeating the Name of God
As prescribed in the ancient texts
Devote yourself to God
By following the True Teacher
All afflictions and sins depart
By great good fortune
The name of God becomes sweet
Endowing the soul with bliss
Nanak, the disciple, says,
In the first round
Initial preparations are made.*

II

*In the second nuptial round
Teacher speaks of the immanence of God
And reveals to the disciple
Knowledge of divine presence
Fear of the fearless enters the mind
And the dirt of egoism departs
The mind becomes limpid
By the fire of the fear of stainless.
It fills the heart with song of praise
And the Lord of Bliss is seen
In Atman, soul, God Himself pervades
Lord himself pervades everything
Within and without is one God
And His devotees, joined together
Sing the song of rejoicing
Nanak, the disciple, says
In the second round
The song of the soul is heard.*

III
In the third nuptial round
With a feeling of exultation
Mind is merged in Vairag
[detachment]
In the company of Sants
By great good fortune
God Himself is found
The omnipresent God is found
Song of praise arises in the heart
Lips murmur the word of God.

By great good fortune
Sants find the Omnipresent
Sound of the divine name echoes
Indescribable story is beyond telling.
They who have inscribed
The letters of good fortune
Repeat God's name
Nanak, the disciple, says,
In the third round
The mind awakens with Vairag.

IV
In the fourth nuptial round
Mind becomes peaceful
Self is realised
All-pervading God is found
The True teacher is met
Who gives his sweet message
Its sweetness pervades
The mind and the body
God has made His Love
The sweet breath of life.

Mind is now fixed on Him
Heart's desire is fulfilled
The desired fruit is obtained
Song of joy breaks forth
Ringing with His Name
God is united with his bride
The bride is full of bliss
With her heart filled with His Name
Nanak, the disciple, says,
In the fourth round is found
The Omnipresent, Immortal God.'

The recital of the fourth Lav Shabad completes the ceremony. Immediately thereafter, the short Anand Sahib are recited to indicate Guru's blessing at the conclusion of the holy ceremony.

The Raagis then sing two Shabads to mark the successful conclusion of Anand Karaj. These are Chhants composed by Guru Ram Das and Guru Arjan Dev respectively.

The bride (devotee) addresses her father on the joy of her finding a true husband (God).

'I

My marriage is performed, O Father

I have found the Lord

Darkness of ignorance is dispelled

Divine light is revealed

Spiritual wisdom shines forth

Pain of my ego is dispelled

Guru has revealed my true search

I have found a husband in my Lord

Ever lasting, never dying, never leaving, all pervasive.

II

My desires are fulfilled.

I have no virtues

You are goodness itself

How can I praise you

You are the Lord.

My good and bad deeds

You did not consider

You have forgiven them

Nine treasures are gained [Vedic allusion]

Songs of rejoicing are sung

Endless trumpets are blown

All sins have vanished

Says Nanak

I have found the bridegroom

My wish has been fulfilled

By the grace of God.'

The Sangat stands up for Ardas, Hukam is taken and Karah Parsad is distributed. The religious part of the wedding ceremony is complete.

There follows the informal celebration of the marriage, with decorum as we are still seated in the presence of Guru Granth. The parents first garland their children followed by close relatives. The Sangat then set the couple on their future life by gifts of money, which are put in the laps of the bride and bridegroom. The Sangat donates money to the musicians for having sung the Lavan. The money usually goes to the Gurdwara fund. The Gurdwara management offers their congratulations and announces the donations made by the marriage parties to the Gurdwara and other charities.

The bride and bridegroom proceed to register their marriage with the Registrar of marriages.

The marriage parties then disperse and the bridegroom's party is treated to a festive meal either in the Gurdwara or at an outside venue.

The girl goes home for the next stage. The groom and his party arrive to take the bride home. The bride changes into clothes brought to her by her mother-in-law. The bride is received with great ceremony at her new home.

The simplicity and elegance of the Lavan service adds lustre and dignity to the marriage. Readers know that celebrations are by no means over but let us congratulate the bride and groom and depart from the scene.

CHAPTER 38
Antam Sanskar (Funeral Rites)

The Sikh Rahet Maryada sets out the funeral rites, which are carried out in conjunction with local traditions in accord with Sikh faith principles.

Once, Guru Nanak asked his musician companion, Bhai Mardana, to go and buy truth for one paisa (penny) and falsehood for another. Bhai Mardana bought death as truth and life as falsehood. Guru Nanak said,

'Death is real and life is unreal'.

Sikh religion considers life transitory. It is a journey to end in union with God. Death is the reality in this world. Of one aspect of life alone are we certain, that the days of a human being's stay on this earth are numbered from the day of birth. One who is born is sure to die.

To accept reality, we should not be afraid of it, but we still fear death. Gurbani says,

'The people in this world fear death
And (try to) hide themselves from it
Lest death's courier should catch and take them away'.

Gurbani then says,

'One should only worry
If a phenomenon, not expected, comes to happen
This (death) is the way of the world
O Nanak, no one lasts forever'.

The moment of our departure from this world is predestined. Gurbani tells us,

'O Nanak, mortals come when they are sent [by the Almighty]
They depart when called back.'

We do not know how long we are going to live. Every day the span of life decreases by one day, with every breath we lose one moment of our life. Gurbani pronounces,

'By day and night the span of life goes on decreasing.'

And then,

'The day dawns, then sets down
Age diminishes but man understands not
The mouse [of time] daily gnaws
The rope of life.'

In Sikh religion, death is not a matter of sorrow. It is the Bhana, will of God. Death means one has accomplished one's purpose in this world. A life has a finite duration of stay in this world. Hence its conclusion, for a Sikh, cannot be a matter of sorrow.

Completion of one's mission in this world is not measured according to the length of one's span of life. It is valued according to one's allotted purpose in the world. One can accomplish one's role in a short period, others might not be able to perform it in many decades.

Sikhs believe in reward and punishment as part of this life. Having done a wrong, the guilty person is always conscious lest others find him to be a liar, a cheat or a robber. He suffers mental agony. Fear of being exposed haunts him for his entire life. This is a much more severe punishment than society will bestow upon him if brought to justice. God does not give punishment and rewards that people deserve. We are rewarded or punished by our conscience for our deeds.

After death, according to the Sikh faith, there is no 'other' world. The soul of a person leaves their body and is absorbed into the spiritual world. Such a union, for a pious person, is a matter of joy, not sorrow.

According to Sikh faith, there is no place which is reserved as heaven or hell. Gurbani says living in harmony with God's creation is abode in heaven and living in its shadow is incarceration in hell in one's own being. Those who perform evil deeds suffer, however happy they seem in appearance. Sometimes it appears to us that people doing evil deeds enjoy their life and go unpunished. They do receive their punishment without other people knowing it. We recognise reward for the just; equally, we must accept suffering for those guilty of cruelty and unjust behaviour towards their fellow beings.

Gurbani forbids Sikhs to lament the death of a beloved one. Guru Amar Das has issued this command to his Sikhs,

'Let no one weep for me after I am gone
That is not at all pleasing to me.'

And,

'O Almighty, the mortals bewail for the sake of worldly objects
All bewailing is vain. All weeping is sinful
The world is forgetful of the Almighty and weeps for wealth.'

Sikhs cremate a deceased body. However, there is no restriction about disposal of the dead body in any other manner. No method of disposal of the dead helps or harms the soul. Some religions believe in beneficial rituals at time of death. It helps the soul to go to heaven. For Sikhs, disposal of a body with respect and dignity does not signify consideration of the effect on the soul. Sikh prayers at time of death are to thank God for giving us life.

The human body is made of five elements. After death, these elements again become a part of the invisible ether that our universe is made of and the soul becomes a part of its creation. Gurbani says,

'The body is dust, the wind screams therein
Consider O Wiseman! Who is it that is dead
Know that the body is made up of five elements
Be you sure, says Nanak, you shall blend with Him
From whom you have sprung.'

A Sikh must bow before will of the Almighty. We do not forget the love and virtues of our deceased friends and relatives. But with every fond memory is underlined the will of God. Gurbani says,

'This call is being sent to all homes every day
So remember the lord who calls, O Nanak
For the day is drawing near for everyone.'

Antam Sanskar (funeral arrangements)

Sikhs are forbidden to indulge in rituals – burning divas (lamps), organised womanly lamentations and auspicious day rituals outside of the faith ceremony. Grief is natural but ostentatious behaviour such as beating of the chest is unseemly, does not lend to the dignity of occasion, and should be avoided.

The funeral ceremony is split into two parts: Sanskar, the cremation, and the Antam (final) Ardas, the last prayer at the end of the Bhog ceremony in the Gurdwara after the funeral.

At a Sikh's deathbed, relatives and friends read Sukhmani Sahib, the Psalm of Peace, composed by Arjan Dev, the fifth Guru, to console themselves and the dying person. When a death occurs, they chant 'Waheguru, Waheguru', to create a mood of acceptance of God's will. Japji Sahib may also be recited. Death is seen as a time for thanking God for the life led in accordance with the tenets of the faith and to acknowledge that dying is the will of God.

The practice in Britain is for the body to be taken to a funeral home, whether it is from a residence or a hospital. Occasionally, a hospital may need to keep the body for a few days for medical or legal reasons. This is allowed.

However young the deceased may be, the body is cremated, though some parents prefer a burial if a baby has died at birth, soon after or is stillborn. Where cremation is not permitted as in some Muslim or Catholic countries, there is no qualm about the body being disposed of in an accepted local manner. As to the time and day of cremation, no auspicious occasion counts.

The family will arrange for Guru Granth to be installed at home, if one is not already present, for its recitation. If time does not permit, then continuous reading is arranged to be finished in forty-eight hours. This means a Sikh's body cannot be cremated for at least forty-eight hours after death. Most families prefer a Sahaj Paath, reading of Granth Sahib which is interrupted to allow for all family and friends to listen to the recitation when time permits. The family and relatives of the deceased carry out the reading of Guru Granth. If this is not possible, then the local Gurdwara will arrange the reading for them. The reading is audible and clearly enunciated to provide spiritual support and consolation to the bereaved family and friends by listening to the words of the Gurbani. The reading is stopped at Bhog Bani, as this will be recited in a Gurdwara after the funeral at the Antam Ardas ceremony.

Meanwhile the family will bathe and dress the deceased in clean clothes in a funeral home. This task is carried out by the same gender as the deceased. While that is being done the family chants 'Waheguru, Waheguru'. The Sikh symbols – Khanda, Kachera, Kara, and Kirpan – must not be taken off the deceased even during the washing ritual. Thereafter the dressed body, complete with its symbols, is put in the coffin. Ardas is said when this takes place.

The hearse arrives at the arranged time for family and friends to pay their last respects to the deceased. The bereaved should recite Japji

Sahib and meditate on 'Waheguru, Waheguru' while this is taking place. The hearse is then taken to the local Gurdwara for Ardas. Men wear white Pagri or head coverings to the funeral and women wear pale coloured or white dress and dupatta.

The hearse is then taken to a crematorium. The Granthi recites the Kirtan Sohila, the last prayer of the day. Ardas is said seeking the divine blessings for the departed soul, following which the oldest son consigns the body to be cremated. The bereaved then return to the Gurdwara for the Antam, final, Ardas.

Kirtan is sung to comfort the family. Guru Nanak Dev composed Alahnian, dirges, in Raag to be sung to folk tunes. The Bhog ceremony, reading the final pages of Guru Granth, takes place. At its conclusion, the Granthi recites Ramkali Ki Sadd, the call, in Raag Ramkali, a eulogy composed by Baba Sundar, brother of Guru Arjan Dev, in memory of their father, Ram Das, the fourth Guru. During the Antam, final, Ardas, the blessing of God for the departed soul is sought and the Sangat is reminded that Gurbani emphasises remembrance of God as the best means of consolation for a bereaved family. Sikhs are always exhorted to submit to and have complete faith in Bhana, the will of God. Hukam is taken, and Karah Parsad is distributed.

In the case of the death of a father, the oldest son is presented with a Pagri and declared the head of the family. It is usual to say a few words about the life of the deceased. The family contributes funds to the Gurdwara and other charities.

The ashes are collected after cremation and disposed of by immersion in the waters of a river, lake or sea. Some families prefer to take the ashes to the Punjab, to be disposed of there.

The Rahet Maryada recommends that all ceremonies should be completed within ten days to allow the family to return to normal life and not be burdened with unnecessary extended rituals. However, the period may be extended if desired.

PART NINE
Gurpurbs, Gurpurb
Melas, Festivals and
Folk Festivals in
Punjab

CHAPTER 39
Gurpurbs associated with the Lives of the Gurus

Gurpurbs, Gurus' days, commemorate anniversaries related to the lives of the Sikh Gurus in Gurdwara. Sikhs celebrate Gurpurbs with great fervour throughout the world.

The anniversaries include the birth, Gurtagaddi (accession to Guruship) and death. Anniversaries are celebratory and festive for joyful occasions. Others which commemorate tragic events such as martyrdoms are more subdued, but even these carry a joyful air as they celebrate heroic sacrifice in the preservation of the Sikh faith. There is no change in the service, just its tone.

There are thirty-one Gurpurbs in the Sikh calendar, marking the births of the Gurus, assumption of Gurtagaddi (except for Nanak Dev, Guru from birth) and death. Two added Gurpurbs are the inaugural installation of Guru Granth in Harmandir Sahib and the foundation of the Khalsa Panth by Guru Gobind Singh. During 2008, these fall on twenty-two days as some share the same date. Not all Gurpurbs are celebrated with the same pomp and ceremony; some are traditionally marked more than others, though all are important to Sikhs. The anniversaries celebrated are benchmarks in the progress of the Sikh faith. The Sikh Sangat is free to celebrate any Gurpurb, and indeed do so to meet local traditions

The word Gurpurb had already come into use in the times of the Gurus. Bhai Gurdas (1551-1636), contemporary with Guru Arjan, says,

'I am a sacrifice unto Sikhs
Who with love and devotion
Observe the Gurpurbs'.

All Sikhs celebrate the following Gurpurbs:

Birthday of Guru Nanak
Inaugural installation of Guru Granth Sahib in Harmandir
Martyrdom of Guru Arjan Dev
Martyrdom of Guru Tegh Bahadur
Birthday of Guru Gobind Singh
Vaisakhi, anniversary of the creation of the Khalsa

Gurpurbs are an integral feature of the Sikh way of life. It is a day to pay homage to the life of Gurus. Sikhs were not always free to mark their Gurpurbs. They were persecuted for doing so during the Muslim rule of India. Thus, celebration of Gurpurbs is very dear to Sikhs.

Gurpurbs are a mixture of the religious and festive, personal and communal. Over the centuries, a standardised pattern of celebration has evolved, now codified in the Rahet Maryada. Gurdwara are decorated with flowers, flags and historical posters and pictures. They are also illuminated. Celebrations often include fireworks.

Akhand Paath is commenced forty-eight hours before the Gurpurb. On the appointed day, the atmosphere in and around the Gurdwara is like a fair, as Sikhs enter and leave the premises throughout the day.

On the morning of the Gurpurb, the day begins with the ceremony of Bhog of Akhand Paath, Ardas, Hukam and distribution of Karah Parsad. Next comes Kirtan Darbar. Asa Ki Vaar is sung, followed by Shabads suitable for the occasion throughout the day. Interspersed are lectures, sermons and katha, discourse on Gurbani, in praise of the Guru whose anniversary is being celebrated. Karah Parsad and Langar are served to devotees in their thousands in major Gurdwara throughout the day.

Another feature of Gurpurbs is Nagar Kirtan (Nagar means town) when Sikhs in their thousands march in Jaloos, processions, through towns and cities in India. The processions are organised a day before the Gurpurb. Panj Pyarae, five Amritdhari Sikhs, lead these Jaloos.

One of them holds the Nishan Sahib, the Sikh flag; the other four have naked swords held aloft in their hands.

Then follows the Granth Sahib, carried in its Palki on a float decorated with flowers and flags. Kirtan Jatha, school bands with their marching pupils, eminent citizens and brass bands playing martial tunes follow in large numbers. Gatka parties, martial arts practitioners, display mock-battle with the traditional Sikh weapons, devotees follow singing Shabads in chorus.

As the procession winds its way through the streets, a continuous chant of the sacred music or Shabad singing is heard, which is occasionally broken by mass shouts of 'Bole so Nihal' answered with the salutation 'Sat Sir Akal' ('Whoever answers will be blessed' – 'Truth is eternal').

The Nagar Kirtan route is decorated with flags, flowers, religious posters, decorated gates and banners depicting various aspects of Sikh faith. Free refreshments, including Langar, are offered on the procession route. Local shopkeepers, community organisations and the Sangat provide these in a spirit of Seva.

Nagar Kirtan has also become a common feature in major centres of Sikh population in Britain, usually on Vaisakhi day or the birthday of Guru Nanak. The processions end in an open space where a Mela, fair, would be in progress.

As part of the Gurpurbs, Amrit Sanskar is also conducted for devotees wishing to become Amritdhari on the day.

Sikh fervour for Gurpurbs was demonstrated at recent special anniversary celebrations evoking widespread enthusiasm and renewal of faith. The tercentenary of Guru Gobind Singh's birth in 1966; the fifth centennial of Guru Nanak's birth in 1969; in 1975 the third centenary of the martyrdom of Guru Tegh Bahadur; in 1977 the fourth centenary of the founding by Guru Ram Das of the city of Amritsar; in 1979 the 500th anniversary of the birth of Guru Amar Das; the tercentenary of the establishment of the Khalsa Panth celebrated in 1999; and the 400th anniversary of the installation of Guru Granth in the Harmandir in 2004 have been memorable events in the Sikh calendar.

2008 will see the tercentenary of the Gurtagaddi of Guru Granth towards the end of October.

Gurpurbs

Janam Divas (Birthday) of Guru Nanak
Historians are of the view that Guru Nanak was born on 15 April 1469 but the date of this Gurpurb is still calculated in the Bikrami calendar. The birthday of Guru Nanak falls on Kartik Puranmashi, full moon day of the Kartik month. The day moves with the moon. It currently falls in November but is tending towards the end of the year. It is the most important Gurpurb in the Sikh calendar and celebrated all over the world wherever there are Sikhs.

Gurdwara Janam Asthan or Nankana Sahib is the shrine built at the site where Guru Nanak was born to Baba Kalu and Mata Tripta. Before the partition of India, Sikhs from all over the world would gather here and celebrate the Gurpurb every year with great devotion and enthusiasm.

Since the division of India in 1947, Nankana Sahib has become part of Pakistan. Sikhs do not have unrestricted access to their holy shrine. Sikhs gather here annually but the numbers vary depending on the current political relationship between the two countries of India and Pakistan. Even then, numbers of Yatris, pilgrims allowed from India is limited. There is usually no restriction for British passport holders to enter Pakistan and visit Nankana Sahib.

Janam Divas of Guru Gobind Singh
Because of the historical complexities of establishing dates, the Gurpurb is celebrated on 5 January. Guru Gobind Singh, the tenth Guru was born in Patna Sahib in central India on 22 December 1666.

Shahidi Divas of Guru Arjan

Arjan Dev, the fifth Guru, was martyred on 16 June 1606. It is commemorated as Shahidi Divas, Martyrdom Day. Before the partition of India, millions of Sikhs would visit the Samadhi, Gurdwara on the site where Guru Arjan Dev was martyred. Sikhs no longer have open access to the site. It was customary to set up sabils, refreshment centres, where sweetened iced milk-water was served to every passer-by in memory of the very hot days when the Guru was tortured with burning sands for days on end without mercy.

The day is now similarly marked all over India and abroad. This day is commemorated with diwans in Gurdwara and Nagar Kirtan. Sabils are set up outside Gurdwara and on the route of the processions to serve sweetened iced milk drinks free to all passers-by.

Shahidi Divas of Guru Tegh Bahadur

11 November is the day when Sikhs commemorate the time that Guru Tegh Bahadur was martyred by Aurangzeb, the last great Mughal emperor, in Chandani Chowk in Old Delhi in 1675. Gurdwara Sis Ganj marks the site. Sikhs helped the British imperial army to capture Delhi in the Indian mutiny in the year 1857. This was the opportunity for Sikhs, more than 150 years after their Guru's execution, to pay homage to him and raise the Sikh flag, which still flies today in memory of the martyrdom. The day is commemorated with Gurdwara divans and Nagar Kirtan in Delhi and all over India.

CHAPTER 40
Parkash Utsav (Installation of Guru Granth in Harmandir Sahib)

It took three years to compile Guru Granth. Its site is called Ramsar, near the Harmandir in Amritsar. The task was completed on 1 August 1604. Bhai Gurdas, the transcriber of the Granth, marks this date at the end of the Granth. The completion of the Granth was celebrated with much jubilation. Karah Parsad was prepared and Sikhs in large numbers came to partake of Karah Parsad and seek Darshan, holy sight, of the Granth.

Guru Arjan had already prepared the Harmandir to house the Granth. For he said,

'There is nothing like it in all the three worlds
Harmandir is the ship
For devotees to cross over the worldly ocean
A new joy daily pervades
A sight of it annuls sins.'

On 16 August 1604, the chosen day of installation, Guru Arjan Dev woke early in the night before the hours of dawn. The Sangat had begun to gather too, ready for the procession to march to the Harmandir for the historic ceremony. In front were Sevadars, sprinkling water over the ground to be traversed, followed by Bhai Buddha with Guru Granth held aloft over his head and Guru Arjan Dev walking behind ceremoniously waving the Chor Sahib, ceremonial fan, over the Granth. Raagis were singing Shabads and the Sangat were repeating the refrains. The procession would make frequent stops to allow devotees gathered on the route to pay their respects to Guru Granth. Baba Buddhaji, carrying the Granth, crossed the Causeway over the Sarovar to enter the Harmandir where Sevadars had already prepared the Manji, palanquin, in the middle of the Harmandir, on which the Granth was to rest. The Guru appointed Baba Buddhaji as the first Granthi, reader, at the Harmandir.

Bhai Buddhaji said the Ardas and sought permission of the Guru to open the Granth. With tears flowing from his eyes and with great reverence, he opened the Granth at random and then recited the Hukam, divine command, to the Guru and the assembled Sangat with their heads bowed in respect. The Hukam read,

'He [God] Himself aids his Sants in their task
He Himself sees the task accomplished
Blessed is the earth, blessed the Sarovar
Blessed the Sarovar of Amrit
Amrit overflows the Sarovar
Eternal is the perfect being
His praises the world sings.'

Guru Arjan was standing behind him waving the Chor Sahib all the time over the Granth.

Guru Arjan directed that Guru Granth should remain open throughout the day. During the second watch of the night, on the orders of Guru Arjan, Bhai Buddhaji recited Kirtan Sohila, the concluding Nit-nem Bani for the day. Guru Arjan and the Sangat joined in the last refrain of the Sohila,

'Listen to me, friends
Serve the holy One
Earn divine blessings
Bring comfort in the hereafter.'

After Ardas, the Granth was closed and wrapped in silks. Baba Buddhaji then once more carried the Granth on his head and began to walk towards the room of repose for the night that Guru Arjan had had specially prepared in his residence, just across the Causeway.

Guru Arjan and the Sangat followed, singing Shabads, their faces glowing in the darkness with the lanterns lighted up to show the way.

As Baba Buddhaji entered the room of repose, Guru Arjan stepped forward to help place the Granth on its Manji, bed. Baba Buddhaji retreated but the Guru stayed that night and every other night prostrate in the presence of the Granth reciting Bani, only interrupting this to allow himself a few hours of rest. Baba Buddhaji returned early in the morning to prepare to take the Granth to its daily place in the Harmandir.

The rituals inaugurated on that day have become fixed for Sikhs for all times and repeated daily in Gurdwara all over the world. The original residence of Guru Granth with its place of repose is now within the Akal Takht shrine.

The ritual in the Harmandir continued for another thirty years. Then, persecuted by their Mughal enemies, the Sikhs with Guru Hargobind had to abandon the Harmandir. His oldest son, angry at not being given the next Guruship, removed the first Granth Sahib to Kartarpur. This Granth followed a chequered history as Maharaja Ranjit Singh, the Sikh ruler of Punjab, forcibly removed it to Lahore, his capital. The descendants claimed the return of the Bir to the family, which the British, who had captured the Sikh kingdom, agreed to do. The first Granth, known, as the Kartarpur Bir, after the name of the village, is still in the possession of the family and is displayed for worship once a month.

After Guru Hargobind left Amritsar, Harmandir fell under the control of different factions whose observance of Sikh ritual was arbitrary. It was not until Mata Sundri, widow of Guru Gobind Singh, commanded Bhai Mani Singh to install there a copy of the second recension of Guru Granth that the suzerainty of the Khalsa Panth was to be restored again in the Harmandir. This version of Guru Granth had been inscribed by Bhai Mani Singh, a learned Sikh, under the guidance of Guru Gobind Singh. This Bir was lost to the Sikhs during the turbulent times of the early seventeenth century. Baba Dit Singh Shahid, a close companion of Guru Gobind Singh and a revered protector of Harmanidir Sahib, had prepared a number of copies, with permission of the tenth Guru, at the same time as the original recension was being made ready. One of these recensions was installed in the Harmandir. We do not know the fate of this original volume.

Harmandir Sahib was to suffer much tribulation over the next fifty years but whenever the Sikhs could they would return to Harmandir to resume their worship of the Granth.

The day of the first installation of Guru Granth in the Harmandir is marked with a Gurpurb all over the Sikh world. The centre of celebrations, on a grand scale, is the Harmandir itself. Devotees in their hundreds and thousands attend to pay their respects at the Sikhs' holiest shrine on this auspicious day.

At sunset, the devotees light oil lamps and candles on all sides in rows upon rows along the Parikrama around the Sarovar. This is in addition to the lights strung throughout the Darbar Sahib. As myriads of lights flicker in the deepening dusk and weave patterns of light, a truly magical display of illumination takes place. Devotees have come here for hundreds of years, through wars, persecution and danger to celebrate the inauguration of Guru Granth at the Harmandir.

On this day, the original ceremony is re-enacted. Guru Granth is carried ceremoniously in its golden palanquin from Ramsar Gurdwara, where Guru Arjan had compiled the Granth, to the Harmandir where it was installed.

CHAPTER 41
Khalsa Sajna Divas (Vaisakhi Day Celebrations)

Vaisakhi Gurpurb, anniversary of the creation of the Khalsa, is usually coupled with processions and Jore Melas (public fairs) especially as Vaisakhi Day also combines the celebration of the spring in Punjab. Jore Melas and processions take place, particularly in Punjab. Guru Nanak's birthday may be celebrated similarly. Melas will have funfair rides, stalls and traditional music and dancing, sports and stalls selling Sikh artefacts.

The word Vaisakhi comes from the name of the month, Vasaikh. The day falls on the first day of the month. The day varies in the Western calendar year. Vaisakhi is the most colourful event in the Sikh calendar, next in importance to the celebration of the birthday of Guru Nanak, founder of the Sikh faith.

Vaisakhi had been chosen as a date for the meeting of the Sikhs because it was easy for the Sikhs to know about this date, a day reserved for celebration since ancient times. As the Bikrami calendar was in use in those days the people could know about the main events and dates. The calendar is based on the movements of the moon, hence the variation in the dates of the month.

In Punjab, India, Vasaikhi day also marks the time for the harvest of the spring wheat and the two events are combined as a day of celebration of the founding of the Khalsa Panth and the beginning of the harvest season. It is a time for family and community celebrations. Vaisakhi Day is also of importance in other ways in the Sikh social and cultural calendar.

Sikhs mark Vaisakhi all over the world with great enthusiasm. Religious services are held and Akhand Paath is carried out to celebrate the occasion. The Jore Mela (Jore means crowds and Mela festival) is a time for Sikhs to come together and show their commitment to their faith. In Punjab, it is of course celebrated additionally as the time of the arrival of spring after the hard days of winter.

Sikhs celebrate Vaisakhi by going to Gurdwara for prayers and holding processions and Melas to commemorate the creation of the Khalsa by Guru Gobind Singh and to celebrate the spring harvest festival. Young Sikhs often choose this day to be initiated into the Khalsa Panth.

Amrit Sanskar

The Vaisakhi occasion is especially favoured by the young to be initiated into the Khalsa Panth. Others wishing to renew their vows may also do so again. These ceremonies are held in Gurdwara all over the world.

The people who are to enter Khalsa bathe and put on the five Ks. During the ceremony, they kneel and receive Amrit in their cupped hands. They imbibe it five times. Amrit is also sprinkled in their eyes and hair. Once initiated into the Khalsa brotherhood, they promise to follow the teachings of the Gurus.

Raising of Nishan Sahib (the Khalsa flag)

The Sikh flag is called Nishan Sahib (the sign). It flies from the top of a tall steel pole –flag mast – outside Gurdwara and other Sikh institutions. The flag is triangular and bright saffron in colour. The pole is also wrapped in yellow cloth, chola.

There is a black khanda symbol imprinted in the centre of the flag. The khanda is made up of a double-edged sword, a symbol of God's power to annihilate evil. There is a surrounding circle to show that God has no beginning or end. The two crossed swords on the outside of the circle symbolise the earthly and spiritual power of the Sikh faith. The Nishan Sahib was a gift to the Sikhs from the sixth Guru, Hargobind.

The flag and the chola are changed every year on Vaisakhi day. The pole is lowered, stripped of its coverings and washed with yoghurt. The congregation take part in the washing of the pole. Sikhs have to do it in bare feet. As it is still early spring in the UK, other helpers flood the floor with hot water to keep the feet warm.

Once the pole is washed, it is clothed once more with new coverings. There are loud cheers and calls to the Almighty as the pole slowly goes up again, in its new glory but old sentiments with the Nishan Sahib at the top. Everybody shouts 'Waheguru', 'Waheguru'.

It is a very emotional time for Sikhs. Sikh families vie with each other to provide the flag cloth.

Processions

Processions are held in all towns in Punjab and abroad wherever there are sizable populations of Sikhs. The processions are mainly held on Vaisakhi day in the West but also on the birthday of Guru Nanak in India. The procession usually starts from a Gurdwara, going through streets and ending up either at a fairground or another Gurdwara.

At the front, the procession is led by Panj Pyarae wearing the Sikh uniform of orange or yellow robes and blue, dark or orange Pagri. They also wear full-length swords. Each holds a Nishan Sahib. Behind them comes a beautifully decorated float, which carries Guru Granth Sahib, with musicians singing hymns and the congregation – men, women and children – following the float, also singing to the accompaniment of musicians.

People lining the route are given sweets and dried fruit. Free drinks and food stalls are set up on the route by devout Sikhs to serve people taking part in the procession or standing on the route. These processions are also held in the UK, USA, Canada, Australia, New Zealand, Malaysia and Singapore where there are substantial Sikh populations.

CHAPTER 42
Sikh Faith Festivals: Bandi Chhor Divas (Sikh Divali), Hola Mahalla and Maghi Jore Mela

Apart from Gurpurbs, Sikhs celebrate three festivals linked to their Gurus. One, before the harvest is ready, is the time for the farmers and their families to rejoice and relax as Vaisakhi festival time comes around. The Vaisakhi Gurpurb is combined with the harvest time festival.

Fairs are held in all big towns in Punjab and abroad. Fairs are most popular for the performance of Bhangra, the folk dance of Punjab. Bhangra is a very popular form of entertainment, not only in Punjab but also all over the world wherever there are Sikhs. It is based on a dhol, a big barrel-shaped two ended drum. Teams of both women and men perform the Bhangra. It is vigorous form of dance. Popular Indian sports are also played.

For fairs with a religious orientation there will be a temporary Gurdwara installed in the fairground. Prominent musicians provide Kirtan. Smoking and drinking are strictly prohibited at such Mela, but free Langar is served to all visitors to the fair. Sports and games are played, Bhangra dancing takes place. Speeches are made, fairground funfair rides provide for the children and shops and stalls sell Sikh memorabilia.

Bandi Chhor Divas (Sikh Divali)
Festival of Light at Harmandir Sahib

Divali has a deep resonance with Harmandir Sahib. Sikhs have gathered here on the day since the time of Guru Ram Das. Baba Buddha, the first Granthi, completed the first reading of Guru Granth on this day. Guru Ram Das commended Sikhs to visit the Harmandir on Divali to pay their respect to their Gurus. As Bhai Gurdas says, 'Night of Divali, burn the oil lamps'. The Harmandir, on Divali night, presents a spectacular sight, with hundreds and thousands of oil lamps, candles and electric lights, glimmering in the Sarovar, lending an enchanted air to the shrine. Divali is celebrated on the last day of the dark half of the lunar month in Katik, which usually falls in October or November.

Divali and Vaisakhi had become days to be together in the absence of means of communication; it was easy for the Sikhs to know about these dates and hold gatherings at their shrines. While Vaisakhi is a big day in the Sikh calendar and celebrated all over the world because of its association with the founding of the Khalsa Panth, celebration of Divali is mainly confined to Harmandir Sahib, Amritsar. It is on this day that Jahangir, the Mughal emperor, released Hargobind, the sixth Guru, from prison after five years of incarceration for refusing to renounce his faith. Guru Hargobind had refused an earlier release until fifty-two Hindu princes imprisoned with him were also set free. Only when they were set free did he leave the prison. Guru Hargobind is known as Bandi Chhor, liberator, for freeing the princes of their chains of captivity. It was on Divali in 1620 that he arrived in Amritsar, hence the celebrations in Harmandir on Divali day, which Sikhs call Bandi Chhor Day.

Harmandir Sahib is illuminated on Divali in his honour. It symbolised freedom to practise one's faith and to stand steadfast against persecution. Divali has come to hold a special meaning for Sikhs for this and many other events associated with the Sikh faith on Divali at Amritsar.

Divali holds for Sikhs a test of their resolve in their faith during the turbulent eighteenth century. Roaming warrior bands of Sikhs would converge upon Amritsar braving all hazards. It was on this day in 1738 that Bhai Mani Singh, a companion of Guru Gobind Singh and the Granthi at Harmandir, was martyred fighting to preserve the sanctity of the Shrine. Bhai Mani Singh was torn limb from limb and his body cut to pieces on the orders of the Muslim governor of Lahore. It was for Sikhs an event of deep sorrow.

When Ahmed Shah Abdali, an Afghan marauder, plundered Delhi in 1756, Sikhs began to attack his army on its return to Afghanistan. So angry did Ahmed Shah become at this continuous haemorrhaging of his loot and army that he desecrated Harmandir Sahib and filled its Sarovar with dead animals. He then deployed his vast Afghan army in the genocide of the Sikhs.

Baba Dip Singh, a companion of Guru Gobind Singh, was so outraged at the news of the desecration that he set out for Amritsar with as many Sikh warriors as he could gather, vowing to either liberate the shrine or die in the service of his faith. Baba Dip Singh fought a heroic battle, killing scores of Muslim soldiers, but he was in the end outnumbered by the vast Afghan army. All his followers were slaughtered on the battlefield. Eyewitnesses describe Baba Dip Singh holding his partially decapitated head in his left hand and his sword in the right hand fighting his way through the enemy and expiring at the foot of the steps of Harmandir Sahib. A shrine stands in the Harmandir at the spot where he perished.

The martyrdom of Baba Dip Singh shocked the whole Sikh Panth. Jathedar Jassa Singh, a Sikh chieftain, challenged his fellow chiefs to stand up for the rights of their faith and avenge the death of fellow Sikhs at the hands of the Afghans.

The Sikhs could only deal with the Afghan army by guerrilla action and reduce its strength by attrition. The repeated attacks reduced their own strength with great loss of life. While Afghans were to return repeatedly to try to annihilate the Khalsa Panth, the Sikhs slowly gained the upper hand and made sure no Muslim army was ever to enter Punjab again after 800 years of Muslim invasions from Central Asia, Iran and Turkey.

On Divali day Sikhs gather in Darbar Sahib in great numbers. At night, the Harmandir Sahib is illuminated with candles, oil lamps and electric lights. The reflection of illuminations in the Sarovar adds to the beauty and grandeur of the Harmandir. Firework displays also take place. Sikh treasures are displayed with pride and honour. There is no more moving sight for a Sikh than to witness Deepmala, the festival of light, at the Harmandir. For Sikhs it is a night of wonders. Each twinkle reminds them of the sacrifice of their Gurus and their devotees to make it possible for Sikhs to visit their holiest shrine whenever they wish to.

Sikhs all over the world visit their Gurdwara to commemorate the tragic and celebrate the glorious past of the Harmandir, at the heart of this struggle, on Divali day.

The origin of Divali is shrouded in antiquity. It was celebrated even before the arrival of the Aryans in India. It then became associated with Hinduism as its most important religious day. Although Sikhs do not like the excesses sometimes seen in Hindu celebrations, they too rejoice on Divali to share in this the most ancient of Indian festivals, especially since it has played such a historic role for their faith.

In ancient India, Divali was time to take account of their wealth and display it ostentatiously. Divali in its earliest forms was also celebrated to ward off malignant spirits of darkness. Aryans in their turn adopted it all and then extended it to the celebration of Lakshmi, goddess of wealth. It then added the return of Ram, the king and god, to his capital after an exile of fourteen years. Hindus celebrate this day by burning earthen lamps, letting off fireworks, festive eating, gambling and having fun. It is also the day of the birth of Mahanvir, founder of the Jain faith. The birthday of Raja Bikramjit, creator of the Bikrami calendar, is marked on this day. It is also on this day that Lord Krishna murdered his uncle Kensh to take revenge against his evil acts against his parents. Pandav, Lord Shiva and Parbati have links with Divali.

The story of India and of the Sikhs is encapsulated in Divali, which is rightly celebrated to remind them of their ancient history.

Hola Mahalla

Hola, of Arabic origin, means attack and Mahalla, of Persian origin, means a place.

The festival of Hola Mahalla is celebrated all over the Sikh world but chiefly in Anandpur Sahib and other shrines associated with Guru Gobind Singh as an annual event. It coincides with the festival of Holi. It is held on first day of the lunar month of Chet, which usually falls in March. Hola Mahalla is a Jore Mela, a colourful, lively festival in the Sikh calendar.

It commemorates the day Guru Gobind Singh summoned the Sikhs to gather at Anandpur Sahib in the foothills of the Shivalik Mountains in Northern India. The precise date of the first Mela, which became an annual event, is not known but it is generally accepted to have started about two years after the foundation of the Khalsa Panth in 1699.

The Nihang, formerly a Sikh warrior class founded by Guru Gobind Singh, live a colourful life dressed as in the time of the Guru Gobind Singh. They speak Punjabi laced with martial words, analogy and metaphors.

Guru Gobind Singh set the day for Sikhs to hold military manoeuvres to allow the warriors to show their skills and prowess on mock battlefields. In those times, thousands would gather for the occasion to take part and witness Sikhs at play and merry making, there being perhaps too few such occasions in their tragic but brave history.

There was a purpose too in these gatherings. Guru Gobind Singh organised war games to prepare his Sikhs to defend their faith in troubled times. Warriors showed their prowess in the use of different weapons and equestrians in full battle regalia would rush across the mock battle theatre with such ferocity as to shake the very ground under the feet of the spectators.

The warriors would bring their own weapons and horses. At the end of the day, the Guru would lead an attack on a model fort, to sharpen their skills as they competed with the best swordsmen, archers, expert shooters, riders, foot soldiers, and others who attended such gatherings.

It is not surprising that the occasion is very popular with Sikhs, who hold great affection for it. Thousands of Sikhs from Britain, Canada and the United States travel to Anandpur Sahib every year to take part in the three-day festivities.

This day reminds Sikhs of the valour and preparedness of Sikh warriors under the command of Guru Gobind Singh, battling the might of the Mughal Empire. Sikhs like to remember the fun, festivities and colourful celebrations that must have taken place surrounding such gatherings as Guru Gobind Singh had so little time to be celebratory in those dire times for his Panth.

A vast temporary camp city is organised by the local Sangat and Gurdwara to accommodate visitors. Langar at many sites provides free meals. It is a glorious gathering of the Panth as it pays homage to their Guru. It is the day when the Sikhs fulfil their promise to the Guru to uphold their faith and feel proud that it had prospered despite all the adversities it has had to face in the past five centuries.

Sikhs also hold martial displays to celebrate Hola Mahalla in Britain. Prince Charles and Lady Camilla attended one in London in 2007. Both participants and onlookers gather in close proximity. There are no barriers. Both the Prince and the Lady would cover their faces with their hands in mock horror when the displays came too close to them for comfort. Both claimed to have enjoyed themselves, that it was a long time since they had had such clean fun and good time.

On this three-day festival mock battles are held, martial music played and stirring Shabads of the Gurus recited. It is the day of the Nihang Singhs, who carry on the martial tradition with displays of swordsmanship and horse-riding and perform daring feats in encounters such as Gatka, tent pegging, bareback horse-riding and standing erect on two speeding horses sporting shining swords, long spears, and conical Pagri. The Nihangs present a fierce picture as they gallop past the crowds on horseback.

One of the most popular field sports is Kabadi, an Indian game. The area of the game is divided into two halves. There are two teams of players. The aim of the game is for one player to break through a row of members of the other team, to touch or wrestle one of them the ground. At the same time he has to take a deep breath and repeat 'Kabadi, Kabadi' for as long as he can. He must return to his side before his breath runs out.

On the last day Panj Pyarae carrying Sikh flags followed by a float carrying Guru Granth lead a long, colourful Nagar Kirtan. Following them is an organised procession in the form of army columns accompanied by war drums and standard-bearers. It starts from Takht Keshgarh Sahib, the site where Guru Gobind Singh founded the Khalsa Panth, and passes the shrines in Anandpur Sahib, including Qila Anandgarh, Lohgarh Sahib and Mata Jitoji shrine, and then returns to the Takht. It recreates the martial parades conducted to celebrate victories during the Sikh Raj in the nineteenth century.

Maghi Jore Mela: Festival of Muktsar

Sikhs celebrate Lohri but do not follow Hindu traditions. On the day after Lohri, Sikhs go to their Gurdwara to commemorate Magh, January, Sangrand in memory of the forty Mukte, the liberated ones, who all died in the battle against the Mughal to protect Guru Gobind Singh. These martyrs had previously rebelled against the Guru. At the end of the battle, in which the enemy retreated from the battlefield, Guru Gobind Singh tore the letter the rebels had written to their Guru renouncing him. The Guru forgave them and made them mukt, blessed with eternal life.

The town of Muktsar is the scene of Maghi Jore Mela. Huge celebrations are held every year attended by thousands of Sikhs to commemorate the martyrdom of the forty Sikh Mukte. A procession starts from the main shrine, marking the site of the battle, to Gurdwara Tibbi Sahib, sacred to the memory of Guru Gobind Singh. Devotees take a dip in the Sarovar, sacred pool, built in memory of the Mukte to symbolise their respect for them.

Glossary of Sikh faith terms

A

Adi Granth – Original name of what is now called *Guru Granth*, the sacred scripture of the Sikhs, compiled by Guru Arjan Dev in 1604. The second recension, compiled by Guru Gobind Singh, is now accepted as the holy book of the Sikhs

Akal Takht – Eternal throne, the oldest of the five *Takhts*. Established by Guru Hargobind, the only one by a Guru. Principal seat of temporal and religious Sikh authority, located adjacent to the *Harmandir Sahib, Amritsar*

Akhand Paath – Uninterrupted recitation of *Guru Granth* from beginning to end, lasting forty-eight hours

Amrit – Holy nectar, sanctified water, used in Sikh Amrit ceremony, introduced by Guru Gobind Singh

Amritdhari – A Keshdhari Sikh who has taken *Amrit* and been initiated into the *Khalsa Panth*

Amrit Sanskar – Initiation ceremony of the *Khalsa*

Amritsar – Holy city of the Sikhs. *Harmandir Sahib*, the Golden Temple, is located here. The largest city in Punjab, centre of commerce and education

Amrit Sarovar – Reservoir around the *Harmandir*

Anand Karaj – Sikh marriage ceremony

Anandpur Sahib – City of Bliss. Guru Gobind Singh spent most of his life in this holy city. It is here he introduced the *Amrit* ceremony and fought many battles to preserve the faith

Anand Sahib – Composition by Guru Amar Das. The first five and the last *Pauris* (short Anand Sahib) are recited to conclude Sikh service

Ardas – Personal prayer of supplication to God

Arti – Shabads that are recited after the Bhog ceremony at the end of the recitation of *Guru Granth*

Asa Ki Vaar – *Gurbani* set to *Raag* composed by Guru Nanak with *Saloks* by the second Guru, Angad Dev. It is sung to music in the morning service. It then includes *Saloks* by Guru Amar Das

B

Bandhan – Bond. Analogy used to suggest ties to God. The arrival of Guru Hargobind on release from prison on *Divali* day in *Amritsar* is celebrated as Bandhan Chhor, Liberation day

Bani – Speech. In Sikh faith, the Word, the scriptural compositions. See also *Gurbani*

Barah Maha – Compositions about the twelve months first by Guru Nanak in *Raag* Tukhari and then by Guru Arjan in *Raag* Majh. The appropriate composition by Guru Arjan is recited in *Gurdwara* on *Sangrand*, first day of the Nanakshahi calendar month

Benati – Appeal, a *Shabad* with an element of prayer for mercy

Bhagat – Devotee of God, saintly person. Term applied to holy people, Hindus and Muslims, whose compositions are included in *Guru Granth*

Bhagat Bani – Compositions by Hindu and Muslim *Sants* included in *Guru Granth*

Bhai – Brother, friend. Used in Sikh faith as a title of honour for *Gurdwara* Sevadars or devout Sikhs

Bhatts – Bards. In Sikh history a group of poet-musicians who sang *Shabads* in the times of the Gurus and whose compositions are included in *Guru Granth*

Bhog – Ceremony which concludes a Sikh service. Also ceremony after complete reading of *Guru Granth*

Bole So Nihal – Sikh salutation meaning 'anyone who answer will be blessed', the answer is 'Sat siri Akal', truth is eternal. It is used at the conclusion of *Ardas* and as a Sikh greeting. Also indicates a sign of agreement and collective shout of Sikh sentiment

Buddha, Baba – Contemporary of six Gurus. First *Granthi* of Guru Granth in *Harmandir Sahib*

C

Chakar – Quoit. A circular steel weapon; an emblem of Sikh faith depicted on Sikh artefacts including *Nishan Sahib*, the Sikh flag

Chamkaur – The site where Guru Gobind Singh fought his last battle against the Mughals. He lost his two eldest sons here

Charan – Feet; touching feet symbolises devotion, humility

Chaunki – A division of each day from sunrise to sunset in the shrines, in which a particular set of *Bani* is sung. Historically, there were five Chaunki in each day. Also historic choirs that moved from one *Gurdwara* to another singing *Shabads*

Chaupad – As in *Shabad*, consisting of four verses

Chaupai – A four-line stanza form. Benati Chaupai, composition of Guru Gobind Singh, is recited with *Reheras* as part of daily *Nit-nem*

Chaur/chauri/chawri/chor – Ceremonial fan like a fly whisk, usually made of yak's hair with a wooden, silver or golden handle, which is waved over the *Granth Sahib*

Chhant – A lengthy composition in *Guru Granth*, commonly of four or six verses

Chimpta – Tongs. Tong-shaped musical instrument used in folk music and singing of *Shabads*

Chola – Clothing, a term applied to the coverings of *Guru Granth* and to the coverings of the *Nishan Sahib* at a *Gurdwara*

D

Damdama Sahib – Guru Gobind stayed here for a year and produced the last recension of *Guru Granth*. Damdama Sahib was nominated the last of the five *Takht* by the Sikh *Sangat*

Dar – Door, portal [to God]

Darbar Sahib – The shrine complex at *Amritsar* which includes *Harmandir Sahib*, Golden Temple

Dasam Granth – Purported compositions of Guru Gobind, now accepted as only part true. Accepted compositions of Guru Gobind Singh are part of *Nit-nem* and *Shabad Kirtan*

Darshan – Vision [of Divine Light]

Daswandh – Donation of one-tenth of one's earnings for religious and social causes

Dhadhi – Musician who sings praise of Guru, using an instrument called a dhadh. Guru Hargobind introduced dhadhi music

Dharam – Righteous actions, duty, religion

Dharamsala – Originally place of worship for the Sikhs from the times of Guru Nanak without *Guru Granth* in place

Dhol/Dholak/Dholki – A wooden two-sided drum. Dholki is its smaller version

Divali – Indian festival. From the time of Guru Amar Das Sikhs have gathered on this day in *Amritsar*. In 1577, the foundation stone of the *Harmandir Sahib* was also laid on this day. Sikhs celebrate it as the day Guru Hargobind arrived here after release from prison

Diwan – Congregational worship in the presence of *Guru Granth*

Doha/Dohira – *Gurbani* verse form consisting of stanzas of two rhyming lines

E

Ek Onkar – There is one God (also *Ik Onkar*)

G

Gatka – The Sikh martial arts form

Ghar – Home. Also a musical term, refers to rhythm or beat in *Gurbani*

Gian – Knowledge, realisation

Gobind – God. Also first name of the tenth Guru

Granth – A compilation of the sacred scriptures

Granthi – Custodian of the *Gurdwara* and *Guru Granth*

Gur – Of Guru, affixed to designate faith institutions or devout Sikh. Example: *Gurdwara, Gursikh*

Gurbani – Guru compositions. Teachings of the Gurus and *Bhagats* enshrined in *Guru Granth*

Gurdas, Bhai – Companion of the Gurus who transcribed *Guru Granth* under the supervision of Guru Arjan

Gurdwara – Gur – Guru, dwar – house. The Sikh place of worship

Gurtagaddi – Seat of authority of Gurus, invested in *Guru Granth* in perpetuity

Gurmat – Teachings of the Gurus

Gurmata – A resolution adopted by the *Panth* acting in prayer to resolve faith issues. It is symbolic of the will of the Guru, expressed in a formal decision

Gurmukh – Pious person

Gurmukhi – Script used by Sikhs to write Punjabi

Gurpurb – A Sikh festival associated with Gurus

Gursikh – Pious Sikh

Guru – In Sikh faith, refers to the ten founders of Sikh faith and the Granth. It is forbidden to apply the term elsewhere

Guru Granth – The *Adi Granth*, scriptures of the Sikhs, prepared by Guru Arjan Dev and then by Guru Gobind Singh in its second recension

Gutka – Handbook of *Nit-nem Bani*. Most Sikh homes will have several copies of the Gutka

H

Har – God

Harmandir Sahib – Golden Temple, *Amritsar*. Principal Sikh shrine

Haumai – Self centredness, ego, pride. One of the five sins in Sikh faith

Hazare Shabad – The name given to a selection of seven *Shabads* from *Guru Granth*. In addition, Shabad Hazare Patshahi 10 refers to a compilation in the *Dasam Granth*

Hola Mahalla – Annual spring gathering of Sikhs at *Anandpur Sahib* for war games, sports contests, music and poetry recitals, inaugurated by Guru Gobind Singh in 1701

Holi – Hindu festival

Hukam, Hukamnama – Command. Hukamnama is a randomly selected *Shabad* from the Granth recited at the end of a Sikh service after *Ardas*. Other terms are Hukam laina, Vak laina, awaz laina. Also an edict issued by a religious authority on matters that affect Sikh faith

I

Ik Onkar – There is one God. First two words of the *Mool Mantar*, Sikh creed of faith, and the first two words of the Granth (also *Ek Onkar*)

J

Jaap Sahib – Morning prayer, composition of Guru Gobind Singh

Jaloos – Outdoor procession

Janam – Birth

Jap – Repetition of the divine name of God; also recitation of *Bani*

Japji – Morning prayer, composition by Guru Nanak

Jatha – A party of Sikhs, formed with a religious purpose in mind
Jathedar – Leader

K

Kaccha/Kachera/Kacch – Pair of drawers, one of the five Ks of the Sikh code of dress
Kakars – The five Ks, symbols of Sikh religion
Kamal – Lotus
Kara – Bracelet. One of the five Ks
Karah Parsad – Sacramental food distributed at the end of a Sikh service
Karaj – Affair, task. Anand Karaj, wedding ceremony
Karta Purkh – God, the Creator of the universe
Katha – Exposition of *Gurbani*
Kaur – Last name given to Sikh females
Kesh/kes – Untrimmed hair, one of the five Ks
Keshgarh Sahib – Place where Guru Gobind Singh founded the *Khalsa Panth*
Keshdhari – A Sikh who maintains the five Ks
Keski – Small *Pagri*, usually worn by children, sportsmen and women
Khalsa – Pure, Amritdhari Sikhs, brotherhood of *Amritdhari* Sikhs
Khalsa Panth – Men and women who belong to the brotherhood of *Amritdhari* Sikhs
Khanda – Double-edged sword. *Khalsa* emblem, comprising a vertical double-edged sword over a chakar, quoit, with two crossed *Kirpan* on the outside
Kirpan – A sword, small or full size, one of the five Ks
Kirtan – Singing of *Gurbani* in *diwan*, *Gurdwara* service

L

Langar – Serving of free food in Sikh tradition. Chiefly in *Gurdwara*
Lavan – Circumambulation of *Guru Granth* during a Sikh wedding
Lohri – An Indian festival

M

Maghi Mela – Sikh festival held annually on 14 January to celebrate the memory of the martyrdom of the forty Immortals in battle at Muktsar

Mahala – Each Guru used the name Nanak as the author of their compositions in the Granth. Numbers in Mahala showed their identity. For example, Mahala 2 was the second Guru, Guru Angad; Mahala 5 was the fifth, Guru Arjan; Mahala 3 the third Guru, Guru Amar Das

Mahant – Head of a historic Gurdwara until disestablished in 1925

Maharaja – King, Emperor

Mala – A beaded string like a rosary

Manji – Cot-like structure on which *Guru Granth* is placed. Also a preaching office in the times of the Gurus

Mantar – Verse, phrase or syllable of religious import. *Mool Mantar* is the creed of Sikh faith

Masand – Sikh representatives appointed by Guru Ram Das, later disestablished by Guru Gobind Singh because of corruption

Mata – Mother. Also a prefix showing respect for elderly woman

Mela – A fair or festival

Miri and Piri – Miri is the temporal authority in the Sikh religion. Guru Hargobind introduced the concept of the balance between *piri*, spiritual matters, and *miri*, worldly matters. To illustrate, he wore two swords

Misl – A Sikh confederacy of the twelve Sikh sects, disestablished by Maharaja Ranjit Singh

Mool Mantar – Prologue to *Japji*. Sikh declaration of faith (also Mul Mantar)

Mridanga – Type of drum; a single piece of wood that is hollowed out and with playing heads on both ends. Used in South Indian music in preference to a tabla, more popular in North Indian music.

Muktsar – Town where forty Sikhs sacrificed their lives, having previously deserted Guru Gobind Singh. The Guru forgave their sins and declared them spiritually liberated. See also *Maghi Mela*

Mundawani – Seal. Concluding *Shabad* by Guru Arjan describing the spiritual jewels in *Guru Granth*

N

Naam – Name, name of God

Naam Japna – Devoutly repeating *Naam*, the divine name

Naam Simran – Meditating on the divine Name

Nadar – Grace

Nagara – Large drum. Beaten at the end of *Ardas* in some *Gurdwara*, especially shrines

Nihang – Devout Sikh sect. The Nihangs trace their origin to Guru Gobind Singh who robed his warriors with a blue battle-dress. Nihangs have continued this mode of dress. They lead an ascetic life. Now dwindling in numbers

Nirgun – God, without form or material attributes, beyond human knowledge and comprehension

Nirmala – A sect of celibate, intellectual Sikhs, who commanded particular sway over the faith in the eighteenth and nineteenth centuries. In a small minority now

Nishan Sahib – Saffron flag with Sikh symbols of the faith

Nit-nem – Sikh daily prayers

P

Paath – Recitation of *Gurbani*

Paathi – Reader of *Gurbani*

Palki – Palanquin to house *Guru Granth* as it moves from one place to another in ceremonial processions

Panj Pyarae – First five Sikhs to be initiated into *Khalsa Panth*. Also any five *Amritdhari* devotees chosen by *Sangat* to perform duties

Panth – Sikh commonwealth, nation

Parchar – Missionary work

Parsad – Sacramentally offered food

Patka – Cloth which fits snugly over the head, worn by boys and sportsmen. See also *Keski*

Pauri – Ladder, stanza in *Gurbani* as in *Japji* and *Vaars*

Pothi – A book of *Shabads*. Guru Nanak kept Pothis to write his compositions in

Purkh – Person, being, God

R

Raag – Musical mode. The classical system of Indian music, as in *Guru Granth*

Raagi – Musician who performs *Gurbani* in music in *Gurdwara*

Raag Mala – The last composition in *Guru Granth Sahib*. It is a listing of eighty-four *Raag* used in Indian music. Most Sikhs believe it to be a fake insertion

Rahau – Pause. Marks chorus or main theme in a *Shabad*

Rahet – The code of belief and conduct of the Sikh *Panth*

Rahet Maryada – The official Code of Conduct for Sikhs, produced by the *SGPC* (also Rahit Maryada)

Reeheras – Evening *Nit-nem* prayer

Roomala – Silk cloth to cover *Guru Granth*

S

Sabad/Shabad – Word, compositions in *Guru Granth*

Sabha – Society, association

Sagun – Temporal realm of human existence. See also *Nirgun*

Sahaj – State of peace, tranquillity

Sahaj Dhari – A Sikh who does not wear a *Pagri*. The word suggests he may do so in future

Sahaj Paath – Interrupted reading of the *Granth* over a period, usually a month or two

Sahib – Master, term of respect applied to Sikh Gurus and places and institutions connected with them

Salok – A short composition, usually a couplet, in *Guru Granth*

Sanatani – People who proclaimed to be Sikhs, as part of Hindu religion. Belief is no longer sustained

Sangat – Congregation. Also Sadh Sangat

Sangrand – First day of the month in the Nanakshahi calendar. The portion of the composition Barah Maha by Guru Arjan Dev relevant to the month is recited in *Gurdwara* on *Sangrand* day

Sanskar – Ceremony

Sant – Saintly person, a rare title bestowed on a devout Sikh

Sant tradition – A devotional tradition pertaining to the reverence for a Sant and following in his footsteps

Sarbat Khalsa – Formal gatherings of Sikhs to discuss matters of faith

Sardar – Chief. Leader of a *misl*. Sardar is now used as a title for all *Keshdhari* male Sikhs. The corresponding title for a Sikh woman is Sardarni

Saropa/Siropa/sripao – A gift or honour bestowed by the *Sangat* for services to Sikh faith. Usually a *Roomala* or a saffron cloth

Sarovar – Sacred pool in shrines

Sat – Truth. In *Gurbani* truth equals God

Satnam – Divine truth

Sat siri Akal – Truth is eternal. Sikh greeting

Seva – Voluntary religious service

SGPC – Shiromani Gurdwara Parbandhak Committee, Amritsar. It controls the Sikh shrines and is the supreme body of the Sikhs

Shabad – Word. A composition in *Guru Granth*

Shabad Kirtan – Vocal and musical renditions of *Gurbani*

Shahid – Martyrs. Often used as a prefix to the name of a person who died in the cause of Sikh faith

Sikh – Follower of Sikh faith

Sikh Panth – Sikh nation, often used interchangeably with *Khalsa Panth*, brotherhood of *Amritdhari* Sikhs. Not all Sikhs are *Amritdhari*. See also *Sahaj Dhari*

Simran – Meditation on the name of God

Singh – Lion. Last name of Sikh males. Many Sikh women use it as well

Singh Sabha – Sikh reform movement initiated in 1873. It was a struggle between the conservative, Sanatani, Sikhs and the radical *Tat Khalsa*, true, *Amritdhari* Sikhs. See also *Sanatani* and *Tat Khalsa*

Sodhi – Seven Sikh Gurus (Guru Ram Das to Guru Gobind Singh) were of this clan

Sohila Kirtan – Late evening prayer, said before retiring

Sukhmani Sahib – Composition of Guru Arjan in *Guru Granth*

Swayyae – *Shabads* composed by Guru Arjan in praise of God and by *Bhatts* in praise of the Gurus; also a composition by Guru Gobind Singh

T

Takht – Throne. Temporal and spiritual Sikh authority

Tat (Khalsa) – Sublime, true. Term applied to the reformed Sikhs towards the end of the nineteenth century who abjured rituals, idol worship and other Hindu practices

U

Udasi – Travels of Guru Nanak. Also a sect founded by the eldest son of Guru Nanak, now in decline

V

Vaar – *Gurbani* verse arrangement consisting of a *Pauri* and a preceding *Salok*. *Asa Ki Vaar* is the best known example of a Vaar

Vaisakhi – Harvest festival. It is also the day on which Guru Gobind Singh introduced Amrit ceremony and created the *Khalsa Panth* on 14 April 1699

W

Waheguru – Wonderful God

Waheguruji ka khalsa, Waheguruji di Fateh – Hail khalsa of the wonderful God, who is always victorious. Sikh salutation and greeting

Z

Zafarnamah – Letter of defiance written by Guru Gobind Singh to Aurangzeb, the Mughal emperor